France 1870-1914

R. D. ANDERSON

France 1870-1914
POLITICS AND SOCIETY

ROUTLEDGE & KEGAN PAUL
London, Boston, Melbourne and Henley

First published 1977
by Routledge & Kegan Paul plc
39 Store Street
London WC1E 7DD,
9 Park Street
Boston, Mass. 02108, USA,
464 St Kilda Road
Melbourne, Victoria 3004
Australia and
Broadway House,
Newtown Road
Henley-on-Thames,
Oxon RG9 1EN
Set in 10/12 point Garamond
and printed in Great Britain by
Ebenezer Baylis and Son, Ltd
The Trinity Press, Worcester
and London
Printed and First Published as a
paperback in 1984

ISBN 0 7100 8575 3 (c)
ISBN 0 7102 0175 3 (p)

Contents

Preface *vii*

Introduction *1*

1 The evolution of the Republic 1870–1914 *5*

2 The social foundations *30*

3 The map of opinion *42*

4 Elections, deputies and parties *61*

5 Parliamentary politics *74*

6 Republicans and Radicals *88*

7 The Right *100*

8 The working-class movement *119*

9 France and the world *141*

Conclusion *157*

Appendix 1 Political evolution *163*

Appendix 2 Socialist and trade-union
organizations *175*

Appendix 3 Political geography of Paris *177*

Notes *178*

Bibliography *187*

Index *209*

Maps

1   Provinces and departments   *43*
2   Left and Right in 1876   *54*
3   Left and Right in 1914   *55*
4   Industrial France   *129*

Preface

The aim of this book is to describe political developments in France under the Third Republic between 1870 and 1914, to set them in their social context, and to suggest a framework of interpretative ideas. The student who begins his reading in English has access at present to some fine scholarly works and some sophisticated analytical ones, but no apology is needed, I feel, for presenting a briefer account which attempts to synthesize a wide range of recent work. Historical study of the period is now at a fruitful stage, and I have tried – through the Bibliography as well as the text – to provide the reader with a conspectus of current scholarship and to guide him to discover for himself some of the original work that is being done.

A British historian cannot help being struck by the different approaches of French and British historians to their national histories in this period. Classic political history and biography, so popular in Britain, are neglected in France; biography, indeed, is still regarded as hardly a respectable activity for academic historians, and many of the great figures of the Third Republic still await their historian. The modern French historical school has shown a preference for social and intellectual history, and much original and stimulating work has been done – especially, for this period, on various aspects of religious history and on the working-class movement. There has also been a notable concern with local and regional history, and with the aid of some important theses and of the flourishing regional historical reviews, it is now possible to construct an account of French politics which allows for the country's great social and geographical diversity. However, the history of parliamentary life and of political institutions (apart from the Press) is only now beginning to attract a revived scholarly interest, and this book is therefore perhaps more original than might at first appear.

I have approached the problem of combining narrative and analysis in a fairly radical way: Chapter 1 provides a narrative outline of the whole period, and the subsequent chapters discuss various special aspects. Chapter 1 may be read in conjunction with Appendix 1, which gives more details of election results and governments. Chapters 2–5 build up a picture of political life by looking at the social foundations of parties and ideologies (Chapter 2), at the 'grass roots' variations in political behaviour (Chapter 3), at parties and political leadership (Chapter 4), and finally at politics as played on the parliamentary stage in Paris (Chapter 5). Chapters 6–8 discuss the main political forces: the Republicans and Radicals (the original Left, turning into the Centre), the Right, and the new Left formed by the organized working class. Chapter 9 is a brief survey of foreign and colonial policy.

I first felt the need for a book like this when teaching the subject at the Universities of Glasgow and Edinburgh, and I am grateful to my colleagues and students at those universities for much intellectual stimulation. I should also like to thank St Antony's College, Oxford, for its recent hospitality (and for electing me to a studentship in 1965) and the Travel and Research Committee of Edinburgh University for financial aid.

Introduction

The Third Republic, as its name indicates, was established in a country already rich in political traditions and experience, where opinions were defined by relation to past events and where conflicting political ideals were identified with alternative regimes. In the course of the nineteenth century, the Republic had come to symbolize the ideal of democracy, and the Republican movement under middle-class liberal leadership looked back to 1789 and forward to the full expression of popular sovereignty through universal suffrage. Many of the liberal ideas of the French Revolution had been widely accepted by the bourgeoisie, but for a long time universal suffrage was feared and rejected as incompatible with liberalism; it had been introduced in 1848 as the main permanent achievement of the Second Republic, but the rule of Napoleon III had since shown that universal suffrage did not by itself lead to the triumph of democracy. The aim of the Republicans was now to turn the principles of the Revolution into effective institutional form, and to pull down the remaining strongholds of reaction. The first decade of the Republic's history was to be dominated by the struggle between them and their conservative opponents.

The conservatives in France were divided between three parties (using the word in the contemporary sense of 'bodies of opinion', for organized parties hardly existed). The Legitimists were those who remained loyal to the older branch of the Bourbon dynasty, which had ruled during the Restoration of 1815–30; based on the landed class, they had never really reconciled themselves to the disappearance of the *ancien régime*. The Orleanists, faithful to the Orleans branch of the dynasty and to the memory of the July monarchy of 1830–48, were an upper-middle-class party who accepted the liberal heritage of the Revolution but interpreted it in an elitist, whiggish manner; in the 1870s some of them were to desert the royalist cause and accept the Republic. Both Legitimists and Orleanists believed in a parliamentary monarchy with a property-based franchise. The Bonapartists, on the other hand, accepted universal suffrage, but as the basis of a plebiscitary Empire rather than a parliamentary system. Napoleon III had shown how universal suffrage could be neutralized and reconciled with strong government and social order through a system of managed elections and 'official candidates'. The disaster brought on France by the Emperor in 1870 discredited the Bonapartists for a time, but they were to revive and to remain a significant force in certain areas.

The loyalty of these parties to three rival dynasties was a fatal weakness in their struggle with the Republicans, but in many ways they formed a single conservative block. They all believed that society should be run by a governing class qualified through experience, wealth and social prestige – by the 'notables', to use a contemporary term adopted by many historians. Landowners and members of the wealthy middle class still dominated public life outside the big cities, and provided all three conservative parties with their leaders. The Church also supported conservative social values and the upholding of traditional authority, and the defence of religious interests came to provide the Right with much of its cohesion and drive (the anti-clericalism which Orleanists and Bonapartists had shown in earlier years being submerged). Thus their appeal was wider than that which dynasticism alone could provide, and the monarchist parties took over much of the support which the conservative bourgeoisie had given to Napoleon III.

Napoleon III had also relied on the support of the peasantry, who formed the largest element in the French electorate. The peasant vote was the great prize for which conservatives and Republicans contended in the 1870s, and it was the Republicans who won it. Their position had been a strong one from the start, for they had wide support among the middle class and in the urban masses, who as yet had no socialist alternative – though the Commune of 1871 showed that many workers had an interpretation of the revolutionary tradition which differed markedly from that of the middle-class Republicans.

By 1879 the Republicans had defeated the enemies of the Republic, and were in a position to carry out their programme – a programme, notably, of anti-clerical measures. As elsewhere in Europe, liberal-democratic ideas had become almost inseparable from secularist anti-clericalism, partly for very general reasons – the heritage of the Enlightenment, the progress of science, the anti-liberal and anti-rational direction given to Catholicism by Pius IX. In France, the events of the revolutionary years had already created an almost unbridgeable gulf between the ideas of 1789 and the Church, and this had been widened by the Church's political choices. Rather than maintain political neutrality, it had supported the governments which it thought would give it most freedom to pursue its mission; the Church had supported Napoleon III (especially in his early years) and was now the ally of the Legitimists. The traditionalist values of Legitimism were closely identified with Catholicism, and in general the Church had aligned itself firmly on the side of property and the existing social order.

When the Republicans attacked the Church, therefore, they were also attacking their political enemies. Perhaps, indeed, they preferred to make the Church the main symbol of reaction so that they could envisage their cause in terms of idealistic principle rather than class conflict. But Republicanism did have a class basis, as it came to represent the two classes which had benefited most from the Revolution and which had gains to defend – the peasantry and the bourgeoisie. The fear of peasants that tithes or feudal dues might be restored was still real enough to be exploited against the 'reactionary' Right after 1870, while the bourgeoisie was concerned to defend the 'career open to talents' and the meritocratic State education system against the return of a network of privilege and patronage based on the Church and the old landed families. Broadly speaking, the Third Republic stood for the social aspirations of new and dynamic elements in the middle class who resented the way in which the old governing class, whether aristocratic or bourgeois, hung on to power; they saw themselves as the natural leaders of the classes below them in establishing a social democracy which would give every citizen the chance of developing his natural talents, acquiring property, and moving up the social ladder.

Despite differences of party nomenclature, political developments in France were broadly similar to those in other European countries. The Republicans were middle-class liberals of a familiar type who successfully challenged an established governing class which enjoyed wealth and social prestige, both of which derived partly from land-owning. Having won this struggle, they saw their own position challenged in turn by the rise of the industrial working class, and responded to this threat either by drawing closer to the conservatives, or by rejuvenating liberalism to give it a wider appeal – a process represented in France by the rise of Radicalism. Industrial growth meant that the underlying movement of opinion was to the left, as the old landed and professional classes declined in relative importance and the proletariat grew. Correspondingly, those who had once been on the left of the political spectrum found themselves pushed to the right as their original programme was fulfilled, and as they began to feel their own interests to be under attack. By 1914, the rise of the Socialist party seemed to be the central question in politics: would it too join in the process of peaceful evolution rather than posing a revolutionary threat? The prospect seemed more likely in France, with her successful and flexible parliamentary institutions, than in other major countries.

CHAPTER I

The evolution of the Republic
1870–1914

Between 1870 and 1914 France had sixty governments. In order to make sense of what at first appears bewilderingly complex, many historians have adopted a convenient three-part division of these years: the 'monarchist Republic' of the 1870s, dominated by the attempt of the conservatives to resist the consolidation of the regime and erect barriers against democracy; the 'Republic of the Republicans' or 'Opportunist Republic', running from the definitive defeat of the Right in 1879 until 1899; and the 'Radical Republic' after 1899, when the Radical wing of the Republicans replaced the moderate Opportunists as the dominant force in politics, a shift coinciding and connected with the Dreyfus affair. This division is a helpful one, although of course further subdivisions could be made. In the 1880s, for example, the Opportunists were more or less unchallenged, and carried through their major legislation, while in the 1890s there was a political realignment caused partly by the rise of Socialism: some of the Opportunists moved towards conservatism, and were met half-way by part of the Catholic Right which (in the movement known as the *Ralliement*) reconciled itself to the Republic in order to defend social order.

As the idea of the 'monarchist Republic' indicates, the proclamation of the Third Republic on 4 September 1870 established the regime only provisionally. The defeat and capture of Napoleon III at Sedan created a vacuum of authority in Paris, into which the leaders of the Republican opposition moved swiftly with the support of opinion in the city. As in previous revolutions, the provinces fell in behind Paris, and the new 'Government of National Defence' was immediately accepted. It was determined to carry on the war, but its task was not easy. The Prussian armies advanced rapidly, and by 19 September Paris was surrounded. The government had already set up a 'Delegation' at Tours, and in October Gambetta escaped from Paris to lead it. For the rest of the war, Gambetta was the real government of France. Thirty-two years old, inspired by the patriotic traditions of the Jacobins, he was determined on resistance to the last, and made heroic but ultimately unavailing efforts to raise new armies and encourage partisan warfare in the occupied areas.

The Government of National Defence stayed in Paris, able to communicate with the provinces only by balloon and carrier pigeon, and increasingly unpopular in the city. The fall of the Empire had revived the revolutionary spirit, and political tensions between the Left and the government – there were serious demonstrations on 31 October 1870 and 22 January 1871 – compounded the tensions caused by unemployment, hunger, bombardment and the failure of the city's own military efforts. With few regular troops available, most able-bodied men had been armed and enrolled in the National Guard, whose parades and committees became natural centres for political discussion.

Gambetta's armies were unable to relieve Paris, and an armistice was signed on 28 January. Gambetta and his supporters wanted to fight on, but the majority of the Government of National Defence accepted the inevitability of defeat, and wanted elections so that a new government could negotiate the peace. Fearing the strength of conservative pressures in crisis conditions, Gambetta would have preferred to postpone the elections until Republican authority was firmly established, and he resigned when the government refused to accept his plan to disqualify candidates associated with the Empire.

The new National Assembly, which was to sit until the end of 1875, did indeed have a large conservative majority: 400 of the 650 or so members were monarchists. Public opinion decisively favoured peace, and the Jacobin patriotism of the Gambettists was now popular only in the towns. With half of France occupied, and normal political activity impossible, the voters turned to the 'notables', those whose wealth and local influence made them natural leaders; another factor was that the method of voting, on a single list for each department, allowed rural votes to swamp urban ones. The majority of the deputies who met at Bordeaux were members of the old governing class, many of them Legitimist landed gentry of a type that had played little part in national politics since 1830. Though mostly inexperienced in parliamentary life, they were patriotic, public-spirited, and generally devoted to parliamentary and constitutional methods.

The first act of the National Assembly was to appoint Adolphe Thiers as 'head of the executive power' (in August he became President of the Republic). Thiers was a veteran statesman widely respected in

Europe, a prominent politician under the July monarchy, and leader of the liberal opposition to Napoleon III. Formerly an Orleanist, he now became convinced that a moderate Republic gave the best chance of preserving social stability and national unity – it was, in his famous phrase, the regime which divided Frenchmen the least. His political skill and shrewdness did much to make it permanent. For the time being, however, following an understanding between Thiers and the Assembly known as the 'pact of Bordeaux', constitutional questions were postponed while Thiers was given a free hand in the painful task of negotiating the Treaty of Frankfurt and the cession of Alsace-Lorraine. He also had to deal with the Paris Commune.

Events in 1870–1 followed a similar pattern to those after the 1848 Revolution: a Republican provisional government called elections which produced a moderate majority, creating disillusion and tension among the urban masses, and leading to a working-class rising when it seemed that the gains of the Revolution were to be snatched away again. In 1871, the reversal of Republicanism was more violent, and so too was the reaction. The election and the armistice had brought the tensions in Paris to their snapping point. Paris was still prepared to fight on, and it seemed that both the Republic and France had been betrayed. With the end of the Government of National Defence, the hold of central authority over the city was weak: the National Assembly moved back to Versailles, but not to Paris, because of the fear of mob pressure. Thiers now prepared to restore normality in Paris, ending the wartime freezes on rents and debts, and disbanding the National Guard. Though no longer needed, the National Guard had provided a living for thousands of men who were now thrown back on the depressed labour market. It was an attempt by Thiers to remove cannon belonging to the National Guard which set off the rising on 18 March. From then until May, Paris governed itself. Political direction was provided at first by the Central Committee of the National Guard, later by the Commune, the elected municipal council. Instead of attempting to repress the rising at once (as parallel risings in Lyons, Marseilles and other towns were repressed), Thiers withdrew the government forces to Versailles and waited. A more conciliatory policy, making allowances for the distressing social conditions in the city and for the strained nerves and patriotic susceptibilities of its inhabitants, might have avoided the rising in the first place, and there seems strong evidence that Thiers was content to let the Commune develop so that the final repression could be all the more thorough and break the turbulence of Paris for good.

The government action was certainly savage enough when it came: the Versailles troops marched in in May, those resisting were shot on sight, and the Communards burnt public buildings and shot their hostages. Pacification was followed by summary executions and hardly less summary judicial proceedings, which sent thousands to prisons and penal settlements. One way or another, about 20,000 people were killed during 'bloody week', and the repression of the Commune was notable for the hysterical atmosphere of class hatred which accompanied it. With its social divisions laid bare before the eyes of the occupying Germans, with the centre of its capital in ruins, France had hardly made an auspicious start under the new regime.

The immediate political effect of the Commune was to discredit the extreme Left and rally respectable opinion behind the cause of order. Hardly any Republican deputies showed sympathy with it, and most were anxious to repudiate the Right's attempts to identify Republicanism with anarchy by showing how the new regime could act firmly to repress disorder. In fact, the Commune failed to produce the right-wing reaction which conservatives hoped for, and which had occurred after the similar rising in June 1848. On the contrary, by-election results began very soon to show that the February election result was a product of war conditions, not a popular endorsement of royalism: of 114 seats filled in by-elections in July, 99 were won by Republicans.[1]

The growing popularity of the Republic made the constitutional task of the National Assembly difficult. The conservative majority hoped to bring about a restoration of the monarchy, or at least to give conservative forces an entrenched position in the new constitution, but they were hampered by their own divisions. The Orleanists in particular, a key group at the centre of the political spectrum, lacked the uncompromising loyalty to one man which characterized Legitimism. They believed in parliamentary monarchy, but if a monarchy seemed impracticable they might well accept a parliamentary Republic and make common cause with moderate Republicans. Part of the Orleanists, the 'Centre Left', did just this, following the lead of Thiers, and this eventually allowed the voting of the Republican constitution in 1875.

Until 1873, however, the prospect of restoration seemed a real one, and the majority paved the way for it by removing Thiers, whose Republican inclinations had become too apparent. He was forced to resign on 24 May 1873, a few months before his work as peacemaker was crowned by the final departure of German troops; from then until his death in 1877, Thiers came out openly for the Republic and did much to bring moderate opinion round to it. In his place, the Assembly appointed Marshal MacMahon, a respected soldier. MacMahon declared that his aim was 'the re-establishment of moral order in our country',[2] and the label 'moral order' became attached to the new government; it also reflected the strong Catholic influence on MacMahon and his ministers.

This phase has also been called the 'Republic of dukes': the new prime minister was the Duc de Broglie, a member of a distinguished liberal family who himself stood on the right of Orleanism (other Orleanist dukes active in politics were Decazes and Audiffret-Pasquier). Broglie pinned his hopes of restoration on 'fusion' of the two Bourbon lines: the Legitimist pretender the Comte de Chambord, who was childless, would be succeeded by the Orleanist Comte de Paris. This compromise was agreed on in the summer of 1873, but almost immediately sabotaged by Chambord, who revived an issue which had obstructed previous efforts in 1871: he refused to accept the tricolor as the national flag, and would rule only under the white flag of his ancestors. This was a symbolic repudiation of liberal constitutional ideas, a declaration that Chambord would return only on his own terms; it immediately alienated all the Orleanists and the more realistic Legitimists, ended the hopes of a restoration, and left Broglie without a policy. In November 1873, MacMahon's mandate was prolonged for seven years (the 'Septennate') in the hope that Chambord would die before the term was up (he survived until 1883).

While these manœuvres took place, the Republicans were winning the propaganda battle. In 1872 Gambetta returned to active politics, and launched a series of speaking tours which were a sensational success. Like other Republican orators, he was particularly concerned to win over the peasants and to stress that the Republic stood for moderation and stability. This did not prevent him from being bitterly attacked for his supposed dictatorial and demagogic tendencies, and the moral order government (using powers given by the 'state of siege' still in force) obstructed the Republicans' efforts by banning meetings and closing newspapers. But they continued to win by-elections.

The Assembly now accepted that a constitutional settlement must be reached, and in January 1875 the 'Wallon amendment', which passed by only one vote, paved the way for the three laws which made up the Third Republic's rather unsystematic constitution. The conservatives provided a strong Presidency and Senate to counterbalance universal suffrage; Republican traditions were hostile to these institutions, but

Gambetta persuaded his party to accept them as the price of seeing the Republic established. Events soon showed that the conservatives lacked the unity to use the safeguards which they had established: in the election of the life members who formed part of the Senate, the Legitimists practised a *politique du pire* and voted for Republicans rather than their Orleanist allies. In 1876, the new Chamber of Deputies was elected, and the swing of opinion to the Republicans was decisively confirmed: there were about 340 Republicans and 153 monarchists – and 75 of the latter were not traditional royalists, but Bonapartists, who had begun to make a political come-back.

MacMahon, however, was still president, and took the view that his powers ran parallel with those of Parliament, and that he had a duty to preserve social order as he understood it. He did his best therefore to ignore the Republican majority, and for most of 1876 maintained governments based on the ex-Orleanist Centre Left. He was eventually forced to turn to Jules Simon, the most moderate of the true Republicans, but soon found that the prime minister paid more attention to the Republicans in the Chamber than to the president, especially over anti-clerical policies, and on 16 May 1877 MacMahon dismissed Simon, inaugurating the *Seize Mai* crisis. Broglie became prime minister again, the Republican deputies (the '363') issued a protesting manifesto, and Parliament was dissolved. MacMahon's actions were within the constitution, but made political sense only if the new elections produced a conservative majority. Broglie spared no effort to achieve this, making use in the campaign of all the means of pressure available to a government; the Church also threw its weight behind him. On the other side, the Republicans submerged their differences in defence of the Republican regime, and Gambetta deployed all the resources of his oratory. The result was another Republican victory. Not all the '363' were returned, but Broglie's strategy had failed beyond question.

The *Seize Mai* was of considerable constitutional importance. MacMahon was the last president to use the weapon of dissolution, and the last to see his powers as the foundation of an executive independent of Parliament. Against the intentions of the makers of the constitution, the Republic became a regime of pure parliamentary sovereignty. The crisis was also politically significant, as the last attempt by the old governing class to hold back the progress of democracy. They had pushed the constitution to its limits, but kept within it – some of MacMahon's advisers wanted him to continue resistance even after the 1877 election, but such an enterprise was fraught with the danger of civil war. In the last resort, the French 'notables' sub-

mitted to the decision of universal suffrage, and gave up power peace-
fully. They had seemed to hold many cards in 1871, but had lost the
struggle through their disunity, the difficulty of abolishing the Republic once it was in existence without resort to violence or illegality, and
their failure to convert public opinion to their ideas. They adapted less
successfully than their British counterparts to the new age of democratic politics, and ensured by their opposition to the Republic itself
that they would be excluded from direct political power under the
new regime, and that France would lose the benefit of their political
experience and public spirit.

The year 1879, when MacMahon finally resigned, and when the
Republicans achieved a majority in the Senate, marks the real 'end of
the notables'. MacMahon was replaced by Jules Grévy, a veteran of
1848. The Republic was now truly in the hands of the Republicans,
and they marked their triumph by a number of symbolic gestures – the
return of Parliament to Paris, the adoption of the Marseillaise as the
national anthem and 14 July as the national holiday, and an amnesty
in 1880 for those condemned after the Commune. The 1881 election
confirmed the Republican majority, and in these years the notables
were also losing control of local government, which they had enjoyed
for generations and often valued more than national political power.

Through the 1880s, the gulf between the Republicans and the Right
remained unbridgeable; the conservatives were cut off from participation in governments, and though their opposition was strenuous
(especially to anti-clerical measures) they could not obstruct the Republican programme. The Republicans, however, had their own divisions. There had been a small 'extreme Left' in the National Assembly,
of which Gambetta was considered the leader. But Gambetta moved
towards the centre, and during the 1877 crisis emerged as spokesman
of the whole Republican party. From that time, the Republicans were
divided into Opportunists (so called from their pragmatic attitude to
reform) and Radicals, Clemenceau becoming the leader of the latter.
The Opportunists themselves had two leaders, Ferry and Gambetta,
who disliked each other, and who attracted rival groups of supporters,
a rivalry which weakened the Opportunist dominance and complicated
the problem of forming governments. Gambetta's supposed dictatorial
ambitions and bellicosity towards Germany made him seem a dangerous
leader, and among those who distrusted him was Grévy, who succeeded in keeping him out of office until 1881. Gambetta had much
influence behind the scenes (being denounced for this as the 'occult
government'), but whereas Ferry had two very creative periods of

office in 1880–1 and 1883–5, Gambetta's one administration in 1881–2 was a short-lived failure, and he died at the end of 1882.

In Gambetta's words, the Republic entered in 1879 on its 'organic and creative period'.[3] The work of the founding fathers had several aspects. First, they were very conscious that although Republicans might control Parliament conservatives were entrenched in the bureaucracy and other parts of the Establishment, and they carried out a series of purges with the long-term aim of creating a new Establishment loyal to the Republic. All new regimes reshuffled key officials like the prefects, and to some extent the Republicans were only taking their revenge for the similar purges carried out in 1877. The most controversial aspect of this policy of *épuration* was its application to the judiciary, which traditionally enjoyed security of tenure (*inamovibilité*); a law of 1883 suspended this temporarily and allowed notorious anti-Republicans to be retired.

Second, the Republicans passed a number of laws which complemented the constitution and guaranteed the liberties of the individual, a part of their work which has lasted to the present day. These laws covered the Press (the law of 29 July 1881; one of the best-known of French laws because it also regulates the sticking of posters on walls), the right of public meeting (1881), the legalization of trade unions (1884), local government (1884), and the re-establishment of divorce (1884 – a measure with obvious anti-clerical motives). A partial revision of the constitution in 1884 appeased the hostility of the Radicals to the Senate by making it more representative and abolishing the life members.

Third came the series of educational measures which are especially associated with Ferry, which were inspired both by anti-clericalism and by the real need for educational progress – primary education first became free in 1881 and compulsory in 1882. These laws were controversial from the start: when Ferry first became minister of education in 1879, he introduced a bill on higher education which included a clause ('article seven') banning 'unauthorized' religious orders, which meant chiefly the Jesuits, from teaching in France. This was rejected by the Senate, but the government went ahead and enforced the measure by decree in 1880. In scenes which were to be repeated twenty years later, the Jesuits and nearly all male religious orders were expelled from their houses amid protests and demonstrations. They were able to re-form, however, and the real target of the policy, the Catholic secondary schools patronized by the upper classes, survived virtually unscathed.

Other measures designed to weaken Church influence were the introduction of State lycées for girls (1880), legal restrictions on the Catholic universities which had been set up after a law of 1875, and above all the secularization (*laïcisation*) of the primary schools. The *laïcisation* of the syllabus (1882) meant excluding religious teaching in favour of a programme of 'moral and civic instruction'; the *laïcisation* of the teachers (1886) meant banning members of the clergy and of religious orders from State schools, though this could be enforced only gradually since many girls' schools were in the hands of nuns. These measures often showed the Republicans in an illiberal light, but the policy was claimed to be one of State neutrality rather than hostility towards religion, and the Opportunists (unlike the Radicals) believed in maintaining the Concordat of 1801 under which the State paid the salaries of the clergy.

Fourth, the Republicans sought to create prosperity by investing in the economic infrastructure. This started in 1878 with the 'Freycinet plan', a vast scheme of public investment in railways, canals and ports. The French railways were private companies, but operated under State concessions and with public guarantees of their dividends. The Radicals saw them as monopolies battening on the State, and called for nationalization. Gambetta's government was thought to be considering this, but after his fall the companies secured the revision of their concessions in 1883 (denounced by the Left as the *conventions scélérates*). This episode, along with the Freycinet plan, illustrated the way in which business interests were now gaining satisfaction from the Republic.

The desire to increase France's economic strength was also a motive, though not the only one, for the active policy of colonial expansion, chiefly in Tunisia and Indo-China, which was a feature of Ferry's governments. This too was controversial, the attack on it being led by Clemenceau, who alleged that colonies were a diversion from the patriotic task of revenge against Germany, and that Ferry was betraying France. The fall of Ferry's second government in 1885, after the minor reverse of Lang Son in Indo-China, ended Ferry's political career, and the intense unpopularity which he attracted suggests that Clemenceau was expressing a widely felt frustration at the exclusion of France from European affairs by Bismarck.

Ferry's defeat was indeed symptomatic of a more general disillusion with the work of the Opportunists. Far-reaching though their reforms were, they remained essentially political rather than social, and offered little to the working class, who were suffering from the effects of a commercial and industrial depression which had set in in 1882. At this time the Radicals still drew much of their support from urban workers, and they were able to capitalize on discontent with Ferry's complacency. The Right also profited from the situation: they too were against colonialism, and gathered the support of moderates alienated by the sectarian anti-clerical policies. The result was the 1885 election, which shook the Opportunist dominance and strengthened both Left and Right. The conservatives did so well in the first ballot that Opportunists and Radicals dropped their differences and presented common lists in the second; the Radicals came back stronger than before. After 1885, the Opportunists could no longer rule in defiance of both sides of the opposition. Alliance with the Right was still ruled out, and most governments over the next few years relied on Radical votes and included one or two Radical ministers. Paradoxically, this opening to the Left led to the greatest threat to the Republic since 1877 – the rise of General Boulanger.

The minister of war was normally not a parliamentarian but a general, a practice which encouraged ambitious soldiers to display their political leanings. General Boulanger had become known as a Republican general, and the Radicals demanded his appointment as minister as their price for support of the Freycinet government in 1886. Boulanger soon became popular in the army for his sympathy with the common soldier, and was further tempted towards political ambitions when he became the idol of the jingoistic Paris crowds. He came to be seen as a strong figure who would stand up to Bismarck, especially during the Schnaebelé affair of 1887 (Franco-German tension arising from a frontier incident). His growing popularity alarmed the politicians, and in 1887 he was removed from office and sent to an obscure provincial command. A 'Boulangist' movement continued to develop, and in 1888 Boulanger was dismissed from the army. This in fact enabled him to return to the public eye by standing in by-elections and by winning a series of sensational victories (the law allowed multiple candidatures in simultaneous elections). He won twice in the industrial Nord department, and his successes culminated in a triumph in Paris in January 1889. Boulanger's supporters urged him to seize power, but either from failure of nerve or respect for legality he refused to do so, and his moment passed. The Republicans recovered their own nerve, and decided to act against Boulanger before he could sweep the board in the 1889 general election. Threatened with prosecution for treason, Boulanger fled to Brussels and did not dare to return; in 1891 he committed suicide over the grave of his mistress.

The Boulangist movement was perhaps more significant than Boulanger himself. It became a real force in 1888 because it gathered together the various causes of discontent and disillusion with the regime. Its positive programme was vague, centring on the idea of 'revision' of the constitution – an old Radical slogan, but used by Boulanger to indicate the need for a strong ruler who would sweep away the corrupt politicians. Their corruption had been opportunely revealed by the 'Wilson scandal', which had caused Grévy's resignation in 1887 when it was discovered that his son-in-law Wilson was trading in decorations.

Boulanger's mixture of anti-parliamentarism and nationalism was later to be characteristic of the new nationalist Right, and one of the lessons of the affair which was not lost on the perceptive was that a new sort of popular conservatism might be founded on this basis. But it is essential to note that Boulangism started and in many ways continued as a movement of the Left. Boulanger was disavowed by the orthodox parliamentary Radicals, but the leaders of his movement nearly all had Radical or revolutionary backgrounds, and both his nationalism and his authoritarianism had roots in the Jacobin revolutionary tradition. As his election campaigns continued, however, Boulanger increasingly courted the royalist Right, and came to be largely financed by them, since they saw in him a way of discrediting the Republic and provoking a crisis which would reopen the constitutional options. In the 1889 election, Boulangist candidates worked closely with the Right – many of them, indeed, were simply old conservatives under a new vote-catching label. Some of the new Boulangist deputies, however, including the novelist and nationalist thinker Maurice Barrès, remained true to the distinctive ideas of the movement, and for some years were to work more closely with the Socialists than with the Right.

By the end of the 1880s, with the Boulangist challenge surmounted, the future of the Republic was secure. The 1889 election was the last in which the question of the regime was a real issue, and the bulk of the Right gave up hope of reversing the verdict of 1877; it began to seem more profitable to use their political weight within the Republican system. For their part, the Opportunists had now achieved their principal aims, and could relax their guard against the Right, especially as the rise of socialism was providing a common enemy for defenders of the bourgeois social order. The 1890s were to be a decade dominated by the 'social question', and this was reflected in politics by a move away from centrist governments to a more polarized pattern, with the

Opportunists (now renamed 'moderates' or 'governmental Republicans') on one side, relying on the support of the Right, and the Radicals and Socialists on the other.

The working-class movement had recovered only slowly from the suppression of the Commune, and although there were important developments in the 1880s both trade unions and Socialist groups remained weak and divided. Only about a dozen Socialists were returned in the 1889 election. What attracted public attention was rather the large-scale strikes which appeared in the 1880s for the first time since the end of the Empire, and which sometimes ended in violence after troops were called in. Among the more notable (though really untypical) incidents were the miners' strike at Anzin in 1884, on which Zola's *Germinal* (1885) was partly based; a miners' strike at Decazeville in 1886, in which an engineer, Watrin, was murdered; the shooting of nine May Day demonstrators at Fourmies in 1891; and the strike at Carmaux in 1892 which led to the return of Jean Jaurès to Parliament as a Socialist. In 1893, nearly fifty Socialists were elected. Even more alarming to the bourgeoisie was the anarchist campaign of bomb outrages in 1892–4, which included the throwing of a bomb in the Chamber of Deputies by Auguste Vaillant, and culminated in the assassination of President Carnot. The reaction to the anarchists was one of panic: Parliament rushed through the so-called *lois scélérates,* restrictive laws directed especially against the Press. More significant in the long run was the acceptance of the industrial working class as a force to be reckoned with – the Fourth Estate, as Clemenceau called them. Socialists, Boulangists and Radical-Socialists (the name adopted by the left-wing Radicals) competed to show their awareness of the social question and attract working-class votes. Another sign of the times was Leo XIII's encyclical *Rerum novarum* of 1891, which greatly encouraged 'social Catholic' and 'Christian democrat' movements within the Church.

Leo XIII also stood behind another component of the realignment of the 1890s, the *Ralliement,* or reconciliation of Catholics with the Republic. Both the hierarchy and leading Catholic laymen had so far remained loyal to Legitimism, now obviously without a future. Leo XIII discouraged the idea of a separate Catholic party, but wished Catholics to accept the Republic so that they could join in a broadly based conservative party which could defend the interests of the Church effectively by having a share in power. The Pope's wishes were first revealed by Cardinal Lavigerie in 1890 in an after-dinner speech (the 'toast d'Alger'), and became clear in the encyclical *Au milieu des sollicitudes* (1892). They were accepted very reluctantly; it was difficult for priests and journalists who were used to denouncing the atheist Republic and its 'godless schools' to change their tune, and many of the rich laymen who led Catholic opinion openly defied the policy. In Parliament, however, a number of deputies, led by Jacques Piou, formed a 'Rallié' group, and stood as Republicans in the 1893 election. The way was open for co-operation between the *Ralliés* and the moderate majority.

Another thing which cleared the way for political change was the Panama scandal, which had shaken the political establishment and discredited many individual politicians. The Panama Canal Company had been formed by Ferdinand de Lesseps, the creator of the Suez Canal, and since Suez had proved a highly profitable venture for French investors the new company appealed successfully for the funds of small savers. But the two isthmuses were very different, and the company soon ran into difficulties through the terrain and disease. It began to bribe journalists to conceal its problems and maintain the confidence of investors; it also bribed deputies to get parliamentary sanction for an issue of lottery bonds. All this did not stop the Panama Company going bankrupt, and in the subsequent proceedings the bribes were revealed. The scandal broke in 1892, and provided a field day for the anti-parliamentarian Boulangists. The scandal cast a lurid light on the relations of Parliament, the Press and high finance, and also fed anti-Semitism, because of the two Jewish financiers, Herz and Reinach, who had acted as intermediaries (Reinach committed suicide during the scandal). In the event, only one deputy was convicted, but a number of political careers came to a premature end. The most distinguished victim was Clemenceau, compromised by his relations with Herz. He was the target of a vicious attack led by the Boulangist Déroulède (including the fiasco of the forged 'Norton letters' allegedly showing Clemenceau to be in the pay of the British) and he lost his parliamentary seat in 1893.

The underlying tendency in politics was towards moderate governments which (unlike the Opportunist governments of the late 1880s) were prepared to defy the Radicals and rely instead on the support of the *Ralliés* and even of the traditional Right. This tendency appeared in the Casimir-Perier government of 1893–4, which appealed for *Rallié* support by announcing the advent of a 'new spirit' in Church–State relations, and was consolidated in Méline's government of 1896–8, the longest-lasting the Republic had known. The Méline period was a sort of apotheosis of the bourgeois Republic, whose spirit

Méline himself well represented. He was associated especially with the cause of protectionism, and gave his name to the Méline tariff of 1892, which made France one of the most protectionist States in Europe. Protectionism, patriotism and social defence were causes on which the moderates and the Right could agree; originally demanded by industrialists, high tariffs had also come to be seen as the cornerstone of peasant prosperity, and Méline especially cultivated the peasant voter, using an 'agrarian' rhetoric which exalted the moral virtues of peasant farming and rural life.

Méline was not simply a conservative. He had been an active Republican since his youth, and saw himself with some justification as the political heir to Ferry. His slogan was 'neither revolution nor reaction', and this meant defending the work of the Republic. He skilfully retained the support of the *Ralliés* while making no real concessions to them: none of the existing anti-clerical legislation was relaxed, and no *Ralliés* sat in the Cabinet. The *Ralliement* thus seemed to have failed in some of its essential aims, and did not even benefit the Right electorally, for one of its effects was to make Catholic voters more willing to vote for moderate Republicans.

What kept Méline in office was the Right's fear of the 'collectivist' alternative. The Radicals in this period were rather ineffective politically, being shaken by the Boulanger and Panama episodes, weakly led, and outflanked on the left by the Socialists. But they did seem to be moving towards the idea of collaborating with the Socialists on a programme of social reform, including notably a progressive income-tax. The one left-leaning government of the period, that led by the Radical Léon Bourgeois in 1895–6, proposed to introduce this tax, and was overthrown by the Senate for its pains. French conservatives were to resist income-tax until 1914. The 1890s were a decade of stagnation from the point of view of social reform, and one may see here the beginnings of the malady from which the Third Republic was to suffer in the twentieth century, when necessary reforms were sacrificed to complacency and vested interest.

For a time, Méline's version of Republicanism seemed unchallengeable. But within a few years it was the Radicals who were to occupy the middle ground in politics and have ministers in every government. The occasion of this new realignment, if not its cause, was the Dreyfus affair. The affair reached its height in 1898–9, though the case itself went back to 1894. In that year, evidence appeared that military secrets were being passed to the German embassy, and the army's intelligence service pinned the guilt on Dreyfus on the basis of his handwriting.

He was convicted by a court martial, and condemned to life imprisonment on Devil's Island. For several years, Dreyfus's family fought to clear his name, but with little success. Even when the real traitor, Esterhazy, was discovered by the new head of the intelligence service, Colonel Picquart, senior officers refused to reopen the case. Picquart was transferred, and Esterhazy put on trial and acquitted. It was at the time of this trial, at the end of 1897, that Méline declared 'there is no Dreyfus Affair'. January 1898, however, saw the publication of the open letter 'J'accuse' by Zola, one of the small group of intellectuals and politicians who had now become convinced of Dreyfus's innocence; it appeared in the newspaper run by Clemenceau, who was to make his return to politics through the affair. Zola's forthright accusations against the army forced the government to prosecute him, and this at last brought the details of the case into the full glare of publicity. Zola was convicted, and left the country to avoid imprisonment, but his purpose had been achieved. Successive governments still resisted the reopening of the case, but the 'Dreyfusards' grew in number. One reason for governmental reluctance was that the army had added some impressive forgeries, which seemed to prove Dreyfus's guilt, to the file which ministers of war were shown when they inquired about the case. It was the discovery of these forgeries in August 1898, and the suicide of their author, Major Henry, which proved the real turning-point in the affair.

It did not end it, however, for entrenched positions had already been taken up. The affair is notorious for the way in which it polarized French opinion, setting two incompatible sets of principles at odds, and creating fierce personal enmities. Some historians have questioned this traditional picture, describing the affair as a 'pseudo-revolution of the elite' which hardly affected the masses.[4] Certainly, it had little impact on the elections held in May 1898. Certainly too, the obsession of the Press with the affair and the amazing violence of tone which it adopted were untypical of public opinion, although the developments in the case were dramatic enough to fascinate even those for whom the issues of principle involved meant little. On the other hand, the affair was to set off a new wave of anti-clericalism, which certainly engaged popular opinion, and it was to be almost as important in the evolution of the Socialist movement as of middle-class politics; and quite apart from its direct effects it remains of absorbing interest to the historian because it lays bare the forces and ideals at work in French society.

The initial resistance to reopening the case can be explained by the normal dislike of governments for scandals, and the reluctance of bureaucracies to admit their mistakes – especially since there had been irregularities in the original trial (documents kept secret from Dreyfus had been shown to the judges). But why did the anti-Dreyfusards close their minds so firmly to reason? It was the Right which had first introduced political passion into the question, when the Catholic and anti-Semitic Press attacked the pro-Dreyfus campaign as a conspiracy to undermine the national interest. Anti-Semitism had been profitably exploited for some years by the journalist Drumont, and it was now merging with the Boulangist strain in politics to form a new kind of extreme nationalism. Nationalists found the Dreyfus case irresistible: Dreyfus was a Jew; the Dreyfusards seemed to be attacking the army, an institution cherished by traditional conservatives as well as nationalists; and for nationalist theorists the affair illustrated the 'decadence' of democracy and the way in which individualism weakened the strength and unity of the nation by putting justice to one man above the preservation of social discipline and military morale. The idea that the Dreyfus campaign was got up by a 'syndicate' of Jews, Protestants and freemasons, subsidized by Germany (or by international Jewry), came to be accepted by many respectable and level-headed people.

Some extreme nationalists, mostly veterans of Boulangism, still dreamed of a violent overthrow of the Republic, and thought that the Dreyfus affair provided a new opportunity. Déroulède, leader of the 'Ligue des Patriotes', attempted a somewhat farcical *coup d'état* in February 1899, on the occasion of President Faure's funeral, and it was this incident together with other nationalist agitation in 1899 which finally forced the government into the vigorous action which brought the affair to a close. But extremism was not confined to the nationalists, for parts of the Catholic Press – especially the popular national newspaper *La Croix*, run by the Assumptionist order – were equally violent in their anti-Semitism and their denunciations of the 'syndicate'. The Assumptionists had a marked taste for political activity, and were active in the 1898 election in organizing Catholic campaigns and opposing *Ralliés*. This was perhaps the main reason for the anti-clerical reaction of the succeeding years. It can be argued that this militant minority was untypical of the Church as a whole, and that the hierarchy did its best to remain neutral, but the fact remains that no authoritative voice condemned extremism, and that Catholic opinion as a whole was almost automatically anti-Dreyfusard. One of the strengths of the anti-Dreyfus campaign was that it used themes which, however extreme in their expression, evoked a natural response from the whole of the orthodox Right: patriotism, the defence of the army, respect for legal decisions and the maintenance of the principle of authority.

The divisions caused by the affair widened by a process of reciprocal reaction – how could Catholics, for example, be sympathetic to a cause which was adopted so enthusiastically by the enemies of religion? The Left developed its own conspiracy theory: the conjunction of the army and the Church (the alliance of 'le sabre et le goupillon' was a favourite propaganda theme) with the nationalist agitators seemed to show that the old enemies of democracy were again plotting to destroy the Republic. On the level of ideals, men like Zola thought that the Republic meant nothing if it did not stand for justice, and that the honour of France was in question if injustice went unrighted. On a more political level, the affair offered a tempting opportunity to stir up popular emotion through reviving the anti-clerical issue, root out conservatives from institutions like the army which still resisted democratization, restore the fortunes of Radicalism, and break up the conservative-centre alliance forged by Méline.

Méline's government had fallen in 1898, after failing to improve its position in the elections, and was succeeded by short-lived centrist Cabinets. But 1899 was the real turning-point, when the 'Opportunist Republic' finally gave way to the Radical one. Underlying this, of course, was the steady shift of opinion to the left and the growth of Socialism, which pushed the Radicals to the centre of the political spectrum and made it almost impossible to form a government without them. But the new and decisive factor was that the moderate Republicans who had backed Méline split into two. The more conservative of them finally decided that the defence of social order, especially against Socialism, was more important than their lingering hostility to the Church. This group, which adopted the name Progressist, admitted its own conservatism, and for the rest of the period down to 1914 was part of the parliamentary opposition, along with the *Ralliés* (now renamed *Action libérale*) and the nationalists, never numerous in Parliament. All three groups were at least nominally Republican, and only a handful of monarchists remained.

Those, on the other hand, who felt the atavistic pull of anti-clericalism, and who were alarmed by the activities of the Right, decided that the defence of the Republic was the first priority, and returned to the policy of alliance with the Radicals. These moderates still felt that their basic loyalties were on the left, and adopted the somewhat misleading label 'républicains de gauche'; they were also sometimes called the

Alliance démocratique, after a loose party organization which they formed in 1901. Irreproachably Republican and anti-clerical, they were also conservative defenders of free enterprise, who had close links with business circles. They included a number of younger politicians who had emerged in the 1890s and were now starting on distinguished careers – Delcassé, Barthou and Poincaré. The moderates were almost as indispensable to a government as the Radicals.

It was a typical member of this party, René Waldeck-Rousseau, who formed a government of 'Republican defence' in June 1899 to liquidate the Dreyfus affair. Waldeck-Rousseau had been a member of Gambetta's Cabinet in 1881, but had later retired from politics to make a fortune as a business lawyer. He shared Méline's social ideas, but had no sympathy whatever with the Church or with extreme nationalism, and was happy to preside over a government which appealed to the whole of the Left and which embarked on an anti-clerical programme. In fact, Waldeck-Rousseau and his successor Combes provided a period of exceptional political stability between 1899 and 1905, because they could rely on a coherent majority in Parliament. Under Waldeck-Rousseau the moderates still dominated the coalition, and it was not until after the 1902 election, fiercely fought on the anti-clerical issue, that the Radicals really triumphed. Combes's ministry saw the full flowering of the 'Bloc' (a term especially applied to the Radical/Socialist alliance), with the action of the majority co-ordinated through a steering committee, the 'délégation des gauches', which represented the four groups involved: moderates, Radicals, Radical-Socialists and the Socialist group led by Jaurès.

The Socialists had formed a group of about fifty deputies since the 1893 election; some of them represented organized Socialist parties, but others, like Jaurès, were independents who had gained election through cultivating a local position. At the end of the 1890s, there had been moves towards the formation of a united Socialist party, and the Dreyfus affair came at a critical time because it posed the problem of how far Socialists should defend the 'bourgeois' Republic from its enemies, a problem linked with the question of whether Socialist deputies should ally with other parties and seek practical reforms. The initial reaction to the affair had been that it was a bourgeois quarrel which did not concern the working class, but most of the movement had come round to Jaurès's view that principles were involved which transcended class. Now in 1899 Waldeck-Rousseau offered a post in his government to Millerand, an independent who could be regarded (in the absence of Jaurès, defeated in 1898) as the Socialist leader in

Parliament. Millerand accepted, hoping to carry out some worth-while reforms. His action was repudiated by the other Socialists, not least because the Cabinet also included the veteran general Galliffet at the ministry of war, and Galliffet was notorious for his part in suppressing the Commune. The 'Millerand case' caused debate in the Second International (for the offer of Cabinet posts to Socialists was itself a striking innovation) and put paid for a time to the moves towards unity, two Socialist parties emerging instead: the 'ministerialists' led by Jaurès accepted that the time was not ripe for Socialist participation in governments, but thought it right to give general support to Waldeck-Rousseau and Combes; the intransigents were led by the pioneer of French Marxism, Jules Guesde.

Even before Waldeck-Rousseau took office, the Dreyfus case had been formally reopened. Dreyfus now returned to France, and was put on trial for a second time at Rennes in 1899. So difficult was it for the officers on the court martial to defy their loyalty to the army that Dreyfus was again convicted, though this time with 'extenuating circumstances'. The affair came to an end, however, when the President pardoned Dreyfus, though he was not formally cleared until 1906. The government also ended any threat to the Republic by prosecuting some prominent nationalists and royalists. But could matters be left there? The affair had revealed the disturbing extent of anti-democratic feelings in many of France's institutions, and the demand was for measures which would make a new Dreyfus affair impossible; as after 1877, conservative forces were to be the victims of the 'revenge' of the victorious Republicans. Waldeck-Rousseau's strategy was to concentrate this revenge against the extremist religious orders, the 'moines ligueurs', whose legal position as 'unauthorized' orders was in any case shaky. He introduced a bill to regulate the 'law of associations' (i.e. the freedom of individuals to form societies for all kinds of purposes), a reform which had been postponed for many years. Religious orders would come under its provisions, and Waldeck-Rousseau intended to use the government's powers to dissolve troublesome orders like the Assumptionists while leaving the majority to carry on their work. But this strategy went wrong, and the anti-clerical juggernaut got out of control. The majority in Parliament was less moderate than the government; the bill was amended in an anti-clerical direction before becoming law in 1901, and the power of authorizing religious orders was given to Parliament instead of the government. In 1902, the elections returned the Radicals in greater numbers, and it became clear that the law would be applied vindictively. Although the victor of the election as incumbent prime minister, Waldeck-Rousseau resigned immediately after it, perhaps because he had no taste for working with the new majority, perhaps because he hoped that the policies of his successor Combes would show up his own moderation and help his ambition to become President, perhaps because of his health (he died in 1904).[5]

Emile Combes was anti-clericalism incarnate. A man who had entered the Senate direct from local politics, he was typical of the small-town militants who were the backbone of the Radicals – in his own words, he was 'provincial to the fingertips'.[6] His hostility to the Church (perhaps connected with his own failure to become a priest) was obsessive and sectarian. He began by using the 1901 law to dissolve virtually all the existing religious orders and to confiscate their property. Those engaged in charitable and educational work suffered with the rest, and in 1904 a further law prohibited individual members of orders from teaching in any kind of school, though ten years were allowed for the enforcement of this. The only further anti-clerical measure conceivable was the old Radical policy of separating Church and State, and this was indeed to come about shortly. It was not, it seems, originally planned by Combes, who like most Republicans in office saw the Concordat as a useful way of keeping the Church under control. But relations with the new and intransigent Pope Pius X became strained through a series of disputes (chiefly about the appointment of bishops), and relations with the Vatican were broken off. Combes found himself forced to introduce a Separation Bill, and it was passed at the end of 1905, after Combes himself had left office. Disestablishing the French Church after many centuries proved a complex business, especially where property was involved, and the application of the law did not go smoothly. It had been strongly opposed by the Church throughout, and the Pope (apparently against the wishes of the French hierarchy) refused to accept the system of *associations cultuelles* under which worshippers would continue to use the Church buildings, which remained State property. A compromise on this was worked out through a series of judicial expedients and administrative decisions. A more acute problem was the 'inventories crisis' of 1906, caused by the inventories of Church property by State officials which the law required. As earlier when religious orders were expelled, there were demonstrations by the faithful and occasional violent incidents; this agitation was exploited by the nationalists and lasted until the 1906 elections, which showed however, like those of 1902, that anti-clerical policies undoubtedly had popular support.

Combes had resigned in 1905, after his position was weakened by the 'affaire des fiches', a scandal which revealed another facet of his sectarianism. After the Dreyfus affair, the government had begun a process of purging the higher ranks of the army and favouring Republican officers; Galliffet's successor General André had used the masonic lodges to provide information on officers' political and religious sympathies, and the masonic headquarters, the 'Grand Orient', had become a clearing-house for this system of spying and delation. Its revelation forced André to resign, and Combes followed within a few months. The majority which had sustained him was in any case crumbling away, on both the moderate and the Socialist sides. The Socialists were especially restive, as the Amsterdam congress of the Second International had condemned the policy of the Bloc and called on French Socialists to unite. The new unified party, the SFIO, was formed in 1905, and collaboration with the Radicals came to an end.

The 'ministerial' Socialists had supported the anti-clerical measures partly because they were popular with their own supporters, partly in the hope that the final resolution of the Church–State question would clear the way for social reforms. The anti-ministerialists had argued that anti-clerical agitation was a ploy to divert popular attention from social grievances. In retrospect, it is possible to argue that the years 1899–1905 were an interlude which delayed the emergence of the 'modern' social issues of twentieth-century politics and revived questions that were increasingly irrelevant. It is certainly easy to see why the Radicals wanted to keep anti-clericalism alive: it was an issue on which they were united (unlike social reform), and the only one capable of holding together a coalition as diverse as the Bloc. It was also the only issue on which major legislation was practicable, for the Senate approved of anti-clericalism but was prepared to delay social legislation indefinitely. The alternative to the wave of anti-clericalism was probably not social reform but stagnation, and without the Dreyfus affair the continuation of a conservative-centre coalition would have been more likely than a Radical/Socialist alliance. The post-Dreyfus period did at least bring the Left together for a time, and begin the process of integrating the Socialists into the political system.

Despite the end of the Bloc, the social question dominated politics after 1905 as never before, especially because of the new militancy of the trade-union movement. United since 1902 in the *Confédération générale du travail*, the movement was deeply affected by the doctrine of revolutionary syndicalism, which rejected parliamentarism and saw the strike as the best expression of class action and the general strike as the ultimate instrument of revolution. A wave of strikes began in 1904, and reached a first peak in 1906, when the CGT tried to bring about the eight-hour day by co-ordinated strikes on 1 May. Public opinion was especially impressed by the way strikers were now able to paralyse public services: an electricians' strike plunged Paris into darkness in 1907, and there were major strikes among seamen and dockers, postmen and railwaymen. Governments acted vigorously to repress these movements, and the breaking of the railway strike by Briand in 1910 marked the end of the wave.

A second new phenomenon of these years was the growth of international tension and of nationalist feeling within France. For the first time since the days of Ferry, colonial and foreign policy became real issues in domestic politics. France's expansion in Morocco was the first colonial enterprise to be seriously challenged by the Socialists, not least because it seemed a danger to European peace. The first Moroccan crisis of 1905 revealed the new aggressiveness of Germany, and anti-German feeling was to grow steadily and to become acute after the second crisis in 1911. Nationalism was no longer represented simply by a few extremist deputies, or by the *Action française* movement of Charles Maurras (a product of the Dreyfus affair), which was intellectually influential but numerically insignificant. It was a mood which affected virtually every sector of political opinion, a mood not just of fear but of new-found confidence in national strength. The exception was the working-class movement, which in these same years developed strong anti-militarist feelings (another legacy of the Dreyfus affair); anti-militarism was an integral part of revolutionary syndicalism, and was expressed in another way in the hope of Jaurès that war could be avoided by the solidarity of the French and German working classes through the Second International. The idea that the Left was 'anti-patriotic' brought the social and national questions together, and gave a special virulence to political debate.

The politics of the period after 1905 lack any clear sense of direction – Rebérioux speaks of a 'rotting away' of public life, and of the 'decomposition of the parties'.[7] Because both the Right and the Socialists were excluded from political participation, political conflict took place within the moderate and Radical centre, where there were two basic options: 'pure' Radical governments in the tradition of Combes, carrying out Radical programmes with at least intermittent Socialist support; and governments of so-called 'concentration' which appealed to the moderates and pursued policies of conciliation. Although they had formed a Radical Party in 1901, the Radicals lacked any real unity either of organization or of purpose, and their deputies were divided between two parliamentary groups. The line between Radicals and moderates was uncertain, and most deputies were in practice independents whose first allegiance was to their constituencies. In these circumstances, it was individual leaders who shaped events rather than party programmes.

One of these leaders was Clemenceau, who formed his first government in 1906 at the age of sixty-five. It was to last three years, largely through the force of Clemenceau's personality, for while he frightened the moderates by announcing an ambitious programme of social reforms, he became an enemy of the Socialists through his strike-breaking role as the 'premier des flics'. As minister of the interior in the preceding government, Clemenceau had already shown his mettle in dealing with the coal strike which started in the north after a mining disaster at Courrières in which over 1,100 men died, and with the May Day strikes of 1906. He chose to regard strikes as a challenge to the authority of the State, and was ruthless in using troops to suppress them. He also tried to break the CGT by arresting its leaders, both in 1906 and in 1908, after the shooting of demonstrators in a building-workers' strike in the Paris suburbs.[8] Clemenceau was hardly more conciliatory in dealing with the serious agrarian unrest in the Midi in 1907, a movement of protest by the whole local community over the collapse of the wine market; for once, the policy of repression led to the mutiny of a regiment, the locally recruited 17th infantry. Yet another controversial issue on which Clemenceau took a hard line was the right of civil servants to form unions and go on strike. School-teachers who formed militant unions were disciplined, and a postal strike in 1909 was broken and followed by mass dismissals.

The alienation of the Left by Clemenceau's relish for police operations, and his refusal to seem to be yielding to popular pressures, perhaps account for the nullity of his reforming record. His programme on taking office had included seventeen reforms, but only one of these (the nationalization of the Western Railway) was carried out, in 1908. Some of the seventeen items did reach the statute book later, usually after long delays in the Senate. They included old-age pensions (1910), and the already ancient income-tax proposal, reintroduced by Clemenceau's minister of finance Caillaux, passed by the Chamber in 1909, and finally sanctioned by the Senate in 1914. Progress with social legislation was not entirely absent, but it was painfully slow.

Clemenceau's successor was Aristide Briand, who shared his attitude to strikes, defeating the railwaymen in 1910 by mobilizing them for military service. The irony of this was that Briand had first made his name as an advocate of the revolutionary general strike; of him as of Millerand, whose path he followed, one might say that 'his robust careerism gave unity to his successive positions'.[9] Briand had entered Parliament only in 1902, and had established his reputation as a man of compromise through acting as *rapporteur* of the Separation Bill; his parliamentary skills were such that he was to hold the Third Republic record with eleven prime ministerships. After 1909, he came to incarnate the idea of conciliation or (to use his term) appeasement, appealing to the moderates and to 'men of goodwill' in all parties. This involved keeping the loyalty of Radicals, and exploiting dissensions between them and the Socialists. This was skilfully achieved through promoting the issue of electoral reform through proportional representation, which took up much parliamentary time in 1910–12 (the Socialists were for it, most of the Radicals against).

The rise of nationalist issues and the growing German threat made the idea of a government of consensus more attractive. But it was Raymond Poincaré rather than Briand who came to symbolize the new nationalist spirit, and his election as president in 1913 was generally interpreted as an affirmation of the patriotic mood. The great issue of 1913 was the Bill to increase military service from two years to three, which was opposed vigorously by the Left but accepted by the majority as an urgent necessity in view of the increases in German military strength. The fight against the three-year law tended to bring Radicals and Socialists together again. The Radical Left was now headed by Caillaux, the champion of income-tax, an ambitious and flamboyant politician who had moved over from the *Alliance démocratique*, and who favoured conciliation with Germany; as prime minister in 1911, he had negotiated the agreement which ended the second Moroccan crisis. At the Radical party congress at Pau in 1913, the party activists showed their hostility to the three-year law and the policy of 'appeasement' by choosing Caillaux as chairman. The prospect of a return to the Bloc, based on an alliance of Caillaux and Jaurès, could no longer be ruled out.

The election of April–May 1914 seemed to bring the prospect closer. It was fought essentially over the three-year law and income-tax, and was a victory for the Left. The SFIO had 103 seats, the Radical party 172; a group called the 'Fédération des Gauches', formed by Briand and other moderates like Barthou and Millerand, won only 23 seats. The electorate seemed to repudiate the three-year law, and Poincaré, who was determined to use his presidential powers in its defence, had some difficulty in appointing a government which would not repeal it. In the event, France entered the First World War under a prime minister, Viviani, who described himself as an Independent Socialist, and a majority of whose Cabinet were hostile to the law. Once war was declared, party politics were suspended under the so-called 'sacred union', and within a few weeks there were Socialist ministers in the government. Three leaders of the Left, however, were missing: Jaurès, assassinated on the eve of the war; Caillaux, discredited by scandal when his wife murdered the editor of *Le Figaro*; and Clemenceau, too prickly a personality to be included even in the 'sacred union', and forced to wait until 1917 for his chance to lead French democracy to victory.

CHAPTER 2

The social foundations

Though not established without conflict, the Third Republic was to last longer than any regime since 1789, and by 1914 France seemed to combine social stability, prosperity and the general acceptance of democratic values. Was this because parliamentary democracy was an inherently superior system, as its champions believed, or because its implantation was favoured by the special features of France's economic development and social structure? Gramsci's explanation for the stability of the Third Republic compared with the turbulence of earlier years was that in it the social implications of the French Revolution were finally worked out: 'the internal contradictions which develop after 1789 in the structure of French society are resolved to a relative degree only with the Third Republic.'[1] The Republicans would probably have agreed, and claimed that once the Republic was achieved social conflict was obsolescent. Despite the superficial instability of politics and the depth of ideological divisions, France had in fact one of the most stable, homogeneous and conservative societies in Europe; many observers have commented on 'the spectacle of a tranquil people with agitated legislators'.[2]

One reason why France escaped some of the social tensions experienced by countries like Germany and Russia was that she had already undergone a 'modernizing' social revolution, expressed in such things as the revolutionary land settlement and the opening up of society to bourgeois ambitions. These changes preceded industrialization and prepared the way for it, so that it could proceed without causing too much disruption. Economic growth in nineteenth-century France was in any case a relatively slow and even process, rather than an 'industrial revolution'. There has indeed been much debate among economic historians about the 'retardation' of the French economy and its possible causes, although this concept has been more popular with American than with French historians, the latter being more inclined to point out that French growth was slow only when compared with the rather exceptional cases of Germany or America, and that it occurred at a rate consonant with conditions in France – notably a static population and a productive agriculture which made large-scale food imports and the development of an international trade less urgent.

Nevertheless, many would agree that France purchased political and social stability at the cost of stagnation and of structural weaknesses in the French economy which showed up later in the twentieth century. The ways in which French society was affected by the nature of France's economic growth may be discussed and illustrated under four headings. The first point is that although the crucial stages of industrialization were over by 1870 many of its social consequences appeared only later, since striking advances in industrial production and concentration occurred in our period. French coal production tripled between 1871 and 1913, pig-iron production doubled between 1896 and 1914, steel production tripled between 1900 and 1914; the 5,000,000 metric tons of steel produced by France in 1914 hardly compared with Germany's 17,000,000, yet France's steel industry was an advanced one, and its most modern centre, in Lorraine, had been created from nothing in recent years.[3] The period 1896–1913, after the recovery from the depression of the 1880s, saw especially rapid growth in France, with an average annual industrial growth rate of 2·4 per cent.[4]

Second, while some areas of France were transformed by the development of factories and mines, a large part of the country was unaffected. France became not so much an industrial country as a country with major industrial areas, and the 'average Frenchman' still lived in a village or small town rather than an industrial conurbation. The urban population rose from 34·8 per cent in 1881 to 44·2 per cent in 1911, but it was not until after the war that the half-way mark was passed;[5] by 1911, France had only 15 towns with over 100,000 inhabitants, when Britain had 47 and Germany 45.

The third point is that France showed at an early stage the tendency of industrialization after a certain point to create employment in the tertiary sector rather than swell the ranks of industrial workers. In 1906, the percentage of the active population working in agriculture was 42·7, in industry 30·6, in transport 4·3, in commerce 9·9; but the figure for industry had been 29 per cent as long ago as 1866, and taking 100 as the base for that year the index of growth in 1911 was 105 for industry, 253 for transport, 155 for commerce, 118 for the professions and public service.[6] Since the population grew only slowly (from 36,900,000 in 1876 to 39,600,000 in 1911), the rise of the proletariat was hardly explosive – the number of industrial workers grew by 17 per cent in 1876–1911.[7] If the peasants were losing their status as the 'masses' in French society, they were giving way, at least in the short run, to a more heterogeneous society rather than to a new mass society of wage-earners. The multiplication of petty functionaries and small shopkeepers in France has a certain notoriety, and seems to be confirmed by the statistics: the number of people paying the *patente* (tax on shops and businesses) rose from about 1·75 million to 2·3 million over the period 1870–1914.[8]

This is linked with the fourth point, the survival in France of extensive self-employment. When asked their economic status in the 1911 census, 42·2 per cent of the active population described themselves as *patrons* (employers or self-employed), 44 as *ouvriers*, 9·3 as *employés* (clerks, shop assistants, etc.) and 4·5 as domestic servants. The 8·6 million Frenchmen who thought of themselves as their own masters were almost as many as the 8·9 million workers.[9] Most of these *patrons* were of course peasant farmers, but even in industry 23·4 per cent were self-employed, an index of the survival of artisan production.[10] Taken as a whole, such figures suggest that the individualist democracy of the Third Republic was successful because economic independence was a social reality, and the eighteenth-century ideal of a Republic of responsible citizens controlling their own destinies through the ownership of property had not lost all relevance. Property was the best basis of independence because it gave security (for the same reason, the salaried employments which enjoyed most prestige were those offered by the State), and the social values to which property and independent work gave rise could be shared by peasant farmers, artisans, employers small and large, shopkeepers and professional men.

The distinction between the salaried and the independent existed at all social levels, and is one of the complications in describing the French class system. The gradations of wealth and status in nineteenth-century France were infinite, yet the use of simple class terms and the interpretation of politics in terms of class conflict was a commonplace of the age. One contemporary spoke in 1870 of the 'clear and definitive division of society into two classes, those who possess and want to keep, and those who have nothing and want to take.'[11] This idea of two basic classes was a common one – 'bourgeoisie' and 'people' were the traditional political terms – but within the upper classes the distinction between the aristocracy or nobility and the bourgeoisie had been strongly felt in the first half of the century (as the novels of

Stendhal and Balzac show), and had been intimately connected with the political and religious struggles of that period. For class was not simply an economic phenomenon, but a matter of conscious adherence to particular sets of values, and class consciousness was not attained simultaneously by all social groups, but formed by political conflict; modern class politics in France were the invention of the propertied classes.

By the early years of the Third Republic, one can speak of a single 'traditional governing class' fighting to preserve its power. The term 'notables' is perhaps the commonest among historians today, and is certainly more satisfactory than 'bourgeoisie', for the challengers too were bourgeois, and the line between conservatives and liberals ran through the middle class. In his book *La Grande Bourgeoisie au pouvoir* (1960), Jean Lhomme argues that it was the 'grande bourgeoisie' who held economic, social and political power between 1830, when the aristocracy finally bowed out, and 1880, when it yielded power in its turn to the 'classes moyennes'. This perhaps underestimates the extent to which the aristocracy retained its social influence and remained part of the 'notables'. In the 1870s, the distinction between Legitimism and Orleanism still existed, and was based on the traditional class loyalties of the families concerned, but as the years passed it faded, and the conservative upper class came to think alike.

One element in it which was prominent at the time of the National Assembly was the provincial landed gentry, a class still thick on the ground in certain regions, which maintained a very distinctive set of values well into the twentieth century. They were Catholic, had a strong sense of patriotism and public service (generally frustrated by their reluctance to serve the Republic), and were inclined to see themselves as the last upholders of decency and tradition in a vulgar, materialist society. The romantic hopelessness of the Legitimist cause, especially after 1883, well expressed their social alienation. Some of them were small squires (*hobereaux*), but others were rich, and all retained some influence through their position as landlords. Land-ownership carried with it influence over tenants and other dependants, and a traditional position in the local community, at least in the many areas where there survived 'a conception of daily life and social organization founded on respect for the principle of property and for the hierarchy of ownership'.[12]

The richer Legitimist nobles, however, were absentee landlords who lived in the larger provincial towns or in Paris (traditionally in the Faubourg Saint-Germain) and visited their estates only during the shooting season. At this level, it is difficult to see much difference between the older families and the Orleanist ones, whose wealth came originally from banking or industry but who had also become great landed proprietors. Conversely, the nobility did not shun business activities. The agricultural depression beginning in the 1870s stimulated their movement into the boardrooms of industrial and commercial companies (and their willingness to marry bourgeois heiresses), but the phenomenon was not a new one: nobles had pioneered the development of coalmines, glassworks and ironworks on their estates since the eighteenth century, and in the nineteenth their local influence helped them to become railway directors (30 per cent of whom were noble in 1902).[13] That their role was not purely decorative was proved by aristocrats like the Marquis de Dion, who extended his class's sporting proclivities in a new direction by founding the Automobile Club and becoming a leading motor manufacturer. It seems true to say that by around 1900 landed and industrial wealth were integrated with each other, and that the topmost strata of French society formed a cohesive and powerful social group.

France therefore had something like an 'Establishment', and there are two theories of French society which are based on this idea. One is the notion of the '200 families' who controlled France through the oligarchic power of finance and interlocking directorships. This was a favourite theme of left-wing propaganda in the 1930s, but it was used as early as 1892 by the Radical Camille Pelletan.[14] The figure 200 probably came from the Bank of France, whose annual meeting was confined to the 200 largest shareholders; the Bank, still a private institution, was indeed a stronghold of the Orleanist financial oligarchy, and there were families who sat as Regents (directors) for several generations.

The hereditary power of a small number of families is also the theme of Emmanuel Beau de Loménie's book *Les Responsabilités des dynasties bourgeoises* (1943f.). Beau de Loménie argued that the families who had consolidated their power under Napoleon I had kept it ever since, and through their control of the banks, big business and the administration manipulated the real levers of power behind the façade of parliamentary life. In the 1870s, they were represented by the Orleanist Centre Left, who compromised with the new regime to safeguard their privileges, and perverted it thereafter through corruption in order to head off economic and social reforms. There is a good deal of exaggeration in this thesis, especially as Beau de Loménie explains all the Republic's financial scandals as manœuvres by the 'bourgeois dynasties'. But it can hardly be denied that the established classes retained a great deal of social and economic power, and that on the political side they remained strongly represented in the civil service, and disproportionately so (despite Republican attempts at purging) in such branches as the diplomatic service, the armed forces and the magistrature.

Nevertheless, their influence did suffer an overall decline. The landed wealth of the established classes was especially hard hit, as the agricultural crisis caused rents and land prices to fall, a movement which harmed the landlord much more than the peasant proprietor. In the Loir-et-Cher department, for example, rents fell 55 per cent between 1875 and 1902, and had recovered by only 24 per cent by 1914.[15] The importance of landed income also declined relatively as new sources of wealth grew. The social historians who have studied private fortunes find that, though the gap between rich and poor remained as wide as ever, the twentieth-century rich owned stocks and shares rather than land: agricultural land accounted for 43 per cent of private wealth in 1878, 23 per cent in 1911–14.[16] The smaller landed gentry became less and less representative of the upper class. The notables also lost direct political power, not only in Paris, but also at the local level, where the dominance of traditional authorities had been particularly well-rooted. In the local elections of the years 1877–81, control passed into Republican hands, and in future it was only in conservative areas that the local landowner was the automatic choice as mayor of a rural commune.

It is true that an important part of the upper middle class followed the lead of Thiers in accepting the Republic and working with it. But did they really turn it to their own use, as Beau de Loménie would argue? The episode of Casimir-Perier's presidency in 1894–5 suggests not. Jean Casimir-Perier was a member of one of the oldest and most typical Orleanist families, which still saw itself as 'bourgeois' and had rallied to the Republic. Casimir-Perier was the principal shareholder in the Anzin coal company (Thiers also had a major holding), and was seen by the Left as a symbol of capitalism. He resigned from the presidency after seven months because of his distaste for the political atmosphere of the 1890s and his reluctance to be a figurehead president. Men of Casimir-Perier's class (unlike their equivalents in Britain) no longer felt at home in the political world, and after the 1870s very few of the Republic's leaders came from the classes which had formerly monopolized political experience.[17]

Who then formed the new class which succeeded the notables? Lhomme calls them the *classes moyennes*; other historians speak of the 'bonne bourgeoisie'[18] – the 'middle middle class', prosperous yet distinct from the rich elite which formed the old upper bourgeoisie. At the time, the most celebrated formulation was that of Gambetta, who announced in 1872 that the coming of the Republic marked the entry into politics of the 'nouvelles couches sociales' – new social strata (not classes, for the Republicans disapproved of the idea of class conflict). Conservatives thought that Gambetta meant the masses, and accused him of rabble-rousing. In fact, it is clear from his speeches (he returned to the theme in 1874) that he was referring to those in the middle class and the peasantry who had increased in numbers and in prosperity through the economic growth of the previous twenty years, and who had established their claim to share in power through their hard work, competence and civic sense.[19] One can see here the idea that the responsibilities of citizenship should be associated with property and economic independence, and also the Saint-Simonian view that power should rest with the useful classes, who do the real work of society, not with the parasitic upper class.

The vogue enjoyed by Gambetta's phrase suggests that many middle-class people did indeed feel that their hour had come, and that the advent of the Third Republic did represent a real shift in the social basis of political power. To say that power passed from one layer of the bourgeoisie to another is of course much too simple, for great issues of political and religious principle were involved which cannot be tied to social class. Just as the liberal members of the old upper class rallied to the Republic, so there were many among the *bonne bourgeoisie*, especially if they were Catholic, who opposed it and voted for the Right. The bourgeoisie was not a homogeneous class, and the various occupational groups had their own traditions. Officials and magistrates tended to be conservative, while doctors had long been notorious for their Republican views. The professional classes – lawyers, doctors, journalists, teachers – were to dominate the public life of the Republic, yet it would be wrong to suppose that only they among the bourgeoisie supported it. Businessmen tended to abstain from active politics and were under-represented in Parliament, but there is plenty of evidence for their solid Republicanism. In later years the middle class as a whole drifted towards conservatism, but in the 1870s and 80s the Republican belief in progress and democracy reflected well enough the optimism of a rising class.

The French bourgeoisie was by no means a purely urban class. Land was a popular form of investment, and there were many middle-class people who lived in the countryside on the proceeds of their rents and their stocks and shares, or who looked forward to doing so after an early retirement from business. The countryside thus contained a ready-made set of middle-class notables who were in a position to influence the rural electorate, take the lead in forming local opinion and replace the gentry on the municipal councils. When the depression came, these landlords were more likely than noble ones to sell up and switch to other investments, and it is clear from local histories that by the end of the century the *rentier* class was tending to move from the countryside to the towns. But there remained, at a slightly lower social level, the indigenous professional and commercial men whom the life of villages and small towns sustained, and who were to form the backbone of the Republic's political personnel.

The middle class had been buying land for centuries, for one of the marks of bourgeois status was the possession of capital. The ownership of income-yielding property was still the only effective form of security against illness and old age; the bourgeois who had only his salary to live on was in a precarious position, and saving was a first priority. It was also essential if bourgeois status was to continue in the next generation: daughters would not secure husbands of the right social status without dowries, and sons had to be provided for either by handing on a flourishing business or practice, or by establishing them in professions which required an expensive education. The idea of the family as a continuing unit was central to the bourgeois ethos, and with their determination to create a 'patrimony' for their descendants the middle class shared many of the attitudes of those peasant proprietors who spent their lives saving and scraping to add a few hectares to their holdings. Property and its defence was a cause around which many elements in French society could rally.

Its importance as a political issue appeared at times when it was threatened: after 1848 and 1871, when the fear of the 'red peril' was coupled with the spectre of revolutionary violence, and when peasant fears of the communist *partageux* could be stirred up; and in a more subtle form from the 1890s, as hostility to Socialism and 'collectivism' became the main concern of conservatives. Many of the practical issues in politics involved property, and the bourgeoisie were alert to anything that threatened the flow of dividends or the accumulation of personal wealth. Hence the emotion aroused by railway questions (dividends being guaranteed by the State), by financial scandals which engulfed the savings of individuals, and by the question of income-tax. Foreign policy was also involved, for the French invested heavily in foreign government bonds; the defence of French interests in Egypt, or the maintenance of the Franco-Russian alliance, served financial as well as patriotic interests.

The upper and middle classes not only had a well-developed class consciousness, but were 'national' classes who thought and behaved in much the same way wherever they lived. Their secondary education, whether given by the State or the Church, gave them a common culture and made it easy for them to subscribe to political movements conceived in ideological terms. As one goes further down the social scale, local allegiances and diversities become more significant, and class consciousness appears to weaken. The group which came nearest to the middle class in its possession of a national political culture was the urban working class; the tradition of popular politics, though forced underground for long periods, had existed continuously since the 1790s both in Paris and in other older urban centres. It was a class tradition, in that it wished to take power from the bourgeoisie and give it to the 'people'; but the 'people' were not so much the factory proletariat (still rare in Paris at the time of the Commune) as the old working-class elite, and the popular democratic ideal was especially related to the way of life and the craft pride of the educated and articulate artisan.

This tradition was carried over into the new labour movement, but there was often a hiatus between the old popular politics and the new. Much of the industrial working force was recruited from the peasantry rather than the existing working class, and industry grew up in new centres without a tradition of political activity. Nearly all workers supported the Republic, but in the 1870s and 80s they still accepted bourgeois political leadership, though the working-class votes given to Boulanger showed the extent of their disillusion. It was in the 1890s that the breakthrough of distinctive class feeling seems to have taken place, and as the working-class movement developed French workers came to support trade unions which were rather aggressively class conscious, and political parties which fitted well into the national tradition of ideological politics.

No such breakthrough was achieved by the urban lower middle class, a rapidly expanding but still amorphous group. The unique rootlessness of this class and its susceptibility to the fomenting of extremist passions by demagogues have become historical clichés. The rise of anti-Semitism and nationalism provided some evidence of this phenomenon, but in France before 1914 the bulk of the lower middle class was prosperous and on the optimistic side in politics, forming the backbone of Radicalism. Those who were economically independent –

shopkeepers and the owners of other one-man businesses – shared the property ethic of the bourgeoisie and its political analogue, the belief in individualist democracy. Those who were salaried – clerks, shop-assistants, primary teachers and other white-collar employees – while aspiring at a middle-class way of life shared much of the insecurity of the working class, and their hopes of saving and building up capital were limited. Like the working class, therefore, they began to turn to collective action and to demand that the State should help guarantee their security; one of the most significant movements of the years before 1914 was the formation of trade unions by teachers and other State employees, and their increasing attraction towards Socialism.

The largest group of all, the peasants, do not fit into any horizontal scheme of social stratification. In a well-known passage, Marx explained how the peasants[20]

form a vast mass, the members of which live in similar conditions but without entering into manifold relations with one another . . . the great mass of the French nation is formed by simple addition of homologous magnitudes, much as potatoes in a sack form a sack of potatoes.

Marx was correct in showing why the peasants did not act as a class, but misleading in his implication that they were an undifferentiated mass. The true picture is complex, and demands some preliminary definitions. The term 'peasant' was commonly applied to all who worked on the land, and even to rural artisans and the inhabitants of the countryside generally. 'Peasant farming' in the more limited sense of a system of family holdings worked with little outside labour was characteristic of France, but by no means all the 'peasants' were 'peasant farmers' – there was a substantial force of landless or near-landless labourers. Moreover, the peasant farmer was not necessarily a peasant proprietor: much land was rented, and peasant farming could co-exist with large-scale landownership. The units of farm working (*exploitation*) did not coincide with the units of ownership, but over-lapped in a manner so inextricable as to make French landholding statistics notoriously unreliable and difficult to interpret (as well as infrequent).

The statistics for 1892 show that 75 per cent of all farms were farmed directly by their owners; but because many of these holdings were small, they accounted for only 53 per cent of the land area. The remaining 47 per cent was owned by landlords, who let it out either for a cash rent (*fermage*, 36 per cent) or on a crop-sharing basis (*métayage*, 11 per cent).[21] Many of these landlords were bourgeois with one or two farms, or squires with an estate confined to one commune, but there were also rich landowners with an accumulation of estates which made them leading figures in their departments, although the British style of landed magnate holding sway over a vast tract of territory was unknown in France.[22]

Agriculture occupied some 6,662,000 people in 1892. Of these, 3,604,000 were self-employed farmers, either owning all their land (2,199,000) or renting or both. But almost as many (3,058,000) made a living by working for others. They were divided between *journaliers*, labourers paid by the day, about half of whom had their own small patches of land, and *domestiques*, farm servants hired for longer periods and usually living in, often in very primitive conditions. There were 1,832,000 of the latter, though many of them would be young or single people rather than heads of families.[23] To this rural proletariat one should add itinerant and seasonal workers (an increasing number of whom came from abroad) and such marginal figures as the woodcutters and charcoal-burners who worked in the forests. The landless rural labourers were a silent and forgotten class, and they were the first to take the opportunity to migrate to the towns: the number of *journaliers* and *domestiques* had been over 4,000,000 in 1862.[24]

The 'rural exodus' was a significant movement of population, but in this period it did not undermine the social structure of the countryside. The population thinned out, and the labourers who remained could demand much higher wages – according to one authority they nearly doubled between 1880 and 1914[25] – but the landowning peasants stayed put. Indeed, it seems that in many areas the position of peasant proprietors was strengthened, as they were able to buy up the land abandoned by urban investors during the depression or the minuscule plots of departing *journaliers*. Thus France was able to develop as a modern industrial country, yet to retain at the same time a strong agrarian base dominated by peasant farmers.

Rural society was thus not homogeneous, but had its own gradations of wealth and status. The peasant proprietor might be regarded as the norm, but this term itself embraced many variations in the type of agriculture (winegrowers formed a very distinctive group apart) and in the size and fertility of holdings. There were also important regional variations in tenurial arrangements: in some areas, especially south of the Loire, peasant proprietors were the great majority; *fermage* was more common in the north and west; *métayage* was on the decline and usual only in certain areas. There were regions, too, where farming was being transformed on capitalist lines, with large farms employing many labourers, as in the wheat and sugar-beet country of the Paris basin, or in the new wine industry established in Languedoc after the phylloxera epidemic. As the next chapter will show, these local variations were reflected in political behaviour in an extremely complex way.

Peasants do not fit conveniently into the pattern of class conflict characteristic of modern industrial societies, nor is it easy to say whether they stand on the left or the right. They were not rich, yet they believed in property and order; they were not revolutionary, yet they looked back to the Revolution of 1789 as the source of their prosperity, and were ready to defend it against its enemies on the right. Their position was perhaps best summed up by Méline's slogan, 'neither revolution nor reaction'. The peasants had supported Napoleon III because he too seemed to straddle left and right; now the Republic won and retained their loyalty. A country in which contented peasant proprietors form one of the largest occupational groups is likely to enjoy social stability, and because of the French social structure the individualist outlook of the peasants was widely shared, so that the social foundations of democracy were securely laid. They were only foundations, for the success of democracy also depended on a super-structure of beliefs, ideals and historical experience.

One cannot explain the evolution of the Third Republic simply in terms of class, but one can suggest a schema which helps in understanding it. In the early years, the middle class and their peasant allies were still fighting to assert the liberal-democratic ideal against a traditional governing class whose power depended on the maintenance of a more hierarchical and authoritarian political structure. This struggle was won, and the parliamentary system which was established satisfied the desire for participation and allowed conflicts of interest to be resolved without the basis of society being called into question. But the alliance of bourgeoisie and peasantry soon found itself defending its essentially negative conception of the role of the State against new classes – the industrial proletariat and part of the urban lower middle class – who could find little meaning in the ideals of individualism and property-based independence, and who looked instead to the State to provide security and redistribute the nation's resources to their own advantage. By 1914, the older democratic forces were on the defensive, but they were far from defeated.

CHAPTER 3

The map of opinion

Class membership is only one of the determinants of political behaviour, some of which are so local or personal that only detailed empirical study can explain them. The analysis of political opinion during the Third Republic is complicated by marked and enduring regional variations, which are the main subject of this chapter, and by the lack of clear party divisions. The apparently simple terms Left and Right were constantly used at the time, but there has been much debate among historians and political scientists about how adequate they are, how they should be defined, and – in the absence of a historic two-party system – to whom they should be applied at any one time.

One common view, apparently supported by the polarization of opinion during crises like the Dreyfus affair, is that in the last resort the French divided into two parties, those who were for the Revolution of 1789 and those who were against it; Left and Right represented rival and incompatible 'ideas of France'. It is true that the terms were still used in this retrospective fashion in the 1900s, and even the most moderate Republicans felt that there was a sense in which they belonged to the Left. This was illustrated by the seating arrangements in the semi-circular Chamber of Deputies: by the 1900s, the Progressist heirs of the Opportunists were on the right of the political spectrum, but they refused to give up their traditional seats in the centre. The left-hand benches became overcrowded, and the Socialists were forced to sit on the right, where there was now plenty of room. Only new standing orders in 1910 forced the conservative Republicans to shift over and acknowledge their own conservatism.[1]

By then, new issues were cutting across the old politico-religious ones, and a 'dualist' interpretation of party divisions was becoming difficult. Most students of twentieth-century French politics explain the multi-party system in terms of the intersection of conflicting issues, 'the non-coincidence of a number of different dualisms of opinion'.[2] Such a concept seems essential for understanding the

Map 1   Provinces and departments

relations in the 1900s between the Socialists and the Radicals, the latter being left-wing on traditional political issues but more conservative on social ones, or for explaining movements like Bonapartism and Boulangism which seem to contain elements of both Left and Right.

For the nineteenth century, however, the dualist interpretation on the whole still holds the field. This reflects the influence of the pioneer of the study of French electoral behaviour, André Siegfried. Siegfried's classic *Tableau politique de la France de l'Ouest* (1913) was a study of western France based partly on Siegfried's own observation and experience; he was the son of a prominent moderate Republican politician, and stood unsuccessfully in several elections. Siegfried was especially struck by the continuity and stability of political allegiances. When studying election results in the west since 1876, he found that the percentage of votes cast for Left and Right fluctuated, but around an unchanging baseline. The stability was also geographical: the political frontiers between the west (which was conservative) and the rest of France, and between areas within the region which voted differently, remained the same over several generations. These observations were the basis of what is today called 'electoral sociology', a technique applied to the study of contemporary elections as well as the past. Siegfried's influence has meant that the question of interpreting election results and describing changes in party strength has become inseparable from the study of regional variations, and some of the most important scholarly contributions to the political history of the Third Republic have taken the form of local studies.

In order to compare election results over a long period, Siegfried introduced the notion of 'political temperaments'. Parties might come and go, but behind them lay permanent temperaments, represented by different parties in turn. Siegfried used this idea to link local and national politics, and to connect underlying structural factors with the political behaviour of individuals: each local community, in his view, had its own local temperament formed by the social and geographical features peculiar to it, and this determined which forces on the contemporary political scene its inhabitants chose to support. As a way of getting behind shifting party labels, Siegfried's concept of temperaments is obviously useful; contemporary political scientists speak in a similar way of 'political families' or 'spiritual families' – intellectual traditions and strains of social thought which have a clear history of their own, but which are incarnated by different parties at different historical periods. Siegfried becomes a little more obscure when he says that social classes too can shift from one temperament to another, and when he seems to attribute collective personalities to local communities (he also favoured the concept of 'national character').

Both the idea of temperaments and the dualist interpretation of politics were taken up and developed by the most influential figure in modern electoral sociology, François Goguel. In his *La Politique des partis sous la IIIe République* (1946) Goguel claimed that temperaments were more important than parties, and that there were only two of them. Parties can be numerous because they are based on abstract ideas, but 'temperament corresponds to simple attitudes, which are often unconscious and always irrational. . . . Temperaments are necessarily less diverse than ideas'.[3] The division between conservatives and men of the Left, pessimists and optimists, reflects a deeper psychological reality. Like Siegfried, Goguel was impressed by the way the relative strength of Left and Right remained stable over the years, and thought that in the last resort there were only two temperaments, which he labelled the parties of 'movement' and 'established order', rather than Left or Right. The advantage of Goguel's concept is that imposing a dualist classification on parties makes statistical comparison of electoral behaviour possible over long periods, and it has been used fruitfully by many historians.

Others have found it inadequate, however, because it does not leave much place for the 'Centre'. Most governments, after all, were coalitions of the Centre, and one may wonder why if the two temperaments had such a powerful hold there was no movement towards a two-party system. An alternative 'Centrist' or 'tripartite' interpretation has been suggested by Georges Dupeux. In his study of the Loir-et-Cher department, Dupeux found that under the Third Republic the bulk of the electorate were the moderates or *satisfaits* who voted for the *status quo*. There was opposition on the right from the old upper class, and on the left from those who still felt excluded from power. But it was only at moments of crisis that politics became polarized, and that the great mass of *satisfaits* were pulled to one side or another.[4] Since local conditions varied so much, there is no reason why this pattern should not have prevailed in one area while a more polarized one was found elsewhere where passions ran higher and class or religious conflict was sharper.

The practical choice before the electors was usually between two, three or at the most four candidates; if none got an absolute majority, there was a second ballot which was normally a straight fight between two candidates. In broad terms, there were four sorts of candidate:

conservative (what sort of conservative depended on the region), moderate Republican, Radical and Socialist. In the 1870s and 80s, the struggle would be either between a conservative and a Republican, or a tripartite one also involving a Radical; in the 1890s, the Right gave up standing in the areas where they were weak, and there would often be only moderate and Radical candidates. The appearance of the Socialists complicated the picture (though they too only stood where they seemed to have a chance), and elections with three or four candidates became more common in the 1900s. This was, at any rate, the pattern in the Isère department, whose historian Pierre Barral has provided a complete set of election statistics.[5] There were other departments, like the Haute-Saône, where neither Radicalism nor Socialism took hold, so that a simple two-party system prevailed throughout the period.[6]

There were some elections which centred on a single national issue, and which tended to create polarization everywhere – as in 1877, when in most constituencies there were only conservative and Republican candidates, or 1902, when opinion divided on Catholic/anti-clerical lines. But most elections were not like this, and because of the way the parliamentary system worked the voter could not generally feel that he was choosing a government or voting for a party programme or a national leader. Elections tended rather to be occasions for expressing one's underlying identification with a particular 'political family' or party. This is perhaps why the division of opinion between parties appears so stable, and it brings us back to Siegfried and the question of local divergences. Siegfried himself was fascinated by continuity: in his study of the Ardèche department in the south, he found that the geographical division between left-wing and right-wing voting corresponded in many areas to that between Protestant and Catholic villages; this division could be related to the diocesan boundaries of the *ancien régime*, and these in turn went back to tribal divisions among the Gauls.[7] To discover 2000 years of political continuity was no doubt exceptional; but it is not at all uncommon to find patterns of voting that have been stable since the first expression of universal suffrage, a continuity which is understandable in a rural society, but which is likely to be broken by urbanization.

Siegfried naturally tried to explain as well as describe the variations which he found. Having plotted the distribution of opinion on maps, he investigated how far it coincided with variations in geographical and sociological factors. (He was helped in this by the French system of counting votes at each polling place, which allows election results to be analysed for every village and for quarters within towns.)

Siegfried classified the factors whose combination produced the distinctive political character of a community under four headings, which remain as useful a way as any of approaching the subject: the 'structure of property', religion, the pattern of settlement and the influence of the State.

By the structure of property Siegfried meant the pattern of land-ownership and the relations between landlord and tenant. Western France was a right-wing stronghold, and Siegfried explained this primarily by the survival and influence of the landowning nobility. As one would expect, this element in the strength of the Right was limited in France by the predominance of peasant ownership, and Siegfried found that the areas in the west where peasant proprietors owned most of the land were those which voted for the Left; indeed, he laid it down as a general rule that such areas would vote for Republicans or Bonapartists, but never for conservatives who represented the *ancien régime*. For in parts of the west feudal society seemed to linger on even in 1913, and Siegfried gave a striking description of the 'inland west' – Maine, Anjou and Poitou – where the nobility survived in strength, the *château* and the Church were indissoluble allies, and deference to these traditional authorities was still the rule. The strength of conservatism seemed to vary directly with that of the landlord/tenant bond: the resident landlord had far more influence than the absentee, small tenants were more dependent than large, and *métayers* (still fairly common in the west) were the most subservient of all.

Comparison with other regions shows that the property factor cannot alone explain the regional variations in political behaviour. Some of the largest concentrations of property were in areas of central France (Berry, Bourbonnais) which were known for left-wing views based partly on agrarian discontent. But Siegfried's interpretation seemed convincing, for the area he studied was that of the Vendée revolt in the 1790s, when the peasants had fought against the Revolution under the leadership of the nobles. Recently, however, it has been challenged by Paul Bois in his study of the Sarthe department. The Sarthe department is on the frontier of the western region: its western half has been on the Right ever since the Revolution, its eastern half Republican. Bois argues that this division arose from the experience of the Revolution itself, and had political and ideological roots. The prosperous peasants of the west turned against the Revolution because they resented the pretensions and the land purchases of the urban bourgeoisie, while the poorer inhabitants of the east, who included many weavers, were more open to urban ideas. Bois claims that the

influence of the nobles was not a major factor, and particularly criticizes
Siegfried for seeing the peasants as passive material to be manipulated
by landlords or priests, without opinions of their own. Siegfried did
indeed deny that conservatism enjoyed real popular support, and
implied that the peasants would have voted Republican if they had not
been intimidated. Bois finds this implausible in view of the secrecy of
the ballot, and prefers to believe that the right-wing views of the
western Sarthe were a conscious and rational option. 'Siegfried was
the victim of an illusion: behind the apparent power of the great
landlord and the submission which he inspires, there is hidden a popular
consent whose origin is not in a bond of economic dependence but
comes from far in the past.'[8] The influence of landlords did exist, but
had to be earned in each case, and was an individual thing, not a network whose meshes kept a whole region in subjection. The work of
R. Arambourou on south-western France suggests a similar conclusion: the influence of notables depended on traditional loyalties and
the right psychological climate rather than their position as landlords.[9]

Bois considers that Siegfried's structural approach neglects the
weight of history, and criticizes him for falling back when other
explanations failed on 'the mystery of ethnic personalities'.[10] But there
is a certain mystical quality in Bois's own idea of a 'collective
personality' embodied in an 'inherited ideology' passed on over many
generations. As Maurice Agulhon says,[11] 'for a choice made in 1793
to be still perceptible in the twentieth century, the country must indeed
have a strong inclination to stability.' Yet it does seem true that memo-
ries of the events of the Revolution, and of who had gained and lost
by the revolutionary land settlement, were lively enough in the
nineteenth century to have a real political influence. The influence of
landlords has to be put in this context; perhaps it was only effective
when social conditions and local tradition favoured it, but one does
not have to suppose that peasants were directly intimidated by the
threat of eviction to see why the holders of landed wealth could
influence those dependent on them, and how habit and custom could
make deference to their views natural, especially when reinforced by
the influence of the Church.

Religion and the influence of the clergy formed Siegfried's second
determining factor, and even the rule about peasant proprietors
voting Left broke down where the clergy were powerful. An example
of a 'clerical democracy' was Léon, in the north-western corner of
Brittany, where fervent piety made the priests the masters of public

life. It was they who chose the candidates, and between 1881 and 1911 one of the constituencies in the area was represented continuously by priests – first the ultramontane bishops Freppel and d'Hulst, then the 'Christian democrat' *abbé* Gayraud; a neighbouring constituency was held by the great Catholic orator Albert de Mun. With popular support, the clergy could make their wishes prevail even over the notables. Elsewhere in the west, priests and landlords generally worked together in the Legitimist cause, and it is difficult to separate the two influences, though religious faith was by its nature a deeper and more permanent factor than the sentiment of deference.

In his study of the Ardèche, a department divided between Catholics and Protestants, Siegfried found that where the two faiths were in conflict religion inevitably determined voting, the property factor coming into play only where religious feeling was weak. This would no doubt apply too to the other parts of this region with substantial minorities of Protestant peasants, like the Gard and Drôme: the Protestants of the south had cause to be grateful for the Revolution and traditionally voted on the Left, just as the Protestant bourgeoisie were nearly always liberal or Republican. Protestantism was an exceptional factor significant only in a few areas, but since religion was the basis of old party divisions in France, and was the central political issue for long periods of the Third Republic, it is not surprising that historical religious allegiances should be intimately connected with political behaviour.

Here the findings of electoral sociology overlap with those of 'religious sociology', a discipline (established in France by Gabriel Le Bras) which seeks to estimate the intensity of religious life by studying such measurable data as attendance at mass, the recruitment of the clergy, or the popularity of Church schools, and to explain the variations that are found. Like electoral sociology, it can be used to study the present as well as the past, and has taken the form of numerous local studies. The map of religious practice in France is as complex as the map of political opinions, and there is a broad but far from total correspondence between the two, with the most Catholic areas tending to be the most conservative.

The religious sociologists define three sorts of area: actively Christian; those where there is religious indifference and only a minority (typically the women) attend church, but where Catholic traditions and forms are respected; and 'dechristianized' areas detached from the influence of the Church. The loss of religious faith in France was not simply a phenomenon accompanying urbanization, but had long been taking place in the countryside as well, and by the second half of the century a majority of departments fell into the last two categories; one tentative estimate for the 1890s is that only 20–30 per cent of adults (with a leaning towards the higher figure) were practising Catholics.[12]

Another distinction is between Catholic areas which accepted the guidance of their priests in political matters and those, often just as devout, which did not. The historian Jacques Gadille has drawn up a map illustrating this,[13] and it shows that in Brittany, for example, the clericalism of Léon was an exception: the Breton peasants, though celebrated for their piety, refused to allow the clergy to dictate to them on non-religious questions. In such areas, the intervention of the clergy could be counter-productive and produce resentment, and bishops tried to restrain the more zealous of their clergy. The right-wing political positions taken up by the clergy were therefore not necessarily followed by the faithful, many of whom accepted the Republic without question at an early date.

The third factor cited by Siegfried was a more strictly geographical one: the pattern of settlement (*mode de peuplement*). The distinction between 'nucleated' villages and a more dispersed pattern of rural settlement is well established. In France, the compact village was normal in the north and north-east: it was a pattern of life which encouraged communal activity and discussion, especially as these were the classic open-field areas where decisions about farming had traditionally been made in common. The village community of independent peasant proprietors formed a natural foundation for a democratic political culture and for emancipation from dominance by the notables. This was also true of the large 'urbanized villages' characteristic of the south. Many of these were communities of wine-growers – a labour-intensive form of farming which produces semi-urban conditions of life, and which encourages co-operation rather than competition. It was normal for winegrowers to stand on the left, and this was as true of the Burgundy area as it was of the south.

Those who lived in villages and small towns were not only stimulated to discuss public affairs and participate in them, but were also more open to urban influences. Advanced ideas originated in the towns and with the bourgeoisie, and they took time to filter down; it was the village artisans or the minor officials and professional men of the small towns who had a vital role in their diffusion. This is one of the themes of Maurice Agulhon's studies of the Provençal village and its 'sociability', part of an ancient Mediterranean tradition of civic activity.

This sociability was expressed in religious fraternities, in drinking-clubs (*chambrées*) which later gave way to the cafés on which local political life centred, in secret societies which paved the way for democratic party organization. The image of the southerner, passionately devoted to politics, always ready to take sides and to push principles to extremes, easily swayed by oratory (Gambetta and Jaurès are the classic southern politicians) has acquired the status of a cliché. Sociability, however, was not a purely Latin phenomenon. Strong traditions of civic and corporate life existed elsewhere, notably in French Flanders, where guilds, choirs and archery clubs provided fertile soil for the implantation of Socialist and co-operative organizations.[14]

By contrast, a scattered pattern of settlement was found in many upland areas (the Massif Central, the Pyrenees), and in the enclosed *bocage* country which extended in a wide band down the western side of France. In the *bocage*, farms were isolated and communications were difficult, many communes consisting only of scattered hamlets with no real centre. These conditions favoured intellectual backwardness, political lethargy and the influence of the notables – perhaps especially of the Church, which acted as one of the few foci for communal life. Siegfried gave a good deal of weight to this factor in the west, especially as the patches of more concentrated settlement tended to prove the case by being on the left. Since the pattern of settlement was partly dictated by the fertility of the soil, Siegfried was able to illustrate some striking coincidences between the political and the geological maps, and was sometimes tempted by a kind of geographical determinism. In the Ardèche, he emphasized the importance of altitude: 'above 800 and especially above 1000 metres, one votes for the Right, while below 300 metres one votes for the Left.'[15] The Ardèche was typical of a number of departments in this division between a backward and sparsely populated mountain area and the more advanced plains or river valleys.

The significance of Siegfried's fourth factor, the influence of the State, is perhaps less obvious. He argued that whoever controlled the machinery of the State attracted support for that reason, since 'the need to be on the side of the government as much as possible is a very frequent state of mind among the French, especially in the country-side.'[16] Thus once the Republic was established, it rested on this as much as on Republican conviction. The Second Empire had had the same advantage, and in a few areas able administrators had built up a support for Bonapartism which survived 1870 for a time, but whose crumbling away could only be delayed. Support for the State as such operated in two ways. First, there was the mentality of those who lacked strong political feelings but supported any regime that provided material prosperity. The classic case of this, according to Siegfried, were the materialistic Normans, whose temperament was reflected in their moderate and unideological conservatism. Second, and by contrast to this political apathy born of prosperity, was the dependence of poor and remote areas on the State for subsidies, favours and employment. These areas needed deputies who were well in with the government, and who could press the case for roads and railways, defend the local product or industry, and secure promotion in the various public services for local men. All deputies did this to some extent, but there were some constituencies where little else was required. Some of the poorer departments in the Alpine region had a reputation as 'rotten boroughs' which gave their votes to those who delivered most in the way of favours. Siegfried found this factor at work in the Ardèche, and showed how poor communities looked to jobs in the civil service, the post office or the railways as outlets for their sons, and how these petty officials were among the most enthusiastic supporters of the Left. Southern France as a whole provided more than its proportionate share of the nation's officials;[17] but Siegfried found dependence on the State in the west too, and described the special case of Brest, a town entirely dependent on its great naval dockyard and a Republican outpost in conservative Brittany.

After analysing the geography and social structure of the different local communities, Siegfried gave subtle, impressionistic and often memorable descriptions of their psychological atmosphere, their character and 'spirit'. In this he was really following the practice of the prefects and other officials whose reports on elections and 'public opinion' are a principal source for historians: encapsulating the attitudes of a town, a region or a social group had become something of a bureaucratic art form. Siegfried's portraits included the towns, although the urban electorate is obviously much less amenable to his methods. It is generally free from the pressure of traditional authorities, and the 'pattern of settlement' varies little. It might indeed be possible to relate the nuances of urban political behaviour to differing patterns of life in street and suburb, but this kind of study has hardly been started. We know far more about rural France than about the towns, though it was in the latter that modern mass politics developed.

Such manifestations of urban politics as Boulangism and nationalism caused difficulties to Siegfried, both because of the problem of classifying them on the Left/Right spectrum, and because their sudden appearance and disappearance seem incompatible with the notion of permanent temperaments. Siegfried therefore devised a special 'eruptive' temperament, which normally existed in a 'latent' state, but surged up from below at times of crisis. At the end of the *Tableau politique*, he suggested that there were five temperaments underlying modern party divisions: the pure Right, the ultra-moderate Left (e.g. the moderate Republicans in the 1900s), the pure Left (e.g. the Opportunists in the 1880s, the Radicals in the 1900s), the extreme Left (Radicals in the 1880s, Socialists in the 1900s), and the independent Left (his name for the Bonapartist-Boulangist-nationalist strain).[18] Four out of five were placed on the Left because they accepted the heritage of 1789. This was the traditional usage, still perhaps valid in the west, where one was either for or against Church and *château*, but somewhat obsolete elsewhere. In 1930, Siegfried was himself to use a more conventional Left/Centre/Right classification of parties. [19]

That Siegfried's approach retains its interest and vitality is shown by its use, in a more sophisticated form, in Barral's recent study of the politics of French agriculture. In order to explain the political attitudes of the peasantry under the Third Republic, Barral takes three variables – class structure, the system of interpersonal relations in the community, and ideology (i.e. religion) – and combines them in different ways to produce seven models of rural society against which the regional differences can be measured. Some of Barral's types recall Siegfried (e.g. clerical democracies), and he incorporates Siegfried's findings into a survey which takes account of the many local studies now available.[20] Barral has provided convenient syntheses elsewhere of recent work in electoral sociology, and Goguel has produced a collection of maps which is an indispensable guide to the subject (see Bibliography, section IIIA). Here one can provide only the most simplified outline of the political map of France and of the ways in which it changed over our period (cf. Maps 2 and 3).

The list of consistently right-wing areas was headed by the west. This block included Normandy, Brittany, the departments around the lower Loire and the northern part of Poitou (the political frontier ran through the Vendée department). There were differences within the region, as we have seen, between the submissive royalism of the 'inland west', the independent Catholicism of Brittany, the clerical democracy of Léon and the cautious moderation of Normandy. Normandy stood a little apart as its Catholicism was of a lukewarm kind, and it was social conservatism rather than religion which placed it on the Right –

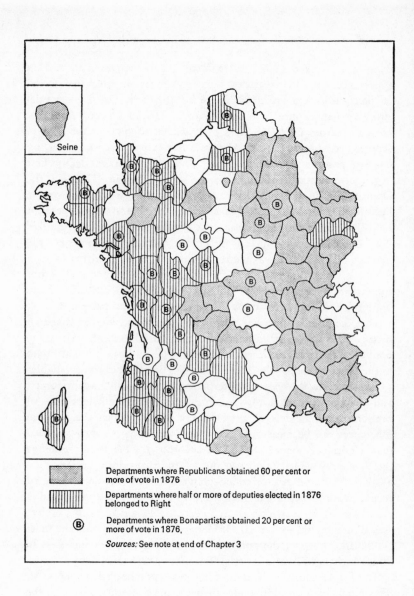

Departments where Republicans obtained 60 per cent or more of vote in 1876

Departments where half or more of deputies elected in 1876 belonged to Right

Ⓑ Departments where Bonapartists obtained 20 per cent or more of vote in 1876,

Sources: See note at end of Chapter 3

Seine

Map 2   *Left and Right in 1876*

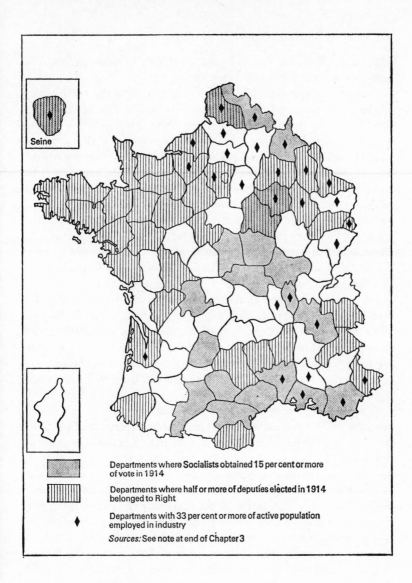

Seine

Departments where **Socialists** obtained **15 per cent** or more of vote in 1914

Departments where half or more of deputies elected in 1914 belonged to Right

Departments with 33 per cent or more of active population employed in industry

Sources: See note at end of Chapter 3

Map 3   Left and Right in 1914

one reason why the area had been receptive to Bonapartism, still strong in some departments in the 1870s.

Support for the Left did exist in the west – in the traditionally liberal and anti-clerical towns, in industrial centres like Brest, among fishermen and quarrymen. But there were not enough left-wing voters to send more than a handful of deputies to Parliament, and neither Radicalism nor Socialism made much impression on the region. On the other hand, moderate Republicanism did make many converts in the early years of the Republic. Siegfried noticed this, and linked it with a distinction which he made between 'quiet' and 'combative' elections. When times were quiet, men drifted into support for the *status quo*, but when passions were aroused opinions were polarized and those who had been moving away from the Right returned to their original allegiance. A particularly combative election was that of 1902, and the anti-clerical legislation of 1901–5 seems to have been a turning point in this region and elsewhere: Catholics who found a moderate Republic quite acceptable were dismayed by the sectarian Radicalism of Combes. There had been a similar reaction to the anti-clericalism of Ferry, reflected in the Right's gains in the 1885 election. Thus in the west, the Catholic departments of Ille-et-Vilaine and Mayenne accepted the Republic very quickly in the 1870s, but later returned to the right-wing camp.[21]

A second right-wing block was the southern part of the Massif central – the Aveyron, Lozère and Haute-Loire departments, and parts of some neighbouring ones. This was an area of peasant proprietors, but it was also one where the clergy retained their political influence, and this was perhaps the decisive factor. Geography was also important, for the political frontier followed the line of altitude: the area voting for the Right included the upland parts of neighbouring departments like the Ardèche and Gard whereas the parts which lay in the Rhône valley or the plain of Languedoc voted for the Left. Another right-wing area which resembled this one was the Basses-Pyrénées department, which included France's strongly Catholic Basque minority. The rest of south-western France, however, belonged to the Right in the early years but later deserted it.

As the west was the classic land of the Right, so the Midi was that of the Left. From the area around Marseilles (the Bouches-du-Rhône and Var departments) left-wing voting extended along the Mediterranean coast through Languedoc and inland to include Toulouse, and (leaving the Midi proper) up the Rhône valley as far as the industrialized area surrounding Lyons and Grenoble. It was a region of peasant proprietors, of religious indifference often turning to anti-clericalism (in turbulent cities like Marseilles, events like the inventory crisis could stir up violence), and with a tradition of political participation. In Provence and Languedoc, even Legitimism had not been an affair of landlords but had taken a popular and democratic form, reflected in the 'white terrors' of the revolutionary period. Some traces of this survived in the 1870s, but in general the Midi had demonstrated its Republicanism at an early date, by voting for the démocrates-socialistes (the ancestors of the Radicals) in 1849, by armed resistance to the coup d'état of 1851, and by voting No in Napoleon III's plebiscite in 1870. The fall of the Empire had unleashed a Republican zeal which the Government of National Defence had some difficulty in controlling (a 'Ligue du Midi' was formed by the Republicans of Lyons, Marseilles and other towns to organize their own military effort), and it was here that the Paris Commune found imitators. There were briefly successful Communes in 1871 in Marseilles, Lyons, Toulouse, Narbonne and the industrial centres of Saint-Etienne and (the most northerly case) Le Creusot. With this tradition (less deeply rooted, it would seem, in Languedoc than in Provence) it is not surprising that the Midi and the south-east became the stronghold of Radicalism, and by 1914 were adopting Socialism as the latest manifestation of the left-wing tradition.

Another consistently left-wing area was formed by certain departments in central France – Corrèze, Creuse and Haute-Vienne (which formed the Limousin region) and Cher, Nièvre and Allier. None of them was strongly Catholic, and some (Creuse, Allier) were 'dechristianized'; anti-clericalism was an important element in left-wing feeling. In the Cher-Nièvre-Allier region, there were many large landowners, whose hold was especially resented, as they applied an oppressive system of métayage through bailiffs called (with an echo of the ancien régime) fermiers- généraux. These métayers were almost the only true peasant farmers to engage in social agitation before 1914, and were joined in this by the proletarian forestry workers. Since this region also contained coalfields and industrial centres, it followed the south in passing from Radicalism to Socialism, and by 1914 the Socialist party was getting some of its highest votes there. The Limousin departments, however, where land was in the hands of peasant proprietors, did not continue to move leftwards in the same way, except the Haute-Vienne, which had an industrial centre in Limoges.

There were many departments which were Republican from the start, and which might evolve towards Radicalism, but would not go

further and accept Socialism. Typical in this was the large area surrounding Paris – the Orléanais to the south, Champagne to the east,
Picardy to the north. The southern and eastern parts of this region
were decisively 'dechristianized' and anti-clerical Radicalism flourished.
In Picardy, Catholicism was stronger, and there was more industry,
though it was dispersed rather than concentrated in large centres, so
that Socialism did not get much hold. This region as a whole remained
Radical until 1914, and was to become more conservative later in the
twentieth century. The Loir-et-Cher was part of it, and the 'centrist'
mentality described by Dupeux seems to have been widespread.[22]

An area which evolved rather faster, so that it was already on the
Right by 1914, was the east: the industrialized area of French Lorraine,
the Franche-Comté, Burgundy. It was a region of peasant proprietors
with a long democratic tradition – the east had not been won over by
Napoleon III, and royalism had no deep roots there. But the east was
Catholic, and it rejected Radicalism in the 1900s. Other factors were
the German frontier, which made the region susceptible to the new
patriotic appeal of the twentieth-century Right, and peasant conservatism. Ferry, Méline and Poincaré were the characteristic politicians of
the east, and it became a bastion of Progressist or moderate Republicanism. This was a significant development, for this modern form of
conservatism had greater staying-power than the traditionalism of the
west; the adhesion of the east rejuvenated the Right and helped it to
adapt to democratic conditions.[23]

What the Right gained in the east, it lost in the south-west, a region
with a less sharply defined political character than others. It was
conservative in the early years of the Republic, but Bonapartist rather
than royalist. This was an area which had benefited (especially the
wine trade) from Napoleon III's free-trade policies, and where
Bonapartist magnates like the Cassagnac family in the Gers or
Eschasseriaux in the Charente-Inférieure had constructed powerful
political machines which ran on for some years;[24] in the two Charente
departments, Bonapartism seems to have had genuine popular appeal
among an anti-clerical peasantry. By 1914, however, most of the south-
west was converted to Radicalism, a transition which may be explained
either in terms of an underlying temperament (democratic, socially
conservative, anti-clerical) which both Bonapartism and Radicalism
could satisfy, or as reflecting the dependence on the State of a region
which was beginning to decline economically as industry shifted to
the north and east.

The major towns and urbanized areas stand a little outside the regional pattern. Where the region had a left-wing tradition they fitted into it (Lyons, Marseilles, Grenoble), but elsewhere the towns usually stood to the left of the areas surrounding them (Nantes, Bordeaux). Two cases are of special interest – Paris, and the northern industrial area. Paris was, of course, the traditional headquarters of the Left, but it lost that position at the end of the century. In the 1890s, Radicals and Socialists still dominated its politics, but the popular nationalism which arose at the end of the decade found strong support in Paris, and in 1900 the nationalists won a striking victory in the municipal elections. The nationalist upsurge did not last, but orthodox conservatism was also growing stronger, and in 1909 the Right gained permanent control of the municipal council.[25] This changeover was due partly to the lower middle class turning away from their former Radicalism, partly to demographic change: the working-class population was moving from the old centre to new suburbs, and if the Left was declining within the old boundaries it was growing in the communes of the 'red belt', several of which had Socialist mayors by the 1890s.

The textile centres and coalmines of the Nord and Pas-de-Calais formed the nearest thing in France to an industrial conurbation, and by 1914 they were strongly Socialist. But this was due essentially to the growth of a new working class: there was no old history of Republicanism, and both royalism and Bonapartism had formerly been solidly established. The rural society of the area was Catholic, and part of it, in the Flemish-speaking corner of the Nord, was of the 'clerical democracy' type, electing the 'democratic *abbé*' Lemire. The industrial employers were also Catholic, and developed an elaborate network of paternalistic and charitable institutions which kept many workers within the Catholic fold. But in this area, the traditional pattern of politics was simply swamped by the growth of industry – by 1906 63 per cent of the employed population in the Nord were workers, and over 70 per cent lived in towns.[26] In the north as in Paris and other major cities, a twentieth-century pattern was emerging: an organized working class on one side, an urban and conservative middle class on the other, with liberal Republicanism and even Radicalism coming to seem irrelevant and being squeezed out.

One general conclusion of this survey must be that such 'modern' politics were uncommon. France was a rural society of great geographical and social diversity, and the political map was equally complex. Both Left and Right had their roots in history, and this profoundly influenced their development in the new democratic age. In particular, left-wing traditions were already strong among peasants and rural workers in many areas, and the geography of Socialism was as much influenced by this as by the growth of a proletariat: Map 3 shows clearly the divergence between industrialization and the strength of the Socialist vote.

The idea that voting was a collective phenomenon in which individuals were influenced by the character of the community, and that regional 'temperaments' can be identified with particular political attitudes, does seem to have some validity. But not all regions were as unchanging as Siegfried's west, and if the balance between Left and Right remained broadly stable on a national scale there was much change going on in the regions: the Right gained in the east and lost in the south-west, some regions moved steadily through Radicalism to Socialism, others remained fixed in moderate Republican or Radical positions. Demographic and social change played a part in these evolutions, as did the reactions of opinion to what governments in Paris were doing. But there was another influence of great importance which has not yet been looked at: political leadership and party organization.

Note on sources for Maps 2 and 3

MAP 2   Left: *Atlas historique de la France contemporaine 1800–1965* (1966), Map 213. Right: F. Goguel, *Géographie des élections françaises sous la Troisième et la Quatrième République* (1970), Map 3 (deputies classified by votes on installation of Broglie ministry, 1877). Bonapartists: J. Rothney, *Bonapartism after Sedan* (1969), Map 7.

MAP 3   Left: Goguel, op. cit., Map 27 (votes given to SFIO and the small *Parti ouvrier*). Right: ibid., Map 15 (deputies classified by votes on installation of Ribot ministry, 1914). Industrialization: C. Willard, *Le Mouvement socialiste en France (1893–1905). Les guesdistes* (1965), p. 331.

CHAPTER 4

Elections, deputies and parties

Universal suffrage was introduced in France in 1848, but before reaching maturity had to pass through a stage of tutelage by governments and notables. Under the Second Empire, there were 'official candidates' endorsed by the Emperor, and the influence of the State and its employees was thrown on their side in the campaign. In the Third Republic the pressure of the administration, though still important, was more discreet, but many voters continued to submit to the pressures of their social superiors, or follow their guidance willingly. The electorate was progressively emancipated from the influence of the notables, and the Republicans saw this as a natural consequence of the development of democracy, seeing the conversion of the masses to Republicanism (and to religious disbelief) as historically inevitable, and delayed only temporarily by the malign influence of the Church and the landlords. Maurice Agulhon speaks of the transition from a traditional 'vertical' socio-political structure based on patronage and deference to a modern 'horizontal' one based on the free association of individuals.[1] But, as he says, there was an intermediate stage of 'democratic patronage', and one may distinguish three phases in the process of democratization: voting under the guidance of traditional social authorities; their replacement by a new generation of Republican notables, who sought to take over rather than abolish the traditional means of influence, and whose political position was personal, not party-based; and voting for parties, with the programme and party label mattering more than the individual candidate. The shift from one phase to another could be quite rapid, and associated with specific propaganda campaigns or the influence of local leaders. Many areas were 'converted' to the Republic within a few years in the 1870s (Gambetta's speaking tours perhaps having a catalytic effect), and the new notables soon established their power after 1877. In the same way, the growth of Socialism can often be traced to the influence of individual propagandists or to agitation arising from major strikes. The degree of

61

evolution varied from area to area, but by 1914 most of France was still in the second stage; the formation of centralized mass parties had begun on the left, but still had far to go.

Where conservatives still retained their traditional influence, they did not rely so much on political organization as on their position as an accepted governing class; they expected to be elected, or to have their advice on voting respected, because of their wealth and experience and their prestige in the local community. The maintenance of this customary respect and sense of hierarchy was itself a central part of their political programme, and for Legitimists in particular the community which gave its submission to an active and benevolent landlord was a microcosm of their political ideal. The support of the Church was almost inseparable from the maintenance of this kind of traditional authority, and it was readily given. The relationship was a two-way one, for by supporting Catholic schools and by making his household a centre of charitable activity at times of distress (and election times) the landlord made the Church dependent on him while reinforcing the image of paternal landlordism and building up a fund of gratitude.

As we have seen, there were areas where conservatives succeeded in identifying their ethos with that of the local community, and they did not necessarily have to resort to open intimidation of their tenants, their employees, or others dependent on their wealth like local shopkeepers and professional men. Intimidation was made easier, however, by the imperfect secrecy of the French ballot. The government did not provide ballot-papers, but each candidate distributed ballots with his name printed on them, and the voter decided which to use. Clearly the different ballot-papers were not difficult to identify even when folded, and the votes were cast and counted under the vigilant eye of the mayor, who might well be the local landlord (or, of course, the leading Republican notable). Only in 1913 was the voter given an envelope for his ballot-paper and a booth where it could be inserted in secrecy.

The kind of influence that the landed class could exercise had two serious limitations. One was that men might be known and respected in their own localities, but could not easily transfer this advantage to a wider political arena. It was more common for noble landlords to become mayors or members of *conseils généraux* (the elected councils in each department) than to stand for Parliament, a tendency which had appeared well before 1870. The National Assembly, about a third of whose members were noble, was a special case; by 1910 the proportion was 9 per cent, and most noble deputies were modestly prosperous resident landlords who had no desire to shine in national politics.[2]

It is true that a new version of the politics of deference seemed to appear when industrialists created electoral fiefs in the areas where they employed labour. This was often due to a feeling that the interests of the enterprise and of the local community were identical, but many employers tried also to create an atmosphere of loyalty by allying with the Church and developing charitable institutions for the benefit of their workers. Mineowners were especially successful in this, and one well-known example of employer influence is in the Tarn department, where the Solages family battled for the allegiance of the miners with the Socialist leader Jaurès, often using violent and intimidatory methods. Another example is Le Creusot, a one-company town dominated by the Schneider iron and engineering works. The Schneider family lived in a *château* adjoining the works, and its head was mayor of the town until 1900. Henri Schneider was deputy from 1893 to 1898, when he was succeeded by his son Eugène, who sat until 1910. The family were conservative and Catholic, and since Schneider had become France's leading arms firm it is not surprising to find Eugène calling in his election address for a 'strong and powerfully armed army and navy'. By 1914, however, the seat was in Socialist hands. There are some indications that industrialists could only keep this sort of seat if they bowed to the evolution of opinion: they were more likely than other conservatives to become *Ralliés* in the 1890s, while in the Seine-et-Marne the Menier family of chocolate manufacturers, who held the seat where their factory was situated continuously from 1877, were calling themselves Radical-Socialists by the 1900s.[3]

The second limitation on the influence of traditional notables was that once the Republicans were in power they controlled the State machine and the patronage which it carried, and could dispense electoral favours in a way that the Right could not hope to rival. Siegfried, indeed, says that in the west the Right could keep up an electoral clientele through influence over jobs and promotion in private business, on the railways (until the Radicals nationalized the Western Railway, partly for this reason), and even in the army; but there were few areas where the Right was as deeply entrenched. As a rule, the loss of automatic support from the State authorities deeply undermined the position of those who regarded themselves as the traditional governing class, and even if they retained control of local government, the municipal councils and *conseils généraux* were feeble institutions compared with the prefects who represented the power of the central State and who acted through their executive agents the sub-prefects and mayors (for the latter, though elected, were also regarded as part of the State system).

The centralized State was itself a major social and political force in the French provinces. It had an army of employees who were found in every commune – postmen, roadmen, rural policemen, school-teachers. It was the source of funds on which communes depended for their prosperity – grants to build roads and bridges, to build schools, to repair churches and so on. Above all (from the electoral point of view) it was a source of patronage for individuals. The appointment of minor officials of all kinds, the granting of licences for tobacco-shops and bars, scholarships for promising children, the posting of conscripts to local regiments and the granting of leave at harvest time: all these were within the influence of the local administration, and they formed a powerful electoral currency. In areas hostile to the government, the prefects (whose duties included the preparation of election campaigns) used their influence to try to detach support from the old notables; those of the Second Empire had acted in the same way in some areas, and thus prepared the ground for the Republic.

In areas where the deputy supported the government, he collaborated closely with the prefect and sub-prefects to make sure that patronage was used to the best effect. A powerful deputy, indeed, could virtually make these officials his election agents.[4] Conversely, the government saw the deputy as the natural channel for the dispensation of patronage: 'it was the normal rule for my government,' said Combes, 'that in every constituency represented by a Republican deputy the preponderant influence should belong to that deputy'.[5] The system perhaps reached its height in the Combes era, for the Radicals were notorious for seeing politics as a matter of jobs and favours for their friends. This favouritism was not the only aspect of the system which could be criticized. It meant that the deputy was besieged with requests and pleas from individuals, and could spend so much time attending to these and defending parochial interests that his duties as a national legislator were forgotten. The constituency side of a deputy's work was certainly time-consuming, involving constant contact with the ministries in Paris as well as with local administrators, and requiring frequent watering of the grass roots, especially as elections approached. A conscientious deputy like the influential freemason Desmons dealt with over 3,000 requests in a typical year, and he or his secretary held a weekly 'surgery' in the constituency.[6] It could at least be said that the Republicans 'democratized patronage' by making the favours of the

State available to all through the deputies rather than only to those who had wealth or family connections.

This system of politics based on patronage and the personal influence of the deputy was to last the life of the Third Republic. In the early years, the practical task of Republicans was still to take over the machinery for their own use and create a new set of notables. One illustration of this is the way in which they challenged the traditional elite for the leadership of the agricultural interest. In the 1880s, an important movement began for the formation of agricultural 'syndicates'; these were not trade unions, but societies of farmers for such purposes as insurance, the co-operative buying of fertilizers, and in later years mutual credit. They were frequently sponsored by conservative notables and by the clergy, and it was the large landlords and industrialists allied with them (e.g. the sugar-refiners) who acted as the spokesmen of agriculture; the syndicate movement was one way in which they were able to retain a real influence over the peasants. But the Republicans also entered the field. In 1880 Gambetta created the *Société nationale d'encouragement à l'agriculture* as a rival to the conservative *Société des agriculteurs de France*, and the Republicans created their own syndicate movement patronized by local politicians, officials and school-teachers.[7] It was Gambetta, too, always acutely aware of the need to get the peasant vote, who set up a ministry of agriculture in 1881. One of the first ministers was Méline, who invented a special decoration, the *Mérite agricole*, often no doubt distributed for political as well as agricultural merit.

It was not necessarily difficult for the Republicans to establish themselves as leaders of the rural community, for many of them were landowners or well-off men who lived in the countryside. At Mazières-en-Gâtine, for example, a village whose history has been vividly described by Roger Thabault, the Republican mayor who took over in 1878 was a landowner respected for his wealth and position, and the village accepted his guidance on political matters just because he was a notable.[8] Other local studies confirm that in the first years the Republican leadership did not always differ in social terms from the conservative, and the fact that the Republic was able to win over such men seemed to guarantee its seriousness and solidity. It was only later – as late as around 1895 in the Isère, according to Barral – that the men of the *nouvelles couches sociales* replaced them.[9] In due course, however, political leadership came to be the preserve of a 'political class' of professional politicians with much the same social and intellectual background. This was most clearly true of the deputies.

The deputies were professional politicians in the sense both that they were paid (9000 francs a year, raised to 15,000 in 1906, a move which earned them much unpopularity) and that politics was a full-time career; few deputies gave up their seats willingly, and turnover was slow. The typical politician was a member of the professional classes, and most frequently a lawyer. A study of this subject shows that in 1881 some 41 per cent of deputies were lawyers, in 1906 37 per cent; at any one time before 1914, about a quarter of all deputies were advocates who had been practising at the time when they were elected. This was obviously a good preparation for a political career, and by the 1900s 55–60 per cent of ministers were lawyers.[10] Among the few prime ministers without a legal background were Clemenceau and Combes, both of whom were trained as doctors, another professional group notoriously over-represented in Parliament. As Bodley pointed out disapprovingly in the 1890s, the members of the liberal professions far outnumbered the representatives of industry, commerce and agriculture, which created the real wealth of France.[11]

Whatever their occupations, the deputies were overwhelmingly bourgeois by origin: in 1893, 85 per cent came from families in the nobility or the upper and middle bourgeoisie; there was a slight shift down the social scale in the 1900s, but the change from Opportunist to Radical dominance did not involve a real change in the nature of the political class. Mattei Dogan, the expert on this question, points out that politics was nevertheless a field where men of modest origin could get further than in other sections of the elite, and he describes the roads which led to a political career. One interesting finding is that a hereditary interest in politics was not confined to the Right, where seats might be handed down as fiefs from father to son: there were also Republican dynasties which provided deputies over several generations. Another way of entering politics near the top was through making a name in Paris as a journalist or an advocate in political trials. This was how many of the founding fathers of the Republic came to prominence in the last years of the Empire, and the phenomenon was repeated in the early days of the Socialist movement when advocates like Briand or Laval earned seats in Parliament through defending trade unionists. But for the average Republican, the usual preparation for a seat in the Chamber (or the Senate) was a career in local politics. The *conseils généraux* (and the less important *conseils d'arrondissement*) became politicized during the early decades of the Republic, and were an important political training-ground.[12]

Municipal councils, though part of the *cursus honorum*, were less politicized. At village level, the candidates were well known as individuals, and personal considerations predominated. The local issues frequently meant far more to the electors, and aroused more passion and enmity, than those of national politics, though they were often linked: the conflict between Church and State was mirrored in village quarrels between priests and mayors, and in disputes over such matters as processions, cemeteries, the ringing of bells or the repair of churches and presbyteries. In larger towns, politics were more impersonal and conducted on party lines. One point which emerges from local studies is that businessmen, if under-represented in national politics, were prominent in city administration, both as Opportunists and as Radicals. The urban elector seems to have preferred men of practical experience to run municipal affairs, and might choose more moderate councillors than deputies.[13] In later years, urban and national politics were often to be linked through the *député-maire*, who combined the two functions, but this was uncommon before 1914. The greatest of all *députés-maires*, Edouard Herriot, was only beginning his career in the Radical party; elected mayor of Lyons in 1905 (he occupied the post until 1955), he entered the Senate in 1912.

Herriot had been a school-master, and can perhaps be seen as symbolizing the entry of intellectuals and teachers into the ranks of political notables, a process often dated to the Dreyfus affair; the term 'intellectual' itself came into use at that time. Secondary and primary school-teachers were socially distinct, but shared intellectual convictions which made them natural supporters of Radicalism, and to a growing extent of Socialism. But they hardly displaced the lawyers and doctors from political leadership. Professional men were uniquely well placed to create an electoral following. Notaries, doctors and vets were the natural advisers of country people, and a successful practice formed the basis of many a political career. Some businessmen too shared this position, especially the numerous dealers in grain, wine, cattle and other agricultural products. The professional and business classes of the towns – especially of smaller market towns – were able to keep control of the rural electorate firmly in their hands down to 1914.[14]

The slow development of party organization was caused at least partly by the electoral system, which was a subject of perennial debate. The system introduced in 1875 was the single-member constituency (*scrutin d'arrondissement*), favoured by the Right at that time because it was thought to facilitate the dominance of notables. Gambetta and the Radicals championed the rival system of *scrutin de liste*, in which the department formed a multi-member constituency and the elector voted for lists of candidates; this was held to encourage the formation of democratic party organization and voting on national rather than local issues. Gambetta's attempt to change the system caused the downfall of his government in 1882, but after his death *scrutin de liste* was introduced for the 1885 election, only to be repealed again afterwards because of fears that Boulanger might sweep lists of candidates to power behind his name. *Scrutin d'arrondissement* was restored until 1919, but criticism of it revived in the 1900s. It was held responsible for the parochialization of politics, and for allowing deputies to turn their constituencies into corrupt personal fiefs through the manipulation of patronage. Gambetta had called *scrutin d'arrondissement* a cracked mirror in which France could not recognize herself; Briand in 1909 described the constituencies as 'little stagnant, stinking ponds', and called for a system of proportional representation (an updated version of *scrutin de liste*) to purify political life. Proportional representation was passed by the Chamber in 1912, but rejected by the Senate. The Radicals, who were by now the main beneficiaries of the existing system, were hostile; Caillaux saw it as a device to ensure the permanent rule of the Briandist centre with the support of big business and the Press.[15] It was supported by the conservatives and moderates and by the Socialists, who saw it as a way of increasing their representation and freeing themselves from compromising second-ballot alliances with the Radicals.

The second ballot was a feature of all the elections except that of 1871, and was necessary if single-member constituencies were to work in the absence of a two-party system. If at the first ballot a candidate got an absolute majority of the votes cast (and at least a quarter of the total including abstentions) he was elected; if not, there was a second ballot (*ballottage*) a fortnight later, in which two candidates were usually given a clear run. There was, however, no rule to force candidates to stand down, or indeed to prevent new candidates coming forward at the second ballot. (Electoral procedure was surprisingly casual: until it was tightened up after Boulanger, candidatures did not have to be officially declared, and candidates could stand simultaneously in different constituencies.) The candidates who stood down (*désistement* was the technical term) normally advised their supporters how they should vote in the second ballot, and the advice seems to have been taken. Alliances or informal understandings with a view to the second ballot were therefore an important feature of politics, and parties might be split on the choice of allies. In the early years, Opportunists and Radicals generally observed 'Republican discipline' and stood down in favour of each other against the Right, but in the 1890s this broke down; in the 1900s, some Radicals formed electoral alliances with moderates, others with Socialists, and the national party organization was too weak to impose a common line.

Serious candidates were put forward by committees representing the different parties, and these committees organized the campaign and raised finance. Each candidate issued an election programme explaining his position and stressing the issues he thought important. These declarations were often as significant for what they left out as for what they put in, and relied heavily on vague phrases which nevertheless indicated the candidate's allegiance to the voters (and to historians using modern techniques of linguistic analysis). The ambiguity of these election programmes, and of the party labels adopted by candidates, makes it impossible to express French election results in precise terms; often a deputy's real loyalties became apparent only when he had taken his seat, and votes on key issues are a better guide to the distribution of party strength than election results.

The candidate spent the campaign travelling around the constituency meeting local notables and voters, while his supporters distributed ballot-papers and pamphlets and put up posters. The local Press played a vital part in campaigns, and sometimes newspapers were founded just for the election period. There were no restrictions on expenditure, and much was spent; only on the Left were candidates not expected to dip into their own pockets. As elections approached, the charitable proclivities of deputies were reawakened, and for government candidates the manna of patronage and subsidy fell thickly. Treating voters to drinks was an accepted custom, and more direct forms of corruption were not unknown. The first task of a newly elected Chamber was to validate the mandates of its members, and there were always some disqualifications. Voting on this issue was blatantly partisan, and in the 1880s the commonest case was of conservative deputies invalidated for supposedly improper pressure by the clergy. The highest number of invalidations was after the 1877 election, when the Republicans took their revenge for the Bonapartist methods used by Broglie. In the 1877 campaign the government had revived the system of official candidates (personally endorsed by MacMahon), dismissed or moved unsympathetic officials, dissolved Republican clubs, closed down cafés where Republicans met, and so on.[16] These tactics were not to be repeated, although as we have seen the prefects remained the election managers of their departments, and did their best under the guidance of the ministry of the interior to use the machinery of the State for the benefit of a chosen candidate. Party organization was to grow from the electoral committees, but it was a slow process. It was the Right which was most resistant to the idea, although for a time the existence of pretenders provided the monarchist parties with some impulse towards central direction. Conservatives relied on candidates emerging from among small groups of local notables, and to some extent the influence of the Church provided a substitute for electoral organization. In the elections of the early years, both Left and Right relied on the Press to co-ordinate their efforts throughout the country; in the crisis of 1877, for example, the role of Gambetta's newspaper *La République française* in organizing the Republicans somewhat overshadowed that of the central committee formed by the '363' deputies.[17] Local committees were active enough, but generally dissolved once the election was over. This was the stage reached by Radical organization in 1881, and it was only later in the 1880s that committees began to be permanent organizations and to exist at more than one level.[18] They remained, however, essentially self-appointed bodies run by the deputies and local councillors themselves, and amounting to a system of co-option rather than of democratic participation.[19]

The desire of individuals to participate in politics was partly met by the formation of extra-parliamentary organizations devoted to political or intellectual ideals. These were generally called 'leagues', and the first of them was the *Ligue de l'Enseignement*, formed by Jean Macé in 1866 to support the cause of secular education; this flourished during the Third Republic as a kind of support organization for the State schools, and a defender of the secular (*laïque*) ideal. The *Ligue des Patriotes*, founded in 1882, had a stormier history. Originally sponsored by Gambettist Republicans to encourage patriotic propaganda and education, it came under the control of Déroulède, who turned it into an anti-parliamentary organization which supported Boulanger. The league was dissolved by the government, but revived at the time of the Dreyfus affair; from this time, 'leagues' tended to be right-wing, anti-parliamentary bodies, and they included the *Action française* movement. The Dreyfus affair also produced, however, the *Ligue des Droits de l'Homme*, the organ of the left-wing intellectuals, which became a permanent organization, unlike its conservative rival the *Ligue de la Patrie française*.

The most famous parapolitical organization of all was freemasonry. The power of the lodges was a favourite theme of Catholic propaganda, often carried to obsessive lengths and presented in conspiratorial terms. Freemasonry was certainly a Republican and anti-clerical organization; in 1877, the Grand Orient, the main branch of French freemasonry, deleted belief in God from its statutes. Until the 1890s, the lodges were generally Opportunist, but the movement was then taken over by the Radicals, and reached the height of its influence at the time of the Bloc; all of Combes's Cabinet except Delcassé were masons.[20] Its real importance was at the local level, where its leadership largely overlapped with that of the Radical party. The lodges provided a ready-made basis for Radical organization, and their discussions provided the Radicals with their policies, though in the 1900s some of them were inclining towards Socialism. It was not so much that freemasonry had an occult influence over the party, as that the two organizations attracted the same people.

Freemasonry appealed most to the middle and lower bourgeoisie, but there was also the *libre pensée* movement, which was linked with masonry and had more working-class support. *Libre pensée* societies were originally formed to give civil funerals to their members, and their activities included Good Friday banquets. This is a reminder that anti-clericalism was not a cerebral affair, but a genuinely popular movement with deep roots. As Rebérioux points out,[21] the 'Radical Republic' rested on a whole network of organizations with similar ideals: *libre pensée* societies for the small man, masonic lodges for the middle class, local branches of the *Ligue des Droits de l'Homme* and the *Ligue de l'Enseignement* for intellectuals and teachers, *Jeunesses républicaines* or *Jeunesses laïques* for the young; and, of course, the Radical party itself.

The inaugural congress of the Radical party in 1901, a result of initiatives by both deputies and activists, was attended by representatives of 476 Radical committees, 155 masonic lodges and 215 newspapers, as well as by senators, deputies and councillors.[22] Thenceforth the party held an annual congress, issued programmes, and maintained a rudimentary central organization. It had some of the attributes of a mass party. Individuals could join (though there was no proper system of membership with cards until 1913), and the local Radical committees extended political involvement downwards to such people as shopkeepers, minor officials and primary teachers. The Radical activist was usually a fanatical anti-clerical of the Combes type, and complaints began to be heard at this time about the 'tyranny' of the committees in provincial France. As in the Socialist parties, there was tension between the 'militants' and the parliamentary leadership; the Radical congresses at Tours in 1912 and Pau in 1913 rejected the policy of supporting centrist governments and showed a preference for revival of the Bloc.

However, the control of the party over its deputies was extremely weak. There was not even a single Radical group in the Chamber until 1914; the Radical deputies had always been divided between two tendencies, as was indicated by the clumsy full name of the party, the *Parti républicain radical et radical-socialiste*, and there were many who continued to call themselves Radical but did not join the party. Clemenceau himself had little use for the party, and belonged to it only briefly. All this reflected the realities of French political life: deputies could ignore central party organizations provided that they enjoyed local popularity and were supported by the local committees, which in most cases were firmly controlled by themselves. The Radical party remained (in Duverger's terms) a 'cadre party' or (in Max Weber's) a 'party of notables' rather than a mass party. As Weber pointed out, this sort of party was resistant to charismatic leadership, and it was certainly the case in France that leaders like Gambetta and Clemenceau were deeply distrusted by parliamentarians because of their ability to appeal directly to public opinion, and were kept out of office for long periods.[23]

The formation of the Radical party encouraged the moderates and conservatives to follow suit, but organizations like the moderate *Alliance démocratique* (1901) were even purer examples of cadre parties, hardly existing outside election times. The Catholic *Action libérale* party was rather more effective, building up a network of local committees. But for true mass parties we have to look to the Socialists: the Guesdist *Parti ouvrier*, modelled on the German SPD, had introduced the idea to France, and the united Socialist party formed in 1905 was by far the most advanced party in France, with its annual congress, hierarchical organization, official Press and disciplined parliamentary group. It was also a party of 'extra-parliamentary' origin, with aims which transcended the existing political system, whereas the Radical party really grew out of the activities of Radical deputies.[24] Yet even the Socialist parties were affected by the habits of French political life. The local *sections* and departmental *fédérations* had more real power than the central organization, and leaders like Jaurès built up a personal position in their constituencies independent of party organization. They could carry their committees and their electors with them in the course of action they chose, and the 'independent' Socialists who refused to join the SFIO in 1905 did not lose their seats.[25] In some ways, the Socialists were simply a new sort of notable capturing an electoral clientele from their rivals by appealing to new issues and using more modern political techniques.

The French party system – or rather the lack of one – had a profound influence on the mentality of the deputy, who felt that he had been chosen because he had the confidence of local leaders rather than as the anonymous representative of a political tendency. His first duty was to his constituency, which he served both in a general way (e.g. by getting it roads and railways, or by supporting legislation which favoured its agricultural and industrial interests) and in a multitude of particular ways. His supporters looked to him to channel patronage in their direction, and to help them in their dealings with the bureaucracies of Paris. In Siegfried's words, he was the mediator between the citizen and the distant, mysterious State, and the 'ambassador of his constituency in the capital'.[26] A deputy who performed this role skilfully could build up an impregnable position in his local stronghold. The danger of parochialism existed, but it could also be the case that provided a deputy defended local interests successfully his electors would give him a free hand and trust his judgment over complex national issues.[27] In any case, it was with a marked sense of independence and self-importance that the typical deputy took his seat in Paris.

CHAPTER 5

Parliamentary politics

The constitution of 1875 was both the longest lasting and the least systematic constitution in French history, and it operated in a way rather different from its authors' intentions. The conservative National Assembly had hoped to moderate universal suffrage through the balancing institutions of Presidency and Senate, but in practice the system became one of parliamentary sovereignty, with governments made and unmade by the Chamber of Deputies and lacking independent executive authority. President and Senate were overshadowed, though both retained a good deal of influence. It was the *Seize Mai* crisis of 1877 which was largely responsible for this evolution, by ruling out the concept of a dual responsibility of governments to president and Chamber, and by discrediting the weapon of dissolution. Presidents retained the power to dissolve the Chamber (with the consent of the Senate), but it was never again used, and governments were deprived of a means of disciplining their parliamentary majority.

Presidents were elected for seven years by the Senate and Chamber together (for this purpose, and for constitutional revision, they met in joint session at Versailles and were called the *Assemblée nationale*). The candidacies of leading politicians usually failed (e.g. Ferry in 1887), and obscure but worthy provincial figures were preferred; but there was a reaction against this tendency with the election of Poincaré in 1913. The first Republican president, Grévy, had been one of the leaders of the party, and was no mere figurehead. One of the President's duties was choosing prime ministers when governments fell, and the fluidity of French politics gave him considerable freedom of choice. He could not impose his own candidate on a hostile Chamber (though Poincaré tried this with Ribot in 1914), but he could keep out men he disliked. Grévy acted thus to delay the advent to office of Gambetta, and was able to give three terms of office to his own candidate, the pliable Freycinet. Grévy has been blamed for perverting the parliamentary system from the start by refusing to appoint the natural leader of the majority, but in practice there was rarely a clear majority for the president to submit to. Grévy also encouraged the practice of ministers from one Cabinet staying on in the next, which provided stability but at the cost of the principle of collective responsibility.[1] When governments were short-lived, the presidents themselves formed an element of continuity. The constitution allowed them to preside at Cabinet meetings, and their advice and experience could be important. This was especially so in foreign affairs, where the presidents had certain prerogatives under the constitution and were usually better informed than ministers. The role of Poincaré on the eve of 1914 again provides the example, and Poincaré indeed seems to have hoped to strengthen the executive by systematic use of the powers of the Presidency.

The powers of the Senate also evolved over the years. In order to make it a conservative body, the constitution had provided that a quarter of its members should be appointed for life, and that the rest should be indirectly elected. The senatorial electors were the deputies in each department, the members of *conseils généraux* and *conseils d'arrondissement*, and delegates from each commune, which guaranteed an enormous rural preponderance. The Senate was renewed by thirds every three years, to insulate it from sudden shifts of opinion. Although Republicans were traditionally hostile to the very principle of a second chamber, Gambetta had persuaded the majority to accept this Senate, arguing that it would be a 'grand council of the communes' embodying the democratic spirit of village politics.[2] The Radicals remained hostile, but the issue ceased to be an important one after the method of choosing senators was changed in 1884 (the only significant revision of the constitution in the life of the Third Republic): there were to be no new life senators, and communes were to be represented in the electoral colleges in proportion to their population. The Senate was still biased towards rural France, and the system guaranteed also that most senators were members of the 'political class', local politicians or veteran deputies rather than men of eminence in other fields. This gave the Senate a provincial and old-fashioned flavour, and it struck observers like Bodley as resembling 'a retreat for elderly men of education' rather than an active legislative body.[3]

In fact, the legislative powers of the Senate were co-extensive with those of the Chamber, and there was no machinery to prevent it delaying legislation indefinitely. Financial bills had to be initiated in the Chamber, but the Senate established the right to amend them. Similarly, although the formation of ministries was a matter for the

Chamber the Senate asserted its right to defeat them. The first notable case of this was the Radical Bourgeois government of 1895-6, which the Senate disapproved of because of its income-tax proposals; Bourgeois resigned rather than test the constitutional issue. The Senate was to succeed in delaying an income-tax until 1914, and used its delaying powers in the same way against social measures like the pensions legislation of 1910, first passed by the Chamber in 1906. The way the Senate was chosen meant that it lagged a generation behind the opinion of the country. No Socialist senator appeared until 1906, and although the majority of senators were Radical in the 1900s they were old-fashioned Radicals devoted to private enterprise and the rights of property. They were also firmly anti-clerical, and conservative on constitutional questions; the Senate rejected proportional representation, and in later years it was to oppose giving votes to women. (France had a suffrage movement, but it made little political impact before 1914.)[4] In 1914, the conservative mentality of the Senate was perhaps less unrepresentative of the country than it was to appear after the war, but it was already making much more use of its obstructive powers than in the Republic's early years.

Nevertheless, the Chamber was the real centre of political life. In a parliamentary system, the functions of the legislative body go beyond legislation itself, and include the accurate and sensitive reflection of public opinion, forming governments and providing them with the support needed to govern effectively, controlling the executive, and acting as a forum for the adjustment of interests and the peaceful solution of conflicts. How successful was the French Parliament in performing these functions, and how far was it the real centre of power in view of the influence of pressure-groups, of a powerful bureaucracy, and of rival opinion-forming agencies like the Press?

It is difficult to deny the success of the French system in giving representation to opinion in all its ideological and geographical diversity. In the early years, the Chamber was really a collection of individuals loosely united by their adherence to sets of principles, and (in theory at least) highly responsive to their electors' views. Constitutional purists, indeed, disapproved of parties and parliamentary groups because they falsified the direct operation of universal suffrage and fettered the independence of the deputy. Deputies did form parliamentary groups, but the boundaries between them were clearer in the National Assembly, when they were based on the varieties of monarchism, than in the 1880s and 90s when most deputies thought of themselves primarily as Republicans. Many did not join any group, while others belonged to more than one. In the 1900s, the lines between groups became more distinct, and in 1910 the Chamber decided to recognize groups officially, and obliged every member to join one and only one. In 1910–14, there were usually ten groups, including a 'group for deputies who are not members of a group' (cf. Appendix 1).[5]

With a few exceptions, like the Socialist party group, these groups were not like disciplined parties, and it is not surprising that the French Parliament lacked firm majorities, and that a system of unstable and short-lived governments developed. The only exception was during the period of Waldeck-Rousseau and Combes, when four major groups agreed to work together and institutionalized their co-operation in the *délégation des gauches*. In the 1880s, on the other hand, when a cohesive Republican majority might seem to have existed, personal rivalries and the deputies' sense of independence prevented any permanent leadership from developing. Every government started with a majority, but there was normally nothing to guarantee that this majority would not disappear if individual deputies or groups became disaffected. Parliamentary procedure made it quite easy to defeat governments, the classic weapon being the 'interpellation' debate. The interpellation procedure allowed any deputy to initiate a debate on a particular question, and the vote on it could easily be turned into a vote of confidence or censure. Sometimes governments arranged such debates in order to demonstrate that their majority still existed, sometimes dissidents within the coalition staged them to bring it to an end; sometimes defeat came unexpectedly, opinion being swayed by the emotions and rhetoric of the debate. In principle, governments needed to resign only when the question of confidence had been formally posed, but few prime ministers made much effort to fight back once it was clear that their majority was crumbling, and some even resigned for tactical reasons (with an eye to returning later) when it still appeared intact.

The manifold ways of bringing down governments have been documented in Soulier's detailed study of 'ministerial instability'. But instability did not necessarily mean chaos or the breakdown of government: even at times when the turnover of ministries was high, there were not the long and debilitating 'ministerial crises' of the 1930s or the Fourth Republic. Behind the façade of instability, there were important elements of continuity, notably the fact that 'ministerial instability was accompanied by the stability of ministers'.[6] Ministers were drawn from a small pool, and the same faces reappeared in different Cabinets. When a government fell, it was normal for several of its members to join the next Cabinet, and they might include the prime minister himself, returning to the ranks. Cabinets formed by this process of *replâtrage* were common, while those whose membership was entirely new – e.g. the Bourgeois government of 1895 – were regarded as an unusual phenomenon. The real turning-points in politics have to be sought, therefore, when one 'team' of politicians which has provided the ministerial personnel for a number of years gives way to another.[7]

It was also common for certain ministries to be held by the same person through several governments, providing another element of continuity. This was especially true of the foreign office, where some degree of permanence was obviously desirable. Delcassé, who held the post in six Cabinets between 1898 and 1905, was the best but not the only example of this. The same was true of certain technical ministries, like the ministry of posts, held by the obscure Cochery in eight successive governments (1879–85). The number of ministerial posts available was in any case small – around eleven on average, with a few under-secretaryships. Some posts went to senators, and the ministries of war and marine were frequently held by generals and admirals. The pickings for deputies were therefore not extensive, and this accentuated the monopoly held by the ministerial cliques. It does not seem that the Chamber's readiness to overthrow governments can be explained by hunger for jobs; most deputies were content to remain 'backbenchers' as long as they knew that the government was at the mercy of their votes.

A system of relatively unstable governments based on shifting coalitions has a number of consequences for political life. One is that there is no clear relationship between the majority in the country, as expressed in elections, and the majority in Parliament. Parties which form second-ballot alliances in an election do not necessarily work together once Parliament has met, and the play of alliances can produce governments of quite different political complexions in the lifetime of one legislature (e.g. that of 1893). Governments are made and unmade by the professionals, in manœuvres which fascinate the initiated but tend to produce disillusion and anti-parliamentary feelings among the electorate. To bring about a closer correspondence between elections and the formation of governments was one of the aims of electoral reformers, especially those like Gambetta who looked forward to the growth of a two-party system in France.

The period of the Bloc was one when electoral alliances held through the lifetime of the legislature. At other times, it is possible to discern a real but less direct connection with opinion in the country. Soulier, for example, suggested that the initial majority gradually broke up in the course of a legislature in favour of a coalition of the centres, but tended to reconstitute itself as the next election approached, producing an alternation between polarized and centrist phases.[8] Mayeur, on the other hand, says of the 1893 legislature that the natural 'moderate' majority produced by the election emerged only after some years when various alternatives had been tried and found wanting.[9] One rule that does seem valid is that coalitions of the centre were a natural development within Parliament, but were difficult to translate into electoral terms, the electors preferring to keep the old party divisions alive; the *Ralliés*, for example, found that they could not form alliances with moderate Republicans in the 1898 election, and that the spirit of *ralliement* was not as popular with Catholic electors as with Catholic deputies.

A second consequence of the system of coalition governments is that it gives a special advantage to parties in the centre of the spectrum, whose support is needed for any successful government and who will rarely feel inclined to deny it on grounds of principle. In the twentieth century, the Radicals became the main beneficiaries of this, just as it was they who gained most by second-ballot electoral alliances. In the same way, the system favoured the emergence of a particular kind of leader – or 'anti-leader':[10] the man who was adept at smoothing over differences and working out compromises, affable to deputies in the lobbies and purlieus of the Chamber. Masters of these emollient skills like Briand enjoyed long ministerial careers, and in the long run the system tended to discourage able men in favour of second-rate and inoffensive ones, and to prevent the office of prime minister developing real authority; the prime minister was only *primus inter pares*, and the office was always combined with holding a normal ministerial portfolio.

Another consequence linked with this was that coalition inhibited firm government and the formulation of policy on a long-term basis. Decisive action could always offend part of the government's majority, and it was difficult to impose unpopular but statesmanlike policies on deputies who were always looking over their shoulders to their constituencies. Before 1914, however, France did not face the international and economic problems which made the weak leadership and 'immobilism' of the 1930s so disastrous. The majority of Frenchmen did not want strong governments or reforming legislation, but valued their independence and preferred to be left alone. In Siegfried's words, the system was one which worked and which was 'adapted to the needs, the inclinations and even the failings of the French people'.[11]

The process of legislation took up much of the time of Parliament, and most of the great controversies of the period centred on legislative proposals; yet introducing such proposals was not really seen as a major function of governments. With a few exceptions (e.g. Clemenceau in 1906) governments did not take office with a fixed programme of reforms, and even when they did few of the reforms were carried out. By the 1900s France seemed to be distinguished from other industrial countries by its legislative lethargy, especially on social questions. Lack of political will rather than problems of parliamentary procedure seems the real cause of this, for when the will existed contentious legislation could be carried rapidly against even the fiercest opposition, as was shown by the anti-clerical laws of Ferry and Combes and by the three-year law. But it was true that the legislative procedure gave great scope for the obstructionism of vested interests.

The procedure made a programme of government legislation especially difficult to carry through. The government did not control the parliamentary timetable, and government bills had only limited priority. The central feature of the legislative process was the system of committees (*commissions*). Every Bill passed through a committee before coming to general debate, and might be indefinitely delayed or extensively amended. At the next stage, it was the committee's version of the Bill rather than the government's original proposal that was debated, and the *rapporteur* of the committee who conducted the debate rather than the appropriate minister. In any case, by the time a Bill emerged from committee the government had frequently changed, and Bills could be carried over from one legislature to another. Legislation was therefore a process largely independent of changes of government, and was in the hands of the deputies as a body, not controlled by the executive. Individual deputies also had unlimited power to present private bills, and used it profusely.[12]

Committees were originally appointed on an *ad hoc* basis for each bill, but a system of standing committees for different areas of policy soon grew up, and was officially recognized in 1902; from 1910, members were chosen in proportion to the parliamentary groups. It was in the committees that much of the real work of the Chamber was done, and they were a way for ambitious deputies to gain a reputation as experts and stake a claim to ministerial office. The most powerful of all was the budget committee, which used its position to review the whole field of government policy, and presented elaborate reports, which often delayed the voting of the budget itself. The chairman of the budget committee was an influential figure: in 1877–81, it was Gambetta, and there were certain men who through chairmanship of the Senate or Chamber committees and spells of office as minister of finance built up a reputation as experts in the mysteries of finance. They included Léon Say and Rouvier, both able spokesmen for private enterprise who had the confidence of business interests, and the very different Caillaux, the champion of income-tax, who was able to boast that 'whether in office or out of it, I dominated financial policy between 1899 and 1914, and imposed my ideas'.[13]

Since there was a standing committee corresponding approximately to each ministry, they were a means by which Parliament sought to control the bureaucracy, but were not very effective in this task. The machinery of the centralized State was ancient and powerful, and it has often been said that ministerial instability did not affect the continuity of policy because the bureaucrats did the real work of governing the country. It was obviously difficult for a minister who stayed only a few months to make much impression on policy, and most were perhaps more interested in administering the patronage which their ministry commanded. After about 1900, the development of *cabinets*, private offices staffed by young men outside the bureaucratic hierarchy, was a symptom of the desire for more political control.[14] Historians have neglected the policy-making activities of civil servants, but one may mention a few names: Charles Dumay, director of the *administration des cultes* from 1887 to 1906, who guided the relations of Church and State under the Concordat;[15] Arthur Fontaine, who at the *Office du travail* (which in 1906 became the ministry of labour) inspired much labour legislation between 1891 and 1920;[16] and Ferdinand Buisson, director of primary education from 1879 to 1896 and theorist of the *école laïque*, who later became a Radical deputy and a luminary of the *Ligue de l'Enseignement* and *Ligue des Droits de l'Homme*.

The training and background of the top civil servants gave them a strong *esprit de corps*. Recruitment was by examination, though political influence still counted for much, and for the best jobs it was almost essential to have attended the *Ecole libre des sciences politiques*, founded in 1871. Between 1901 and 1935 this school provided the *Conseil d'Etat* and the *inspection des finances* with 98 per cent of their entry, the diplomatic service with 88 per cent, and the *Cour des Comptes* with 87 per cent (these were the four so-called *grands corps*). Since it was a private and expensive institution, recruitment was virtually restricted to an upper-middle-class elite.[17]

There was one field, foreign policy, where the continuity of policy and the influence of the officials were especially marked. Parliamentary debates on foreign affairs were rare, and the relevant committee (which also covered the colonies) was one of the weakest. Here the constitution gave governments independent executive power, for it was the president who negotiated and ratified treaties, and only certain kinds of treaty required parliamentary approval; where the interests and security of the State were concerned, treaties might be kept secret. Thus the terms of the Franco-Russian alliance, the basis of foreign policy for twenty years and arguably the reason for France's involvement in war in 1914, were known to only a handful of men and were never debated in Parliament. A minister like Delcassé could have a real influence on policy because of his relatively permanent tenure, but he himself virtually ignored Parliament and the Cabinet; foreign ministers were most successful when their ideas coincided with those of the Quai d'Orsay.

The feeling was that foreign affairs were 'above politics', and that a partisan approach would encourage France's enemies. Much of the activity of the army and navy escaped civilian scrutiny for the same reason, at least until the Dreyfus affair. The laws on conscription were a politically controversial matter, but military policy proper was left to the generals, and Parliament generally voted whatever credits were requested for arms and equipment. Civilian control undoubtedly existed in principle (though its chief representative, the minister of war, was always a general until 1888), but in practice the army was seen as an untouchable 'ark of the covenant' and given a potentially dangerous autonomy.

The same was true of the colonies, although here the operative factor was lack of general interest rather than patriotic bipartisanship. After the controversy over Ferry's policies had died down, French colonial expansion went ahead steadily with little interference from Parliament, and in some cases was decided by the initiatives of the soldiers and officials on the spot. One has also to reckon here with the influence of 'one of the most powerful pressure groups in the history of the Third Republic',[18] the 'colonial party'. The core of the colonial party was the 'colonial group' which brought together deputies of all parties interested in colonial expansion, and which at the height of its influence in 1902 had nearly 200 members. It was linked with outside bodies like the *Comité de l'Afrique française*, which organized expeditions in Africa and was supported by imperially minded geographers and propagandists, and the *Union coloniale française*, representing business interests. The man behind the colonial party was really Eugène Etienne, an important *Alliance démocratique* politician who sat for an Algerian seat; Africa was always the party's main interest, and it was behind the expeditions which led up to the Fashoda crisis in 1898, and France's later penetration of Morocco. After France had established herself in Morocco, interest died away and the colonial group of deputies broke up. The active members of the colonial party were few; they were able to wield such influence because nobody else was interested enough to oppose them, and because they were operating from within the system. The colonial party had its sympathizers in the army, the foreign office and the colonial ministry, and the *Ecole coloniale* which trained colonial administrators was inspired by its ideas.

A pressure-group headed by deputies is perhaps not a true pressure-group at all, if one takes this term to mean a lobbying organization putting pressure on Parliament from outside. The formation of such organizations did not go very far in France before 1914, partly because economic and local interests were represented directly by deputies in their legitimate capacity, and the conflict between them was open. One might expect business interests to be to the fore in forming powerful organizations but this was not really the case. By the 1900s there were numerous employers' organizations, but it has been said that very often the annual banquet was their chief activity.[19] The exceptions were coalmining, which had formed a *Comité central des houillères de France* in 1887,[20] and the iron and steel industry, represented since 1864 by the *Comité des forges*. The *Comité des forges* was undoubtedly highly influential, and worked behind the scenes to secure protection and to ensure that foreign policy benefited French industry. Other employers' organizations, however, were often concerned with price-fixing or strike-breaking rather than lobbying, and there was no effective central body to represent business interests. There was a *Comité républicain du commerce et de l'industrie* (the 'comité Mascuraud') tied to the Radical party, but this was not so much a pressure-group as a conduit through which the Radicals (and the *Alliance démocratique*) tapped the funds of their business sympathizers.[21]

The truth is that businessmen hardly needed pressure-groups when the general atmosphere was so favourable to their activities. In the same way, the formal organization of agricultural interests was hardly necessary when most deputies represented rural constituencies and the needs of agriculture could be expressed through the ballot-box. The most articulate spokesmen of agriculture, however, were landowners and the highly capitalized farmers of northern France, and the French

Parliament did remarkably little to help the ordinary peasant proprietor or the rural worker. There were no significant measures, for example, to end the abuses of *métayage*, to give tenants more security of tenure and to compensate them for improvements, or to make agricultural credit more readily available. Attention concentrated instead on tariff protection and maintaining or securing fiscal privileges. Conservatives succeeded in persuading peasants that protection was good for them and income-tax would be bad, though there was reason to doubt both propositions, and in the long run protectionism held agriculture back by delaying mechanization and structural reform.[22]

The tariff issue was important because it brought together industrial and agricultural interests. It was the former who took the initiative: with the exception of a few industries with a large export trade like silk, French industrialists had always been protectionist by instinct, but on the agricultural side the winegrowers had favoured free trade until the phylloxera crisis (which began around 1875 and ravaged French vineyards until the end of the 1880s) made France a net importer of wine. The economic crisis of the 1880s completed the conversion to protectionism, and from then on the movement was steadily away from free trade, with the Méline tariff of 1892 and the tariff of 1910 as the main landmarks; the first significant protection for agriculture came with the wheat duties of 1885. The evolution of these tariffs illustrated some of the defects of the parliamentary system – nothing was easier than to buy votes and satisfy vested interests by adding constantly to the list of protected goods – and the power of the Chamber's *commission des douanes*. It was as head of this committee that Méline made his mark, and it worked out the details of the 1910 tariff while the government tried rather desperately to restrain it in the interest of good relations with other countries, especially Germany.[23]

It was easy for all to unite against foreigners, but over tax concessions rival interests came into conflict. In the early twentieth century, the agricultural interest was divided by the 'war of the beet and the grape', which was a war between north and south. Its origins were in the problems of the wine industry. The recovery from phylloxera had involved the abandonment of marginal production in the older wine-growing areas, and the growth of a large-scale capitalistic wine industry in Languedoc, whose efficiency led to a serious crisis of overproduction and a collapse of prices. The taxes on drink became a controversial issue, and one where the interests of winegrowers diverged from those of the sugar-beet refiners, who were the main source of industrial alcohol, and who formed a very powerful lobby:

they had already succeeded in protecting themselves from the competition of colonial cane sugar, in getting export bounties until these
were abolished by the 1902 Brussels Convention, and in banning
saccharin (just as dairy interests were able to get laws limiting the use of
margarine).[24] All in all, alcohol was a highly political commodity, and
those interested in it included the café-owners, who were forming
their own defence organizations, and the *bouilleurs de cru*, farmers who
distilled their own wine or fruit duty-free. Only the boldest government attacked the privileges of the *bouilleurs de cru*, and an attempt to
cut them down in 1903 was reversed in 1906.

Lower taxes did not solve the problem of wine prices, which
collapsed disastrously in the early 1900s, culminating in the major
social disturbances in Languedoc in 1907. The popular view was that
the root of the trouble was 'fraud', and Parliament responded to this
by passing laws on the quality and labelling of wine (which caused
further rioting in 1911, when the winegrowers of the Aube department
were excluded from the designated champagne area). After 1914, the
government was to buy up surplus alcohol at an agreed price from both
wine and beet growers, but these great days of the alcohol lobby were
in the future; so was the enforced use of alcohol as motor fuel, though
experiments with this had already begun.[25] Before 1914 no real lobby
was needed, because the deputies representing winegrowing areas
acted together in defence of the industry regardless of party, and were
a force difficult to resist.

No account of parliamentary politics or of the propaganda activities
of interest groups would be complete without some consideration of
the Press, which was enjoying a golden age.[26] On the eve of 1914,
Paris had about seventy dailies, and the provinces 250. Three-quarters
of the circulation of the Paris Press, however, was accounted for by
the four so-called *journaux d'information*, popular newspapers which had
developed since about 1880 with the advent of mass literacy. These
newspapers were run on business lines, and sought to entertain and
interest their readers rather than provide ideological guidance; their
political line was usually somewhat neutral, although there were Press
magnates who themselves entered politics, like Jean Dupuy, proprietor of the *Petit Parisien*. These mass-circulation papers contrasted
with the traditional *journal politique*, which was thin on news but acted
as the organ of a party or tendency and gave its readers much political
comment. The circulation of these papers ranged between 20,000 and
70,000: they included the *Figaro*, which evolved from royalism to
moderate conservatism, the old-fashioned liberal *Journal des Débats*,

and *Le Temps*, noted for its foreign coverage and regarded as the semi-official mouthpiece of the Quai d'Orsay. One special tradition of French journalism was the 'one-man' newspaper, read because it expressed the views of either a leading politician, many of whom spent large sums on maintaining unprofitable papers, or a talented journalist. The Socialist newspaper *L'Humanité*, for example, was read by many simply for Jaurès's editorials. It was on the Right especially that a tradition of combative and often brutal personal journalism flourished, represented (in rough chronological order) by the intransigent Catholic Veuillot in *L'Univers*, by Rochefort, who moved from support of the Commune to extreme nationalism, by the Cassagnacs, father and son, who kept Bonapartism alive in *L'Autorité*, by the anti-Semitic Drumont in *La Libre Parole*, and by Maurras in the *Action française*.

One important function of the Paris Press was co-ordinating opinion throughout the country, for it had a high circulation in the provinces, and provided most of the ideas for the provincial Press, which was less influential than the number of titles would suggest. According to the historians of the Press, 'scissors became the main equipment of the journalist' in the provinces;[27] most papers took their news from Paris agencies, and the monarchist parties in the 1870s had pioneered a system of party news agencies which supplied sympathetic newspapers throughout the country. Since local politicians also got the ideas for their speeches from the newspapers, the result was that politics was debated in much the same terms everywhere. Only the largest provincial dailies had offices in Paris, and only one really established a reputation outside its region: this was the *Dépêche* of Toulouse, which under the ownership of the Sarraut family became a great organ of Radical opinion, a French counterpart of the *Manchester Guardian*.

The golden age had its darker side. The Press law of 1881 was perhaps excessively liberal in allowing attacks on individuals, and the tone of the Press was often violent and scurrilous. Moreover, the large number of small and financially unsound papers encouraged venality. Many newspapers were controlled by financial or business interests with axes to grind, but the worst abuses were in the financial pages, where it became normal to accept money for giving favourable publicity to companies' shares and concealing their difficulties. This abuse was revealed but not ended by the Panama scandal. Since so many Frenchmen invested their savings in foreign government stocks, these governments also began buying the services of newspapers to laud the soundness of their economies and the virtues of their rulers. The most notorious case of this kind, though not the only one, was the

Russian Press campaign. Russian subsidies were especially lavish after 1905, when it was necessary to re-establish confidence in the regime, and their distribution was connived at by the French government. These pressures on the Press were familiar to insiders, but not to the newspaper reader, and they were a danger to democracy mitigated only by the multiplicity of choice which the Press offered.

On the whole, the Press focused attention on parliamentary politics rather than diverting it. In classic nineteenth-century fashion, the public discussion of politics centred on the parliamentary arena and on the personalities and the manœuvrings of politicians, and debates and speeches were reported at length. Even those newspapers which were interested mainly in entertainment and sensation were provided with a good deal of material by the politicians, in the form of crises, scandals and duels (the survival of which in the world of politics was one of the stranger aspects of Republican manners). One of the most publicity-conscious of politicians, Caillaux, carried this to new heights in 1914 when his wife shot Calmette, editor of *Le Figaro*; the trial (and acquittal) of Mme Caillaux monopolized the headlines in the weeks when the Balkan crisis was building up to war.

One can conclude, therefore, that in many ways Parliament remained the real centre of interest and the real centre of power. It had to co-exist with a strong centralized State whose organs enjoyed much autonomy, and with numerous interests who used their economic and social power to get what they wanted, yet it remained the forum through which these interests mediated their conflicts. Moreover, it was still the individual deputies who retained much of the control over legislation, and who acted as the channel for the play of interests. Each of the 600 or so deputies used his vote and his influence in a different way, and there was no neat structure of interest groups tied in with parties to give the bargaining process shape and discreet propriety. The workings of such an open parliamentary system were often unedifying, but it could hardly be denied that they were democratic.

CHAPTER 6

Republicans and Radicals

By 1914, the term 'Republican' was virtually empty of partisan meaning, and the Radicals were a party of government whose creative period seemed already to have passed. In the early years, however, Republicanism stood for ideas of democracy and popular political participation which were still radical if not revolutionary, and until 1870 to be a Republican had been to court imprisonment and exile. The Republicanism of 1848 had not been clearly distinguished from Socialism, and at times it had stirred up popular feeling by appealing crudely to the hatred of the poor for the rich. The veterans of the Second Republic had an honoured place in the Third – some of them, like Victor Hugo and Louis Blanc, had returned from exile only in 1870 – but their ideas were not much listened to, for after twenty years of universal suffrage the nature of Republicanism had changed. The Paris Commune showed how a gap had opened up between Socialism and orthodox Republicanism, and how middle-class Republicans now repudiated violence in favour of legal and peaceful methods. The Republican leaders in the 1870s were a new generation formed by the struggle against the Second Empire, and they were anxious to take over the levers of power and show that the Republic could bring prosperity, efficiency and national unity as well as liberty and equality. These leaders formed an unusually coherent group, and since their struggles gave rise to many doctrinal statements and a flood of oratory their ideals and beliefs can be analysed in some detail, as they are in Barral's invaluable collection *Les Fondateurs de la Troisième République*.

In the early years, Republicans disagreed about the timing and emphasis of their programme but not about its content. The classic statement was the 'Belleville programme' of 1869, drawn up by the Republicans in Gambetta's Paris constituency and endorsed by him. Later Gambetta was accused by the Radicals of betraying the programme, but there was only one major demand in it which was not satisfied by the Opportunists in the 1880s, the separation of Church and

State. The programme concentrated on political reforms, and Gambetta's comment on it was very characteristic of Republican thought in its belief that universal suffrage, once allowed to work freely, would open the way naturally to whatever other reforms were necessary, and that the establishment of political democracy itself satisfied a large part of the demand for liberty and equality. For Gambetta believed that 'France . . . will achieve liberty, peace, order, justice, material prosperity and moral grandeur only through the triumph of the principles of the French Revolution.'[1]

The Republicans saw themselves as the direct heirs of the men of 1789, and turned the memory of the Revolution into a sort of cult. They believed that it was France which had given the world the principles of democracy and defined them in a permanently valid way, and that this was in a sense the culmination of French history. This idea derived from the historian Michelet, who had depicted the history of France as the gradual unfolding of the idea of democracy and the emancipation of the People through its own efforts, and this version of historical inevitability, together with a black-and-white view of the evils of the *ancien régime* and the benefits of the Revolution, was to be widely diffused through the Third Republic's schools. It was one aspect of the deep belief in progress, in which of course the Republicans were entirely typical of the liberals and rationalists of their age. Men educated in the 1850s and 60s were profoundly impressed by the achievements of science, which reinforced the optimistic inheritance of the Enlightenment. Many of them, including Ferry, were directly influenced by the positivist doctrines of Auguste Comte, and a few were themselves distinguished scientists, like Paul Bert, one of the architects of the Republic's educational reforms. Others like Clemenceau had passed through the medical schools, which had become strongholds of positivist and materialist ideas.

'To release man from the chains of ignorance,' said Clemenceau,[2] 'to liberate him from religious, political and economic despotism, and having set him free to set no limits but those of justice to his freedom of initiative' were the aims of the Republic. The idea of 'emancipating' the individual and destroying traditional subserviences constantly recurred. It was a negative conception of liberty, which made it difficult for the Republicans to evolve a social doctrine suited to a mass industrial society, but it provided much of the moral force behind their anti-clerical and educational policies. Comte, after all, taught that religious dogmas belonged to a past stage of society, and would disappear in the positivist age which was dawning. The Church was an obsolete as well as a hostile force, doomed to disappear yet still trying to shackle human minds. Youth in particular must be saved from its influence and shown how to make independent use of the gift of reason.

The Republicans had practical and political, as well as intellectual, reasons for their hostility to the Church. Religion in the 1870s, far from being a declining force, was enjoying a revival which seemed to reinforce the anti-rational tendency of the Syllabus of Errors and the Vatican Council. France's defeat in 1871 had been seen by many Catholics as a punishment for her sins, and set off a wave of pilgrimages and pious demonstrations centred on the cult of the Sacred Heart. The church of the Sacré-Coeur at Montmartre was built as a national expiatory monument, and it was at this time that the popularity of Lourdes began. The Republicans saw all this as both a deplorable revival of superstition and a political challenge, for the pilgrimage movement was openly Legitimist. The Church was also blamed for supporting MacMahon in the crisis of 1877, which many saw as the work of a clerical conspiracy. The first wave of anti-clericalism in the 1880s, like the second after the Dreyfus affair, was partly inspired by the reaction of 'republican defence'.

The Republicans were also reacting to the attempts of the Catholics to 'rechristianize' France and to remodel her institutions along Catholic lines during the National Assembly.[3] The Republican view was that the religious beliefs of individuals should be respected, but the Church should be stripped of social influence and reduced to what was seen as its proper role in a secularized society. The Opportunists (but not the Radicals) were prepared to respect the Concordat by continuing State support for the parish clergy, but the religious orders had no place in their scheme. It was the religious orders, it seemed, subsidized and encouraged by rich anti-Republican laymen, which were responsible for stirring up political trouble and for perpetuating the social influence of the old elite. The hold of the Jesuits and other teaching orders over the education of the upper and upper-middle classes was seen as a special danger, and was one of the targets of anti-clerical policy, although none of the measures taken in fact prevented Catholic secondary schools from flourishing in competition with the State's secular lycées.

But it was, of course, on the reform of primary education that the Republicans concentrated. They saw universal education as the principal and perhaps the only social reform which democracy demanded, and it was a social reform that had the advantage of offending no vested interest except the Church. Inequality of education was seen as the main source of other inequalities; removing it would liberate the energies of individuals and equip them to cope with their own problems.[4] The inequalities certainly still existed, and even apart from anti-clericalism the reforms of Ferry were badly needed. In the late 1870s, illiteracy among married couples was around 17 per cent for men and 28 per cent for women;[5] education was still neither free nor compulsory, both reforms being opposed by conservatives, and the more backward areas lagged badly behind. The laws of 1881–2 filled the gaps, and provided for a massive programme of school building; the schoolhouses of the Third Republic have been described as its most permanent and most fitting memorial.

Religious teaching was excluded from the schools, but the catechism was replaced by a programme of moral and civic instruction which according to Ferry was based on the moral ideas common to all creeds and ought therefore to be acceptable to Catholics. The need for a secular or 'lay' morality which would serve to create social solidarity in a world without religion was a problem which preoccupied many Republican thinkers; its philosophical foundations had been worked out in earlier years by Quinet, Renouvier and Renan, and the idea was elaborated by Durkheim (*L'Education morale*) and by Buisson (*La Foi laïque*). For the primary teachers, both men and women, the *foi laïque* was indeed a sort of religion, and they were among the most passionate and influential supporters of the Republic. For the programme of 'civic instruction' was a successful example of a conscious programme of political socialization, and did much to create the popular attachment to democratic ideals which had become evident by the 1900s. The young citizen learnt that it was the Republic which had given liberty and equality to all and was instructed in the civic duties which he owed in return. The programme also instilled the old-fashioned virtues of thrift, hard work, sobriety, and respect for property and for the social hierarchy, and perpetuated the moral vision of a peasant and artisan France long after the reality had changed.[6]

Education also had a strongly nationalist and patriotic bias. It should not be forgotten that until the time of the Boulanger affair nationalism was an attribute of the Left; the democratic and patriotic sides of the revolutionary inheritance were not separated, and creating a national consensus around democratic ideas was seen as one of the functions of the school. It was also in the schools that the cult of *revanche* was to be kept alive, for the schoolboy of today was the soldier of tomorrow: *Tu seras soldat* was the title of one of the popular textbooks of civic instruction produced by the historian Lavisse.[7] Paul Bert, when minister of education in Gambetta's government, gave special attention to patriotic training and encouraged the formation of *bataillons scolaires* which taught boys to drill and handle rifles. These did not last long, but the patriotic bias of the schools remained strong, especially in the teaching of history, where the Republican view was stretched to incorporate the monarchy's work in creating national unity and the Napoleonic *épopée*. Internationalism was suspect to orthodox Republicans: one of the most damaging charges against the Catholics was that they had a loyalty lying outside France, and in later years respectable opinion was alarmed by the appearance of anti-militarism and Socialist internationalism among the schoolteachers themselves.

It was characteristic of the Republicans that while reforming primary education they preserved the elitist character of the lycées – for the scholarship system was of limited scope.[8] Clemenceau once declared that 'democracy is essentially the regime in which the people is governed by *élites*. To find the best method of forming these *élites* is the primary problem which confronts a democracy.'[9] The Republicans' belief in education was bound up with the legitimation of their own rule: an intellectual elite, democratically recruited and devoted to the cause of popular emancipation, was seen as having a moral right to leadership which the old notables lacked, and the Republicans liked to think of themselves as 'elder brothers' guiding those who lacked the privilege of enlightenment, and to speak of the 'alliance of the people and the bourgeoisie'.[10]

The bourgeois nature of the founders of the Republic is hardly in doubt. Even when Ferry told Jaurès that his ideal was to 'organize humanity without God and without King', Jaurès noted how his views were limited by the social perspectives of the 'Republican *grande bourgeoisie*'.[11] Ferry came from a rich middle-class family, followed his father into the law, and married into the industrial elite of Alsace. He was 'a man who had an instinct for government and a love of order',[12] and may be taken as typifying the constructive spirit of the Republicans. His name is especially associated with education, but his other major achievement, pushing through a policy of colonial expansion against strong opposition, also showed the founding fathers' conviction that they were the people best fitted to direct the nation's destinies and lay the foundations of a new national greatness.

Another leading figure of the period, Charles de Freycinet, illustrates the same tendencies, and was equally remote from the *nouvelles couches sociales*. A Protestant of aristocratic origins, Freycinet was a professional

engineer formerly in government service, who helped Gambetta with
the military efforts of the Government of National Defence. He entered
the Senate as a protégé of Gambetta, attached his name to the
'Freycinet plan' as minister of works, and later built up a reputation as
a military expert, carrying out some major reforms as the first civilian
minister of war in 1888–93. Though in some ways 'the ancestor of the
technocrats',[13] Freycinet became a skilled politician whose very lack
of strong party views made him one of the most frequent holders of
office. His example shows how many of the country's functional elite
accepted the Republic and put their talent at its service; their adhesion,
like that of the ex-Orleanist 'Centre Left', gave the Republic a certain
solidity, respectability and sense of participation in national traditions.

Many of the leaders, however, were like Gambetta (the son of an
immigrant Italian grocer) men who had followed the classic path from
a humble home through the lycées and faculties to a professional
career in law, medicine or journalism before trying their luck in
politics. In his study of Waldeck-Rousseau, Sorlin suggests persuasively
that the difference within the Opportunists between the followers of
Ferry and Gambetta was a social rather than an ideological one. Ferry
stood for the well-established bourgeois families with roots in the
provinces and the confidence given by inherited wealth, while Gambetta
attracted young men who had come to Paris to make a career and a
fortune and who were absorbed by the raffish side of political life
which centred on cafés, newspaper offices and billiard-rooms. André
Siegfried suggested much the same thing when he recalled the visit of
Gambetta and his hangers-on to his father's austere provincial household
in Le Havre.[14]

On the other hand, there was no clear social difference between
Opportunist and Radical leaders, though there might be between the
rank-and-file deputies. Clemenceau was every inch a gentleman, and
came from a landowning family in the Vendée, in which both Republican opinions and the practice of medicine were traditional; though not
rich, Clemenceau did not need to apply himself to his profession. His
rival Caillaux, once described by Briand as a 'demagogic plutocrat',
was the son of a *grand bourgeois* who had been a conservative minister
under Broglie, and had started his career in the elitist *inspection des
finances* before turning to politics and simultaneously making a fortune
in international banking. He was hardly a typical figure, but he was
not the only rich businessman in the Radical ranks.

The division between Opportunists and Radicals had become
clear-cut by the 1881 election, when they put up rival candidates. The

term 'Opportunist' was first used in derision by the journalist Rochefort, but was soon used by the men themselves to describe their policy
of cautious reforms carried out in stages as conditions allowed.
Opportunism was the creed of those who (in Gambetta's words)[15]
wanted to make the Republicans a 'party of government' and follow
a 'policy of results'. It was partly a matter of temperament: to the
Opportunists, the Radicals appeared as irresponsible utopians whose
intransigence imperilled the Republican achievement; Clemenceau in
particular, prepared to join the Right to bring down governments,
seemed to be simply a wrecker without positive ideas. By contrast,
Ferry's sense of authority and cold and arrogant personality seemed
to incarnate the Opportunist spirit and earned him the hatred of the
Left. Speaking in 1883, he called for 'a government which governs',
and declared that since the monarchists had ceased to be a threat 'the
peril is on the Left' (a paraphrase of his exact words, but a valid one).[16]

Behind this division lay a real difference in the electoral base of the
two parties. Throughout the 1870s and 80s Radical deputies came
primarily from urban constituencies and relied on working-class votes,
while Ferry and Gambetta were acutely aware of the need to win over
and retain the support of the peasants and of provincial opinion. It
was Ferry who said that 'the Republic will be the Republic of the
peasants or it will be nothing', and he developed this theme in a speech
at Bordeaux in 1885, which concluded that the institution of peasant
proprietorship meant that 'our social edifice is the most solid in Europe,
and the best sheltered against social revolutions. . . . the universal
suffrage of the peasants is a solid base for our society and a foundation
of granite for the Republic'; but Gambetta had been saying similar
things since 1872, stressing especially the need for the Republicans to
present themselves as the champions of order and stability.[17] Sorlin
shows how at the local level the Republican leaders took his advice,
reading up agricultural questions and entering the rural milieu for the
first time to make speeches and political contacts.[18]

The Radicals in the 1880s were actually divided into two groups,
the 'Gauche radicale' who kept open the links with the Opportunists,
and the Radical-Socialists under Clemenceau. 'Socialism' indicated
little more than an interest in social questions, but this in itself was
significant. The Opportunists had defined liberty and equality in
essentially political terms, and were at a loss when confronted with
problems unimagined in 1789. Gambetta thought that there were no
social questions which could not be solved by piecemeal reforms, and
found the idea of class conflict repugnant; the Republic was to be a

single national community in which differences of wealth and status would be irrelevant, and speaking at Lille in 1877 Gambetta welcomed the rallying of the upper bourgeoisie to the Republic and looked forward to 'the fusion . . . between the bourgeoisie and the workers, between capital and labour'.[19] The Opportunists rejected State intervention on principle, and they inherited the orthodox economic liberalism of the Orleanists.

The Radicals, on the other hand, retained something of the Jacobin belief in State action, and their radicalism on economic questions in this period should not be underestimated: they called for a revision of the railway contracts in a sense favourable to the State (the denunciation of railways and other monopolies as a 'new feudality' was a favourite theme of the Radicals, and perhaps comforted them by its echoes of 1789); they demanded a progressive income-tax, and opposed protectionism because it would raise food prices; they encouraged the formation of trade unions, supported legislation on hours of work, and took the side of workers in strikes. The urban, and especially Parisian, character of their support was also reflected in their nationalism, for their opposition to Ferry's colonial policies was linked with the desire for revenge against Germany.

It was this desire which led many Radicals into the Boulangist movement. The Boulanger crisis weakened and divided Radicalism, and accelerated the shift in its centre of gravity away from Paris and towards the traditional left-wing areas in the south, symbolized by Clemenceau's move from a Paris constituency to the Var in 1885. As Radicalism came to depend more on rural votes, the reformist impulse weakened. At the same time, the rise of Socialism posed a new challenge: while the Opportunists slid easily into conservatism, the Radicals were not prepared to give up their working-class support without a fight, and some of them began to think that Republican doctrine itself needed rejuvenation and extension to cover the needs of an increasingly collectivist age. Clemenceau himself had too deep a belief in individualism to change his ideas; it was Bourgeois who provided the Radicals with a new doctrine in his book La Solidarité (1896). 'Solidarism' tried to reconcile liberalism with the need for new social institutions by showing that a just society depended on mutual obligations and on co-operation rather than laissez-faire individualism, and it allowed Radicals to accept social legislation with an easy conscience. Bourgeois's book perhaps had limited direct influence, but it reflected a widespread feeling at the end of the century that a middle way must be found between capitalism and Socialism.[20] In his 1895 government, Bourgeois at least tried to introduce income-tax, and one of his ministers described the government's programme as 'sensible, practical Socialism'; there was also a less timid wing of the Radicals, which had close relations with the Socialists (especially moderates like Millerand) and hoped to join them in a political alliance.[21]

When the Radicals called their first party congress in 1901, they declared that 'the deliberations will not be concerned with the establishment of a new programme. Our programme is known: it was fixed by our fathers.'[22] In fact, Radical congresses did draw up extensive programmes, and that approved at Nancy in 1907 forms the definitive statement of Radical aims in the pre-war period.[23] On the political and religious side, it was mainly a restatement of principles, since most of the Radical aims had been achieved. On social policy, the programme rejected the idea of class struggle, and declared itself 'resolutely attached to the principle of individual property'; but it was also 'resolutely hostile to the egoistic ideas of the laissez-faire school' and affirmed the right of the State to intervene in the relations between capital and labour to secure social justice. The State must also 'discharge the debt of society' (a solidarist phrase) by caring for the old, children and the sick. Among the positive proposals were progressive income-tax and increased death duties, old-age pensions, improved public assistance, measures to help farmers, and a 'labour code' covering hours of work, arbitration of conflicts, industrial accidents and hygiene, sickness and unemployment insurance, and so on. The programme also called for a State takeover of monopolies, especially the railways and insurance companies.

There was much here to attract the working class. What general message did the Radicals have for them? The party 'seeks to give the proletariat full consciousness of its rights and its duties', and encourages trade unions, co-operatives, and

> all institutions through which the proletariat can assert its rights, defend its interests, improve its moral and material situation, obtain control over its means of livelihood (*la propriété de son outil*) and get fair remuneration for its labour, achieve the end of the wage system (*la disparition du salariat*) and obtain access to individual property, which is the true condition of its liberty and dignity.

The ideal of the Radicals was thus less to help the proletariat advance than to help it to disappear, and they hoped that somehow the industrial worker could come to share the independent status of the artisan or peasant. In their belief in emancipating the individual and creating a society of responsible, self-disciplined, property-owning citizens, the Radicals may have failed to measure up to the challenge of a mass industrial society, but they were being faithful enough to the ideals which had inspired Republicans from the start.

Not all the social reforms proposed remained on paper. By British standards, France had remarkably little legislation in the field of public health, housing and working conditions, but there was some progress. There was only one 'factory act' on the statute book in 1870, a law of 1841 on children's labour. The Catholics of the National Assembly showed more interest in this question than the Republicans, and a stricter law was passed in 1874. Another law of 1892 covered both women and children, but the machinery of enforcement was very lax. When Millerand accepted office in the Waldeck-Rousseau government, he hoped to make his mark by a programme of labour legislation, but most of his plans, including a scheme for the compulsory arbitration of strikes, came to nothing. He did, however, get through a law on hours of work (1900) which led by 1904 to the ten-hour day for all workers, including men, in establishments employing women or children. Other legislation of this kind included the law of 1898 on industrial accident insurance and that of 1906 giving a compulsory weekly rest-day. Otherwise, further progress was made only by privileged groups of workers such as the miners and the railwaymen, who enjoyed special protection because their industries operated under concessions from the State, and in the case of the miners because they were numerous enough to elect deputies who fought for their interests. The miners got a pension scheme in 1894 and the railwaymen in 1909, and the eight-hour day was enforced in the mines in 1905.

Social security of the Bismarckian type came late to France. There was a system of public assistance run by the communes, and from time to time new categories of claimant were given a statutory right to receive it – abandoned children and the insane in 1884, the indigent sick in 1893, the aged poor in 1905, large families in 1913 (it was only on the eve of 1914 that social measures to stem the population decline began to be discussed). But the first contributory scheme was the law on old-age pensions of 1910, which went back to a bill introduced by Millerand in 1901. This law applied to workers and peasants, but in practice proved 'a failure if not a fiasco'.[24] Court decisions made the contributory system virtually unenforceable, it was unpopular with workers and the trade unions were hostile. The historian of this subject, Hatzfeld, considers that the real impulse for social legislation came from the solidarist ideas of the Radicals, anxious to keep the support of the masses and outbid the Socialists, rather than from working-class pressure. He also illustrates the power of liberal ideas: the debates on the pensions bill centred on the dangers of undermining individual self-sufficiency. Traditional Republicans, trained in the strongly individualist principles of the civil code, felt deeply unhappy about the compulsory principle, feeling instinctively that its introduction implied the acceptance of a class society and the abandonment of the old order in which every worker might aspire to independence.[25]

Individualism, though of a more selfish kind, was also at the root of the opposition to income-tax proposals. Progressive income-tax was supported by Socialists as well as Radicals, and returned to the political agenda in the 1898 election. As minister of finance under Waldeck-Rousseau, Caillaux was able to introduce the progressive principle into death duties (1901), and when he reoccupied the ministry under Clemenceau he tabled a comprehensive income-tax bill. This was passed by the Chamber in 1909, but the Senate was implacably hostile. Only the three-year law and the heavy expenditure which it involved reopened the issue. Parts of Caillaux's original plan were enacted in March 1914, but the general income-tax was not accepted by the Senate until July, and not actually levied until 1916.

The Left supported the proposal because it would shift the burden of taxation away from the consumer – indirect taxes provided 55 per cent of the revenue in 1913.[26] But Caillaux's plans were less radical, and were designed mainly to replace the existing archaic direct taxes (the *quatre vieilles*), raising the same amount of revenue but more efficiently and fairly.[27] The rates proposed varied between 3 and 4 per cent according to the nature of the income, with a supertax of 5 per cent to give the progressive element. Various objections were raised, including the fact that the State *rentes* would be included, though they had been tax-free since their creation, but it was the idea of an 'inquisition' into income which made *Le Temps* denounce the tax in 1896 as 'something anti-French, and contrary to the customs and genius of the nation'.[28] The old taxes were levied on tangible assets like land, or on external signs of wealth, but the new one would require a declaration of total income, seen by peasants and businessmen alike as an intolerable invasion of privacy.

'Radicalism was not a party but a state of mind', said Caillaux; and he added, 'the state of mind of the petty bourgeoisie and the majority of the rural population'.[29] The problem for the Radicals was that while it was desirable to offer reforms in order to retain the working-class

vote, the larger part of their support came from peasants, shopkeepers
and middle-class people who were content with things as they were,
suspicious of the State, and devoted to the values of individualism.
Why risk losing their essential votes by trying to put the ambitious
programmes into practice? The identification of Radicalism with
the 'small man' and with the forces of economic backwardness only
became clear later in the twentieth century, but one could already
have said in 1914 that 'Radicalism is the party of the average Frenchman',[30] the man with his heart on the left and his wallet on the
right.

CHAPTER 7

The Right

In the 1870s, the French Right was represented in Parliament by old-fashioned and public spirited country gentlemen; by 1914, France had an extreme nationalist movement, anti-parliamentary and anti-Semitic, whose ideas and tactics anticipated fascism. How far was there really a single 'Right', and what elements of continuity can be found in its evolution? In his book *The Right Wing in France from 1815 to de Gaulle*, René Rémond argued (as the title suggests) that the Right had a continuous history, but one made up of three strands embodying characteristic mentalities and attitudes, and represented by different parties in turn – an application, of course, of Siegfried's theory of political temperaments. In the 1870s, the three traditions – the Legitimist or 'ultra' Right, Orleanist liberalism, and the authoritarian or nationalist Right – were identified with the three monarchist parties, but by 1900, argues Rémond, the corresponding parties were the *Ralliés*, the Progressists and the nationalists. The obvious danger of this approach is that it directs attention to the survival of old attitudes rather than the appearance of new ones; the Right evolved with French society, and since political positions are based as much on what men are against as what they are for, the nature of the Right was partly determined by the history of the Left. The appearance of Socialism had a profound effect, and by 1914 anti-socialism (combined with nationalism) had replaced the defence of religion as the principal binding element of the Right and the means by which it attracted supporters in all classes.

The core of the Right was, as always, those who had wealth and influence to defend, and who had a general preference for traditional social authorities and ways of behaviour. This was clear enough in the 1870s, when the three monarchist parties had a common interest in preserving the dominance of the notables against the advances of democracy. Several historians have recently emphasized that the Legitimists were far from being archaic relics of a past order, but retained much wealth and social influence. Their dominance of the

National Assembly was not just the result of a freak election, but a natural reflection of their power, and their efforts to create a conservative constitution and reconstruct France on Catholic lines were seriously pursued and not necessarily doomed to failure. The Right had much support among the middle classes, and it was not unreasonable to suppose that it could retain its traditional influence over rural voters. But when this supposition proved false, and the front could no longer be held against the verdict of universal suffrage, the Right was left without a strategy, and the actions of MacMahon and Broglie were inspired by desperation rather than clear thinking. The Right were in fact caught in a trap. The *de facto* establishment of the Republic meant that it was their plans which seemed revolutionary; the Republicans exploited this against them, and confiscated for their own use that belief in the established order which is normally an essential part of the psychology of the Right. The special feature of the Right under the Third Republic was that it represented a 'natural' governing class permanently deprived of political power – a case unique in Europe, as Halévy pointed out.[1] Frustration at this exclusion could tempt them to contemplate the use of violence and the exploitation of crises against the regime – but in the 1870s the royalists (though not the Bonapartists) were inhibited from this by their own strict constitutionalism.

The three parties differed in their attitudes towards democracy. The Bonapartists accepted universal suffrage, but believed that it could be reconciled with the rule of an elite by the device of a plebiscitary empire, and they looked to an authoritarian government rather than to religion or the habit of deference to maintain order and social stability. Bonapartism had its democratic and anti-clerical wing, and the idea of strong government based on mass support had radical potential, but the Bonapartist leaders in the 1870s were not well placed to exploit this. Most Bonapartist deputies were landowners who had managed to carry the loyalty of their peasant voters over into the new regime, but whose instincts were those of other notables. In the National Assembly they generally supported the common conservative cause and defended the Church, so that Bonapartism became a regional variant of conservatism rather than a political movement of the kind suggested by its slogan *l'appel au peuple*.[2]

Orleanism was to lose its distinctive identity in a similar way, for those Orleanists who stayed in the royalist camp rather than throwing in their lot with the Republic became increasingly difficult to distinguish from their Legitimist colleagues, and the liberal side of their tradition was forgotten. The Orleanist attitude to democracy had been one of distrust but not of outright rejection. Orleanists accepted the principles of 1789 and the secularization of society, but in the tradition of Tocqueville they valued liberty more highly than equality, and feared that universal suffrage would endanger civil freedom by giving power to those without property or education, who would drag society down to a common level of mediocrity. The Orleanist ideal was a property-based franchise, but this was now a lost cause, and it did not seem possible to adapt a party whose essential principle was elitism to the new conditions of mass politics.

The Orleanist spirit was perhaps best represented in the 1870s by the doubts expressed by certain intellectuals about the advance of democracy, and notably by Renan and Taine, two thinkers in the mainstream of the positivist and scientistic tradition. Renan published his reflections on France's defeat, *La Réforme intellectuelle et morale de la France*, in 1871. Like many others, he attributed Germany's victory in large part to her educational and scientific superiority, and called for urgent reforms in France, but he feared that science and culture might not flourish in a fully democratic atmosphere, just as he thought that the martial virtues were best cultivated in an aristocratic society. Renan proposed that if universal suffrage was to survive at all it should operate through indirect election; later he was to recover his faith in democracy, and occupy a position in the Republican pantheon. Taine, however, who started from a similar cultural elitism, pushed reaction much further, producing in his monumental *Les Origines de la France contemporaine* a much-read analysis of recent French history which came to provide the standard conservative view of the French Revolution. With the Commune very much in mind, Taine emphasized the violent and irrational side of the Revolution and blamed it on the Enlightenment thinkers, with their abstract ideas and failure to understand the organic development of societies; as a liberal, Taine thought that the Revolution had destroyed the true spirit of individual liberty and delivered France over to the bureaucratic State organized by Napoleon.

Hostility to the Revolution and what it stood for was at the centre of the Legitimist view of society, to which most of the vital ideas of the Right may be traced. The Legitimists did not, of course, believe that the *ancien régime* could be restored, but they were 'counter-revolutionaries' in that they condemned many nineteenth-century developments and hoped to resist and if possible reverse them. The attitude of the Legitimists tended to be defensive and pessimistic, as they struggled to hold back the decline of faith, the growth of a materialist and urban civilization, and the rise of social insubordination. Their own ideal, which arose naturally from their experience as rural land-lords, was a hierarchical society in which the relations between indi-viduals were based on mutual respect and the acceptance of inherited status, and in which social superiors accepted their obligation to protect their dependants and practise Christian charity. In principle, this vision of a society based on personal relations and on a social interdependence which transcended the cash nexus could lead to a critique of capitalism, but the traditional French Right did not go far along that road; what happened was rather that Catholic employers tried to transfer the ideal to the industrial world, enfolding their workers in a network of pater-nalistic institutions and expecting in return an unquestioning accep-tance of their authority.

The moral view which lay behind this ideal was pessimism about human nature: the individual, it was thought, needed authority to guide him, roots to give him a sense of identity, and strong social insti-tutions like the family and the Church to integrate his life with that of the wider community. The charge against the Revolution was that it had dissolved these bonds and set man adrift. Behind most right-wing social theory was the concept of the organic society: Le Play, for example, a pioneering sociologist who had a considerable influence on Catholic social thought, developed a theory of corporatism based on the paramount importance of the family. Corporatism renewed an idea which went back to Montesquieu, the need for independent social organisms coming between the individual and the State; a special version of it which reappeared in French thought from time to time was the need for the 'decentralization' of government, which would mean in practice more power for local notables at the expense of the agents of the centralized State.

Those who wanted a more thoroughgoing philosophical basis for conservatism could turn to the Catholic tradition which went back to Maistre, and which exalted the principle of authority as represented by both King and Pope. Within the Church itself the ultramontane current was running strongly in the late nineteenth century: the 'liberal Catholic' movement which had tried to reconcile Catholicism with the principles of 1789 had withered in the climate of Pius IX's papacy, and it was ultramontanism which appealed to the younger priests and to zealous new religious orders like the Assumptionists. This intellectual sympathy was only one of the reasons for the symbiosis between Catholicism and Legitimism. For the average Legitimist, the connection was a matter of instinct – loyalty to the Church was of the same unquestioning nature as loyalty to the dynasty. The fact that

the Church taught respect for traditional authorities was of course one
reason why the Right approved of it, but it would be unjust to see it as
the only reason. Conservatives cared deeply about moral questions
(the term 'moral order' summed up the spirit of their governments
well); they tended to interpret social problems in terms of moral
decline, and wished to regenerate France through a programme of
moralization in which the Church would naturally be the main agency.
They talked frequently of 'saving France', and the idea of rebuilding
national greatness through making France a Christian nation again
was perhaps the principal way in which they expressed their patriotism
in this period.

If it is easy to see why the Right defended the Church, it is less
obvious why the Church committed itself so thoroughly and openly to
Legitimism, a political judgment which proved disastrous. Here too
the identification was often instinctive: for the Legitimist de Cabrières,
for example, bishop of Montpellier from 1873 to 1921, 'the preservation of the faith and the conservation of a social order based on hierarchical relations, with landed property as the economic foundation,
were simply the same cause.'[3] But even moderate bishops found it
difficult to resist the pressure of the rich laymen on whom much of the
strength of the Church depended. The leaders of local society, and of
the conservative party, were also the leaders of Catholic opinion, and
often close allies of the intransigent religious orders. It was they who
financed Catholic charities and schools, and the Church depended on
their social influence as landlords or employers for the maintenance of
its hold on the masses.

The loyalty of the monarchists to their pretenders handicapped their
efforts to retain power in the 1870s, and the principle of monarchy itself
had little popular appeal. Bonapartism had profited from the death of
Napoleon III in 1873, but when the Prince Imperial was killed in South
Africa in 1879 the Bonapartists split into two factions, since the immediate successor, Prince Napoleon, had near-Republican views which
were unacceptable to most of the leaders. This was the end of Bonapartism as an effective independent force, though Bonapartists won as
many seats as royalists in the 1881 election. In 1883 Chambord died,
and the long-awaited 'fusion' of the royalists took place. Many Legitimists who had remained in politics from a sense of honour now gave up
the struggle, and provincial Legitimist newspapers closed by the dozen.
But in fact the collapse of monarchy as a cause allowed the Right to
re-emerge as 'conservatives' and rebuild their popularity by exploiting
new issues. In the 1885 election there was a single 'conservative union'

list in most constituencies, and the Right raised its vote from around 1,800,000 in 1881 to 3,500,000 in 1885 (against the Republicans' 4,300,000).

Permanent exclusion from power at least meant that the opposition could benefit from the unpopular aspects of government policy, and the Right attacked the Opportunists over a wide range of questions, including the agricultural crisis, the extravagance of government expenditure and Ferry's colonial policy. It was the religious issue, however, and especially the educational reforms, which gave the Right something to fight for. Conservatives of all kinds were alarmed by the sectarianism of Ferry's policies, and felt that in creating the 'school without God' the government was flouting the instinctive wishes of the majority and destroying a moral sanction on which the health of society depended. The havoc spread by this 'social crime' remained a favourite theme of conservative oratory for many years.

The case of education illustrates how conservatives felt that power was slipping away from them. Until Ferry's legislation, public primary schools could be run by religious orders, and notables could use their power on municipal councils to bring this about. But after the 1880s the school system was directed by Republican prefects, and conservatives who wanted to maintain Catholic schools had to finance them out of their own pockets – industrialists often did so on a large scale, and put pressure on their workers to use them. But even this became difficult after Combe's law of 1904, which excluded from teaching the religious orders on which Church schools depended. Combes did not ban private education altogether (as many Radicals demanded), but conservatives could certainly feel that the law was being used vindictively to frustrate their efforts to fulfil their social and religious ideals.

By insisting on the religious issue, and on the defence of social order generally, the Right was able to attract much middle-class support. Royalism had in any case never been a purely aristocratic phenomenon, but had rested partly on the 'old Catholic bourgeois oligarchy of provincial France'.[4] Many businessmen and professional men were linked by economic relations, social aspirations and intellectual sympathies with the old upper class, and in areas like the west where the general political climate was conservative, middle-class people who might elsewhere have been moderate Republicans were Orleanists or 'liberal Legitimists'.[5] During the lifetime of the Third Republic, the advance of *bien-pensant* tendencies among the bourgeoisie was reflected in the growing popularity of Catholic secondary schools – which by 1899 attracted 43 per cent of all secondary school pupils.[6]

The rich middle class too were alarmed by the undermining of social discipline, and frustrated by the fact that the wrong people were in power. Legitimists like Bishop Freppel might affect a lofty disdain for 'the handful of doctors and veterinaries who today preside over the destinies of France',[7] but for serious men like the Catholic employers of Lyons the situation demanded action.

They could not understand [writes the historian Vaucelles] the reasons for the growing influence wielded by the new elites. Were not the conservatives capable of satisfying all the legitimate interests of the masses? By their public-spiritedness, their integrity, their independence and their experience of affairs, did they not offer the electors all the safeguards they could desire? One could hardly say the same for the Republicans.[8]

The action which these conservatives took was, significantly enough, the foundation of a popular newspaper, the *Nouvelliste de Lyon* (1879). The popular Press was one of the keys to the new mass politics, and an even more important newcomer was *La Croix*, the Assumptionist newspaper, which became a daily in 1883. *La Croix* achieved a large national circulation through a network of committees and volunteer distributors, which enabled the Assumptionists to act as a force at election times – an example of how the influence of the clergy helped to compensate for the Right's lack of strong party organization.

Frustration at exclusion from power and the search for a means of reaching mass opinion were the motives for the Right's attraction to Boulanger, for he seemed to have found the secret of mobilizing opinion against the Republic through the popular themes of nationalism and anti-parliamentarism. These themes were to become identified with the Right, but Boulanger had of course begun as the protégé of the Radicals, and the leaders of the movement remained men in the Radical or revolutionary tradition – several of them, like Rochefort, were followers of the insurrectionary Socialist Blanqui. Boulanger turned to the royalists for finance, and they responded because they hoped to use him to overthrow or discredit the Republic and discard him later. Much of the money for his campaigns came from the royalist Duchess d'Uzès, and the revelation of this in 1890 contributed to the discrediting of the movement.

Over forty Boulangist deputies were returned in the 1889 election – Boulangist and conservative campaigns were generally separate, but with alliances at the second ballot. They were a somewhat heterogeneous collection, for Boulangism was to a considerable extent a negative movement which simply attracted those discontented with Opportunist rule for any reason. There was some geographical continuity with Bonapartism, as might be expected in view of the plebiscitary element in Boulangism, and some Boulangist deputies were orthodox conservatives who had adopted a new label. What was new was the election of Boulangists in big towns, where they attracted working-class support. In the south-west, for example, rural Boulangism took over the heritage of Bonapartism, but the Boulangism of Bordeaux was left-wing and in alliance with Radicalism.[9] Jacques Néré (in an often cited but unpublished thesis) has stressed the way in which Boulangism exploited working-class discontent caused by the depression which began in 1882; Boulangism proved to be only a stage on the road to Socialism, but was important in detaching the workers from their former allegiance to bourgeois Radicalism.

One of the deputies elected in 1889 was Maurice Barrès, who stood as a 'revisionist' at Nancy; his programme included, along with 'abolition of the parliamentary regime . . . which has given proof of nothing but impotence and corruption', a number of social reforms similar to those which appeared in contemporary Radical programmes, though he struck a distinctive note with a demand for the protection of French workers against immigrant competition.[10] Barrès described himself in the 1890s as a 'nationalist Socialist', and he and other Boulangist deputies figured as part of the Left rather than the Right, voting with the Socialists on social questions. It is possible to see in Boulangism, and in the closely connected activities of Déroulède's *Ligue des Patriotes*, the outlines of a new 'radical Right', popular and anti-capitalist, and pointing forward to fascism: 'primitive, but already clearly discernible, the mythic politics of our own century were taking shape.'[11] Two other possible components of a new Right were also developing in the 1880s and 90s: anti-Semitism, and the 'social Catholic' and 'Christian democrat' movements.

The exploitation of anti-Semitism and xenophobia as a political technique was introduced in France by Edouard Drumont, who published his immensely successful *La France juive* in 1886. This described how every aspect of life in France was controlled by Jews in high places, which became the endlessly repeated theme of the anti-Semitic daily newspaper *La Libre Parole* which Drumont founded in 1892. Anti-Semitism had not played an important part in the Boulangist agitation, but *La Libre Parole* was launched just in time to exploit the Panama scandal, which fed both anti-Semitism and nationalist anti-parliamentarism. *La Libre Parole* circulated widely (it was said, perhaps wrongly, to be the favourite reading of country priests) and was scurrilous in tone. It is hardly necessary to dilate on the way anti-Semitism exploits psychological anxieties and economic distress by directing them against a simple target, and at this time the economic crisis and the rise of Socialism provided the necessary material. It was also the case that anti-Semitism was an attractive journalistic technique because it 'personalized . . . the evil forces against which the newspapers were seeking to crystallize the varying discontents of their readers'.[12] In his study of the anti-Semitic campaigns of *La Croix*, Sorlin concluded that they were partly inspired by the need for themes which would appeal to a mass readership, though he also found that anti-Semitism permeated the militant Catholic thought of the time.[13]

The Catholic origins of French anti-Semitism have been stressed by several recent historians, and may be overlooked if the phenomenon is approached with twentieth-century fascism in mind. (There were protofascists among the anti-Semites, like the fantasist Marquis de Morès, or Jules Guérin, who took over the *Ligue antisémitique* originally founded by Drumont; both men deployed gangs of thugs on the Paris streets drawn from the butchers of the La Villette slaughterhouses.) Drumont himself was a racial anti-Semite, but he was careful to adapt his doctrine to Catholic ideas and cultivated traditional conservative themes like nostalgia for the *ancien régime*. The credulity of many Catholics made them receptive to conspiracy theories and to the identification of Jews (and freemasons, for anti-masonism and anti-Semitism often went together) with satanic forces;[14] but anti-Semitism was also endemic, partly for snobbish reasons, among educated and upper-class Catholics. One thing which encouraged it was the bankruptcy of the *Union générale* bank in 1882. This had been founded as a specifically Catholic bank to break the Jewish and Protestant hold over French banking, and it attracted the funds of the Church and the savings of Catholics, both rich and poor; it was also a Legitimist institution, Chambord himself being among the original shareholders.[15] When the bank crashed, therefore, a large number of right-wing families lost heavily; the collapse was due primarily to the bad management and speculations of its founder Bontoux, but the idea soon grew up that it had been engineered by the Jews. Verdès-Leroux, who has studied the Press treatment of the scandal, concludes bluntly that 'anti-Semitic ideology was in France above all the work of the Catholics.'[16]

The story of the various movements of renewal within the Church is a complex one, only partly relevant to political history. In the 1870s, the social conscience of the Church was represented by the 'Œuvre des Cercles', inspired by the aristocratic laymen Albert de Mun and René de la Tour du Pin, which tried to reach the workers through clubs and other social activities under the patronage of the rich. A little later, employers began to set up *syndicats mixtes*, organizations on corporatist lines which brought employers and workers together. The *Association catholique des patrons du Nord*, founded in 1884 by one of the most powerful sections of the *patronat*, remained faithful to this limited conception until 1914.[17] Meanwhile, the encyclical *Rerum novarum* of 1891 encouraged the 'social Catholic' movement and created a ferment of debate within the Church. At a series of congresses in the 1890s, reaching a peak in 1896–7, a 'Christian democrat' movement took shape, though no permanent organization was formed. This movement acted under the 'triple inspiration' of 'religious renewal, social reform, and acceptance of the Republic',[18] and was notable for the leadership of young priests (the *abbés démocrates*) who were anxious to free the Church from its dependence on the propertied classes. The Christian democrats encouraged the formation of unions consisting of workers alone rather than *syndicats mixtes*, though they still rejected the idea of class conflict. They were also, along with the Assumptionists, the main focus of anti-Semitism within the Church. Drumont tried to identify himself with the movement, and appeared at one of its congresses, and anti-Semitism was espoused by two of the *abbés démocrates*, Gayraud and Garnier. It was rejected, however, by the abbé Lemire, who became the best-known figure in the movement after his election to Parliament in 1893. Lemire was to campaign tirelessly for social reforms, his favourite project being the provision of smallholdings for every worker (the 'coin de terre' movement).

The Christian democrats' social ideas were in the conservative tradition – Mayeur calls the movement a 'branch of the traditionalist tree'[19] – but their acceptance of democracy, going well beyond the grudging republicanism of the *Ralliés*, made them a left-wing force within the Church. As such, they were unable to survive the Dreyfus affair, whose polarizing effect made all democratic movements in the Church suspect. This was especially so after Pius X became Pope in 1904, and in the years down to 1914 the Church in France seemed to turn in on itself and reject the chance of breaking away from identification with the established order. Lemire, for example, came under censure, and was suspended by the ecclesiastical authorities in 1914 when he refused to give up his parliamentary seat. In 1910, Pius X ordered the dissolution of the most radical movement of all, the *Sillon*, founded at the beginning of the century by the layman Marc Sangnier. The *Sillon* attracted idealistic young Catholics and devoted itself to social questions, but the hierarchy became alarmed when Sangnier began to make contact with Socialists and stood for Parliament himself. The participation of laymen in Church activities was growing, and the Church spread its social influence through bodies like the *Association catholique de la jeunesse française* (founded in 1886 under the inspiration of de Mun, and revitalized in the 1900s), but the Church's lack of dynamism meant that the energies of young middle-class Catholics were diverted into nationalist movements like the *Action française*.

Nationalism, anti-Semitism and Christian democracy were all ways in which the Right might have captured a popular following, but none of them had much impact on its electoral fortunes. Most of the Boulangist deputies were defeated in 1893, and the group disappeared as a distinct entity, many of its members becoming Socialists. The Right as a whole lost about eighty seats in that election, and whereas in the 1880s it had challenged the Republicans on equal terms it now appeared as a rump: the Right had some ninety seats, but Méline's moderate Republicans, who had now captured the centre ground as the defenders of property and social order, had over 300. The Right was also split by the *Ralliement*, though this essentially parliamentary movement had no direct connection with either social Catholicism or Christian democracy; de Mun was one of the *Rallié* leaders, but most of them were conservatives with business connections and highly orthodox views. The *Ralliés* did not succeed either in capturing seats by mobilizing new support in the country or in getting any tangible reward for their collaboration with Méline.

When the Dreyfus affair began, therefore, the outlook for the Right was gloomy, and it was not surprising that whatever propaganda advantages it might offer were exploited. The anti-Semites naturally fastened on it in order to revive themes in which the public was losing interest, and in the agitated atmosphere which the affair produced the veterans of Boulangism saw another opportunity of overthrowing the Republic by force. Déroulède's attempted coup in 1899 was seriously meant if farcical in execution, but the eventual result of the agitation was the smashing of extremist organizations by Waldeck-Rousseau. Despite the Left's talk of the 'Republic in danger', only a minority of the Right ever put their faith in violent action – the real danger lay in the influence which they retained within the Establishment. But the actions of a minority served to discredit the Right as a whole, just as the Church became the general target of Republican vengeance

through the violently anti-Dreyfusard campaigns of *La Croix* (until
1900, when the Pope forced the Assumptionists to hand the paper
over to laymen).

The most significant result of the affair for the Right was perhaps in
giving it a new coherence and sense of direction, for the issues involved and the actions of the Dreyfusards crystallized the objections of
conservatives to the workings of democracy, and encouraged the
emergence of a new ideology centred on the concept of nationalism.
The affair welded together the different strains which had developed
in the previous decades, fused the traditional and the populist Right,
and ended the confusion – very real in the 1890s – about whether
nationalism belonged to the Right or the Left. And not least, it focused
conservative emotions on the army.

The army had long been regarded as above party, and had been left
to run its own affairs, until the affair brought home the fact that a large
part of the officer corps was out of sympathy with the Republic. As a
whole the officer corps was not aristocratic – many officers were promoted from the ranks, and most led a modest bourgeois existence – but
it had become a refuge for members of old Catholic families, who
thought that in the army they were serving France rather than the
Republic. The higher up the ranks one looked, the more prominent
were men of good family with Jesuit educations: the Jesuits had been
especially efficient at cramming for the military schools, but the idea
that Jesuit confessors pulled the strings of the General Staff was one of
the myths of the Dreyfus affair. Although the army was far from being
a state within the State, the officers did live in an enclosed world, and
one rather alienated from contemporary values. It was tempting for
them to contrast the ideals by which they lived – patriotism, duty,
discipline, professional work patiently carried out for modest rewards
– with the materialism and corruption of the world outside, just as it
was tempting for right-wing theorists to exalt the army as the last
repository of these healthy virtues. It was in part the enclosed nature
of the army that caused the affair itself: as Dreyfus's second conviction
showed, officers found it difficult to repudiate decisions made by their
colleagues or superiors, and the attempts to reopen the case were
resented as civilian meddling in a professional matter.[20]

Few officers, however, drew political conclusions from their views,
for the French army had a very strong tradition of obedience to the
civil power, whatever it might be. The army was the silent service (*la
grande muette*), and serving soldiers were not even allowed to vote.
The etiquette of the officers' mess deprecated references to politics or

religion, and this was one reason why André's attempt to purge the army after the affair had such a bad effect on morale: the army had previously been a field where political patronage was excluded and promotion was not linked to political views. In the same way, officers disliked the use of the army in political disputes, and a number of Catholic officers resigned rather than take part in the repressive measures against religious orders in 1880 and under Combes; the use of the army in strikes, it is true, rarely caused such crises of conscience.

Although most officers shared traditional conservative ideas, they did not have any separate ideology of the kind which is needed to provoke armies into intervening in civilian affairs. The army might have supported the use of force in 1877 by MacMahon,[21] because MacMahon held legitimate authority, but all the evidence is that officers had no sympathy either with Boulanger or with the nationalist agitators at the time of the affair. Nevertheless, the army became a symbol for both sides because of the values for which it was thought to stand.

> The principle of civil society [said Clemenceau] is right, benevolence, justice; the principle of military society is discipline, duty, obedience. The battle is between the two. The whole revolutionary tradition of France against the blind authoritarianism of a caste, that was the whole of the Dreyfus Affair.[22]

The question of nationalism was involved directly in the affair because the main rational argument of the anti-Dreyfus side was that justice to one individual might have to be overridden in the interests of national unity and security. The sacredness of the national cause was preached by the conservative intellectuals of the *Ligue de la patrie française*, and nationalism in the broad sense of emphatic patriotism and concern for a strong army and for the protection of France's international position became a central theme for all conservatives. The use of the word nationalism in the special sense of right-wing extremism appeared at the end of the 1890s, and 'integral nationalism' reached its fullest expression in the writings of Barrès and Maurras (the phrase was Maurras's, but he had much in common with Barrès). These two writers have attracted much attention in recent years, because they can be seen not implausibly as precursors of fascism. Maurras in particular spread his savage critique of democracy widely in the inter-war years, especially in Catholic and upper-class circles, and provided much of the intellectual inspiration of the Vichy regime. But there is a difference between precursors and the real thing, and integral nationalism was in many respects no more than a reworking and modernization of traditional right-wing ideas.

The ideas were certainly influential, but one should not overestimate the significance of the movements connected with them, which included Maurras's *Action française*. The political sociologist Lipset distinguished between 'extremism of the right', or traditional authoritarianism, and 'extremism of the centre', the authoritarianism of the middle class, which is the true basis of fascism.[23] French nationalism seems on the whole to belong to the first category: it was a means by which the Right extended its support, especially among the lower middle class, but it did not turn into a radical, independent movement which sought to mobilize mass support against such right-wing forces as the Church and big business. The 'extremists of the centre' had an outlet, after all, in Radicalism, which in France was able to express the resentments of the 'small man' while keeping him loyal to the democratic tradition. The way in which Boulangism had developed out of Radicalism suggests that there was indeed an organic connection, but the Socialist side of Boulangism was not really carried over into the nationalism of the 1900s. Nationalism might have turned into fascism, says Sternhell, given 'extensive unemployment, impoverished peasants, and a ruined and frightened petty bourgeoisie',[24] but in fact these social conditions were absent, and extremism remained on the margin of politics.

Like other countries, France experienced a 'cultural crisis' at the end of the nineteenth century, in which certain intellectuals turned against the rationalist and liberal tradition. At the level of ideas, this was reflected in the debate over the 'bankruptcy of science' started in 1895 by the critic Brunetière (later a prominent anti-Dreyfusard) and in the philosophy of Bergson, whose lectures enjoyed success in the fashionable world. Politically, it took the form of disillusion with parliamentary government, and the cult of action and violence. The revolutionary syndicalism of the 1900s, with its slogan of 'direct action', was one expression of this 'revolt against reason', and its self-appointed theorist Sorel complained that 'sublimity has vanished from the ethics of both parties, giving place to a morality of extraordinary meanness.'[25] Sorel's 'Jansenist fury against the squalor of parliamentarism and political parties'[26] was shared by one of the most ardent of the Dreyfusards, the poet Péguy. Péguy reacted violently against the way in which the idealism of the Dreyfusard cause was exploited for narrow political ends by the anti-clericals and (in his view) by Jaurès, and in his famous concept of 'mystique' degenerating into 'politique' one can see the common feeling that the compromises of democratic politics degraded the purity of moral passion. As a Socialist who rediscovered Catholicism (the conversion of young intellectuals was itself a sign of the times) and a mystic patriot who died at the front in 1914, Péguy summed up some of the contradictions of the age, and was ideally placed to become a cult figure in later years.

Anti-parliamentarism went back to Boulanger, and was perhaps endemic in France. It became a part of integral nationalism because Barrès and Maurras argued that the parliamentary system encouraged anarchy and dangerously weakened France's will and unity. For their basic premise was that the interests of the nation must be the supreme criterion of policies and institutions. It represented a reality which was higher and more permanent than the individual, and provided him with a loyalty which transcended class and sectional interests. The idea that the nation alone could give meaning to the life of the individual was the special theme of Barrès, whose cult of 'la terre et les morts' insisted on man's need for 'roots' in the community where his ancestors had lived and left their bones. The individual who was uprooted lost contact with the instinctual basis of life, and entered the desert of abstract ideas. In his best-known political novel, Les Déracinés (1897), Barrès traced the fortunes of a group of young men who left their native town of Nancy to make careers in Paris, and went to the bad in various ways. For Barrès also believed that loyalties must start with the region before they could be transferred to the nation, and the cult of his native Lorraine became a vital part of his nationalism. (Maurras started his literary career with the Provençal revival movement, the Félibrige; it is perhaps odd that both nationalists should have been regionalists, but it fitted into the 'decentralist' tradition of the Right.)

Barrès also developed in Les Déracinés his criticism of French education, especially the philosophy taught in the lycées, for teaching an abstract idealism divorced from national realities, a theme which he was to develop in his attacks on left-wing intellectuals and their malign influence at the time of the Dreyfus affair. This was in the tradition of Taine, whom both Barrès and Maurras admired, and there was nothing particularly new in the denunciation of individualism, abstract ideas and deracinated intellectuals. What was new, by comparison with traditional right-wing ideas, was the exaltation of the State and of force, and the way in which nationalism was turned into a doctrine of exclusion. Julien Benda, whose La Trahison des clercs (1927) was an attack on nationalist thinkers for abandoning the values of the French intellectual tradition, saw nationalism as the prime example of that twentieth-century phenomenon 'the intellectual organization of political hatreds'; it brought together anti-Semitism, the hatred of the possessing classes for the proletariat, and the hatred of authoritarians for democracy.[27]

Barrès said that 'nationalism means resolving every question by relation to France. But how can we do this, if we do not have a common definition and idea of France?'[28] In practice, he and Maurras adopted their own arbitrary definition of what true Frenchness was, and declared that those who did not share these values were not true Frenchmen. Both decided that Catholicism was a part of France's organic personality, and gave it a central place in their ideas, although neither believed in it personally. Both too were anti-Semites, arguing that Jews were an alien element in the nation who could not share in its traditions even after several generations – their nationalism was cultural in theory, but in practice used the vocabulary of racialism. It was Maurras who pushed this line furthest with his doctrine of the four 'confederate states' who were plotting to destroy France – the Jews, the Protestants, the freemasons and the *métèques* (anyone of foreign ancestry) – a development of the conspiracy ideas already so popular among Catholics.

Barrès and Maurras differed in their views about what should replace parliamentary democracy. Barrès always called himself a Republican, and was in the Bonapartist plebiscitary tradition which called for strong government but accepted the modern world. He admired Napoleon as a 'professor of energy', and his emphasis on energy and virility and his romantic cult of violent action were among his 'fascist' aspects. He supported Déroulède in 1899, and thought the Dreyfus affair 'the favourable moment for a courageous surgical intervention'.[29] But no iron surgeon appeared to excise the parliamentary gangrene, and Barrès himself pursued an orthodox parliamentary career. Maurras, on the other hand, rejected the Republic and democracy itself, and really belonged to the 'ultra' tradition which wanted to reverse the work of 1789. He too wanted authoritarian government, but decided that the only form of it which suited France's national traditions was monarchy, and he made the *Action française* a royalist movement. It was recognized by the pretender, the Duc d'Orléans (though with strained relations at times), and the *Action française* virtually took over the moribund royalist organization.

The *Action française* was founded in 1898 (not by Maurras himself), but began its active period in 1908, when its newspaper became a daily and when the younger militants were organized as the *camelots du roi*, a force deployed in violent demonstrations, usually against a carefully chosen symbolic target. An example was the campaign against the lectures at the Sorbonne of the historian Thalamas, whose works were held to have insulted Joan of Arc, whose cult was a speciality of the *Action française*. Much of the movement's activity was centred on the Latin Quarter, for it had many student members; the spread of such ideas among students was seen at the time as a striking aspect of the nationalist revival, and the *Action française* differed from the leagues of earlier years in having distinguished intellectual supporters, attracted by the logic and sophistication with which Maurras presented his ideas.

The *Action française* was the only active organization of its kind by 1914, and had come by then to concentrate on anti-German propaganda. At the time of the affair, however, it seemed that a wide-ranging nationalist movement was emerging. Nationalist and anti-Semitic leagues were active in many towns, and helped to organize a wave of anti-Semitic riots which broke out in 1898 at the time of Zola's trial. In the 1898 election, a dozen nationalist deputies were elected, and in 1902 over fifty; it was in 1900 that the nationalists won their victory on the Paris municipal council, and in the 1902 election they gained 37 per cent of the vote in Paris. The nationalist movement in Paris has been studied by Watson, who finds that it was a much less radical affair than Boulangism. The candidates were sponsored by the conservative *Ligue de la patrie française*, and they stood in middle-class areas, gaining seats from the Radicals by adding lower-middle-class support to the traditional conservative vote. Their campaigns stressed anti-socialism and anti-parliamentarism, but not anti-Semitism or military and foreign-policy themes. On the whole, therefore, they were conservatives who adopted a new label and exploited new issues for opportunistic reasons, and they later declined because they were indistinguishable from other conservatives – most of them, for example, supported the Church in the Separation crisis. The same points probably apply to the nationalist deputies as a whole, for by 1910 they had disappeared as a separate group and were absorbed into the other right-wing parties.[30]

There is no doubt that nationalism did appeal especially to the lower middle class, and the activists in the *Action française* and similar movements (including those of the 1880s and 90s) seem generally to have been clerks, shop-assistants or artisans, with a leavening of students and middle-class youths. Membership often overlapped with that of Catholic organizations, for the Church seems to have been especially successful in recruiting its activists in this social milieu, retaining its

influence over young men who had attended Catholic schools; one
of the few genuinely successful and independent Catholic trade unions
was that formed by white-collar employees.[31] Nationalist propaganda
included some points which appealed specifically to the lower middle
class, like the denunciation of chain stores, but anti-socialism was a
powerful enough theme without the need for radical attacks on capitalism. Moreover, nationalists made little attempt to win over the
working class. There was, it is true, the 'yellow' trade-union movement, whose organizer Biétry founded a short-lived National Socialist
party in 1903, but the 'yellow' trade unions were anti-strike organizations which depended on the favour of employers, not offshoots of
nationalism, and one cannot really take them as evidence for the
existence of a coherent 'national socialist section of the Right'.[32]
Barrès was much less of a 'socialist' after the Dreyfus affair than before,
and Maurras was never very interested in social questions – 'politique
d'abord' was his slogan.

It is tempting to exaggerate the importance of extreme nationalism
because of the intrinsic interest of its ideas, but it was only one element
in the Right of the 1900s, which was overwhelmingly 'respectable' and
parliamentary. Maurras's ideas became widely diffused, but his advo-
cacy of violent methods attracted only a handful of extremists. In
Parliament, the Right now consisted of three groups – the nationalists,
the *Action libérale* and the Progressists. The *Action libérale* party continued the *Rallié* tradition, and came in practice to include virtually all
the traditional Right; only a few backwoodsmen still openly proclaimed
their royalism. *Action libérale* deputies were elected primarily as Catholics, but they were more open to nationalist and anti-Semitic ideas
than in the past, thanks to the way in which Maurras had fused together the 'ultra' and nationalist strands of the Right by presenting
new ideas in traditionalist garb.[33] The influence of his newspaper was
especially important, as it provided intellectual stiffening for conservative newspapers throughout the country.

The Progressists, on the other hand, had little sympathy with radical
nationalism, although (with much of their support in the east) they
were keen patriots who defended the army and the colonial empire.
Their conservative middle-class electors were interested primarily in
economic and social issues. It was anti-socialism, after all, which had
pushed the Progressists over to the right in the first place, and this
theme was as important as nationalism in uniting the different sections
of the Right. In day-to-day politics, 'national' issues came up com-
paratively rarely, whereas a constant battle had to be fought against

the Socialists and against social legislation which threatened conservative interests. This was the stuff of urban politics – at Marseilles, for example, anti-collectivism and income-tax played a much larger part in the Right's campaign in 1914 than the three-year law[34] – and in the pattern of modern right-wing politics that was now emerging nationalism had to take its place alongside the defence of the Church and of economic liberalism.

It seems clear that the new nationalist doctrines were the product of internal tensions rather than external threats: the Boulanger movement was linked with fears of Germany, but (despite Fashoda) there was nothing similar at the time of the Dreyfus affair. In the years before 1914, however, there was a more general revival of nationalist feelings which does seem to have been the product of international tensions, and which was clearest after the second Morocco crisis in 1911. It affected the whole of middle-class opinion, and was shown by the renewed popularity of the army and by a revival of interest in military questions; even the growth of sporting activities, a new social phenomenon among the bourgeoisie since the turn of the century, had strong patriotic overtones.[35] This nationalist revival, which seemed to show a new French self-confidence rather than a sense of insecurity, culminated in the passing of the three-year law. The promotion of the patriotic issue by Poincaré, Briand and Millerand no doubt had internal policy motives as well as military ones, because of its wide appeal. On the one side, it could gather support from the Radicals – Eugen Weber has argued that it was the 'bridge' across which they passed definitively from Left to Right, though this seems contestable;[36] on the other, it was a cause to which the Right could hardly deny their support. The moderates succeeded in attracting a section of the Progressists back to the government side, and the Right found itself in much the same position as under Méline: forced to support the government against a common enemy, but powerless to gain any concessions for itself.[37] The chief political beneficiary of the new nationalist mood was not the right-wing opposition, still less the *Action française*, but Poincaré, elected President with the Right's votes. 'The whole of Europe, unsettled and agitated, is preparing for an inevitable war', wrote de Mun after Poincaré's election in 1913; that is why 'the good Frenchmen for whom I speak turn towards him, full of anxiety and of hope'.[38]

CHAPTER 8

The working-class movement

The term 'working-class movement' is used here to cover both the history of Socialist ideas and parties and that of trade-union organization, although it is common in French usage to distinguish between the two and to reserve the phrase *mouvement ouvrier* for the latter. Political and trade-union organizations developed in parallel, neither being an offshoot of the other, and in the early twentieth century the French trade unions were notable for their rejection of parliamentary action and espousal of revolutionary syndicalism. The two histories cannot be understood apart from each other, however, for although the leaderships rarely overlapped every worker was also a voter, and the advance of parliamentary Socialism was closely tied to the discovery of class consciousness through strikes and the formation of unions. The pattern of development, too, was the same for both sides of the movement: reduced to impotence for a decade after the disaster of the Commune, they established themselves as effective forces in the 1880s, and experienced a 'take-off' after 1890 which rooted them solidly in the working class. Both were still divided into rival factions, especially the Socialist parties, but achieved unity early in the new century – the unions in 1902, the Socialists in 1905. The CGT and the SFIO were by 1914 formidable forces in French society, although neither had succeeded in capturing the loyalty of the whole of the working class.

The divisions and the relative weakness of the French working-class movement were connected with the slow development of the proletariat itself; yet France had a longer tradition than any country except Britain of Socialist thinking and conscious working-class politics. Socialist theories had flourished since the 1820s, and popular participation in politics went back to the Revolution. The revolutionary tradition, however, was something distinct from Socialism, being directed towards the seizure of power by (or for) the 'people' rather than towards an alternative vision of society. The chief exponent of insurrectionary Socialism towards 1870 was Blanqui, who was a Socialist because he wanted the revolution to introduce an egalitarian society which would embody the ideals of the working class, but whose practical aim was to build up a small 'conspiratorial' party of determined revolutionaries. Blanqui's aim was really the dictatorship of the proletariat, and this idea was a natural part of the popular political tradition in Paris, where the workers knew that they were a minority in France but assumed a right to rule because of the superior morality and historical dynamism of their beliefs. Thus an interest in parliamentary politics was not a part of the tradition, and French workers had little experience of acting as an interest group within the framework of bourgeois society. Even if they had wanted to, it was not made easy for them: strikes were legalized only in 1864, and unions tolerated (though not fully legalized) only in the last years of the Empire; the working-class militants of the 1870s and 80s were therefore formed in an atmosphere where secret and illegal activity, the recourse to violence and the risk of imprisonment were normal consequences of activities designed to improve the workers' lot.

It is possible to contrast Blanqui with the other theorist who had a real influence on workers at this time, Proudhon (d. 1865), for while Blanqui believed in the authoritarian revolutionary party Proudhon was an anarchist deeply suspicious of all authority. He looked forward to a moral rather than a political revolution, generally recommending abstention in elections. Proudhon's ideal was that the workers should recover their dignity through a system of independent or co-operative production, which would put an end to exploitation and which would also serve as the foundation of a libertarian society: the family and the workplace would be the basic units, and wider social organization would be built up on 'federalist' principles. While Blanqui wanted the workers to take over the machinery of the State, Proudhon wanted to destroy it, for he saw the State and its instruments – the police, the army, the bureaucracy – as a façade for the rule of the bourgeoisie. Proudhon's total rejection of 'bourgeois society' as unjust and immoral was widely shared by French socialists, and was to be a constant element in anti-reformist feeling in later years. Later anarchists abandoned Proudhon's economic individualism, though nostalgia for a society where the worker was his own master was common among a working class not far removed from its artisan or peasant origins – the Radical social ideal was perhaps not so alien to the workers after all. In a general way, Proudhon's libertarianism certainly corresponded to the deeper instincts of many workers. It reappeared in the later anarchist movement, and in the resistance within the Socialist parties to central control and unification; it was the local group, formed of men who knew each other and whose ideas evolved together, which was to form the vital unit in these parties. Here too the working class showed a sturdy individualism which was not so far from the old Republican ideal.

One of the problems of the revolutionary tradition was that it was shared with part of the middle class. In Jean Bruhat's words, 'the French working-class movement oscillated continually between adhesion without reserve to the French Revolution, and the critique of that Revolution as a bourgeois Revolution.'[1] Socialism had to go beyond the principles of 1789; but did workers have to reject the principles themselves because they were 'bourgeois'? Socialists had no use for bourgeois society; but was the bourgeoisie monolithic, or were there parts of it whose participation in the revolutionary tradition made them useful sympathizers and potential allies? These questions were raised in an acute form at the time of crises like Boulangism and the Dreyfus affair, when the Republic seemed threatened. When it came to the point, most Socialists thought it worth saving; thus they 'oscillated' between feelings of alienation arising from class conscious-ness and the workers' position as outsiders, and feelings of integration into a democratic tradition shared by Socialists with other Frenchmen. The problem of national loyalty created the same dilemma, for though hostile to nationalism and militarism, Socialists still had their roots in the patriotic revolutionary tradition, and as they showed in 1914 they saw the French nation, even in bourgeois hands, as a symbol of progress and democracy.

Frustrated patriotism was one of the reasons for the outbreak of the Commune. It is impossible to do justice in this context either to the drama and human complexity of this great tragedy, or to the historical controversies which it has provoked. Controversy has centred on its place in the history of revolution – was it the end of an old song, or the harbinger of a new age? – on the extent and nature of its Socialism, and on the ideological affiliations of those who participated in it. On the eve of 1870, working-class activity in Paris was represented mainly by the trade unions which had sprung up in the late 1860s, and which – like revolutionary traditions generally – were strongest among the skilled workers who formed so large a part of the capital's industrial work-force. Many of them were influenced by Proudhonian ideas, and the majority of the unions had links with the First International founded in 1864; this was the origin of the myth later promoted by the Right that the International had inspired the Commune. During the siege of Paris, the revolutionary Left was active, but its attempts at insurrection were not directly connected with the outbreak of the Commune, which was a spontaneous affair. The direction of the rising was at first in the hands of the Central Committee of the National Guard, but on 26 March elections took place for the 'Commune' in the strict sense, the body which was to hold executive power until the end. Of the eighty-one members of the Commune, perhaps as many as thirty-five were manual workers, mostly artisans of the classic type.[2] Most of those elected were already known as political activists or union leaders, and (according to Rougerie) at least thirty-two were connected with the International.[3]

The leaders of the Commune can be divided roughly into 'Internationals', Blanquists (though Blanqui himself was arrested shortly before, and could not participate) and 'bourgeois' Jacobins. But there is little point in looking for party identifications or for consistent lines of policy: the leaders were men trying to cope with rapidly changing and chaotic conditions, and preoccupied above all with the Commune's survival. Some of the legislation which they passed was Socialist – designed to improve labour conditions, or to encourage workers' co-operatives in a way reminiscent of 1848. But the emancipation of the workers was not thought to depend only on Socialism, and the greatest reforming energies went into secularizing schools and attacking the Church; nuns were ejected from their convents, and priests formed the larger part of the hostages shot in the final stages of the fighting. The Commune was also more 'Jacobin' than Socialist in its concern for a kind of direct democracy, with elected members and officials kept constantly under the eye of the sovereign people. Marx was especially attracted by the idea that the leaders of the Commune were paid only a working man's wage, so that it was a genuine government of the people by the people. Although men of working-class origin were not a majority of the Commune, their presence in such numbers was itself a remarkable phenomenon, and a Socialist one at a time when Socialism was directed towards the capture of power as much as concrete programmes of reform. Marx was surely right to conclude that 'the great social measure of the Commune was its own working existence'.[4]

The class bitterness created by the suppression of the Commune was felt by the working class in Paris for a generation or more, and its immediate result was to stifle all political and trade-union activity. Most of the former leaders were killed or exiled, and in the 1870s the State tried to outlaw all expressions of Socialism – a law of 1872 made membership of the now-moribund International illegal. The few political militants who were still active had to work clandestinely; the most vigorous current seems to have been anarchism, now inspired by Bakunin rather than Proudhon, and there were a number of groups in southern and eastern France linked with the Swiss-based 'Jura Federation'. One of those active in this milieu was Jules Guesde, who became converted to Marxism and in 1877 founded the first Marxist newspaper, *L'Egalité.*

The revival of trade-union activity began in Paris with the reconstruction of the craft unions which had existed in the 1860s. These *chambres syndicales* often grew out of the friendly societies which were the main form of working-class organization before unions became legal, and the unions were at first anxious to demonstrate their moderation. The movement was indeed sponsored by the Gambettist Republicans, who hoped to divert the workers away from Socialism, and the first 'workers' congress' in 1876, attended by representatives of seventy-two Parisian unions and sixteen provincial ones, was confined to unionists in order to exclude 'bourgeois system-makers'.[5]

This was the first of a series of congresses, and the third at Marseilles in 1879 was a turning-point in the evolution of the movement because it committed itself to the principle of collectivism and to political action, creating a Socialist party called the *Fédération du Parti des Travailleurs Socialistes de France* (cf. Appendix 2, which traces the organizational history of the movement in more detail). These decisions were the work of Guesde and his followers, and the next congress at Le Havre in 1880 adopted a 'minimum programme' drawn up by Guesde in consultation with Marx. But neither the unity of the movement nor the apparent fusion of trade-union and political activity lasted for long. Unionists who objected to politicization seceded in 1879, and other anti-collectivists in 1880. In 1882, the FPTSF itself split, the Marxists under Guesde breaking away and forming the *Parti ouvrier.* The moderate majority were called the 'Possibilists' because of their reformist attitudes, and for the rest of the 1880s conflict between Possibilists and Guesdists was the main feature of the Socialist movement. They did not form the whole of it, for there were also independent anarchist and Blanquist groups. The amnesty for the Commune brought many revolutionary activists back to France, and in 1881 (the year of Blanqui's death) the Blanquists formed a *Comité révolutionnaire central,* whose title indicates their adherence to the older revolutionary tradition. The strength of Blanquism was in Paris; its leader Edouard Vaillant had been a member of the Commune, and kept its memory alive in the Socialist movement until his death in 1915, though in later years he gravitated to orthodox Marxism.

The leader of the Possibilists was Paul Brousse, who shared the collectivist aims of the Marxists but believed that worth-while reforms could be obtained within the capitalist framework, especially if power could be captured at the local level. An anarchist in the 1870s, Brousse developed a theory of 'municipal Socialism' which combined some of the federalist ideas of the anarchists with a more prosaic gas-and-water Socialism; linked with it was the 'public service theory', which argued that economic collectivism was an inevitable development of the age, which Socialists could exploit and use for the benefit of the working class.[6] The Possibilists had strong support in Paris, and by 1887 they had nine members on the municipal council, who campaigned on such issues as housing and public transport.

As a party, the Broussists were more effective and better organized at this time than the Guesdists, whose main achievement was the popularization of Marxist ideas through the indefatigable speechmaking and pamphleteering of Guesde and Lafargue. Lafargue was Marx's son-in-law, and his correspondence with Engels kept the group in touch with the international evolution of Socialism. Despite this hot line to the seat of authority, the historian of the Guesdists concludes that their understanding of Marxism was shallow, and they failed to make an original contribution by applying a Marxist analysis to contemporary French conditions. Even Marx's writings on France were little known – his work on the Commune, for example, was not translated until 1901.[7] There was some resistance to Marxism because it was German (the French, after all, had their own theorists), but in fact the basic ideas which the Guesdists spread – class conflict, the theory of exploitation, the state seen as a façade for bourgeois class rule – were very similar to those of Proudhon and other French Socialists, and were comprehensible by workers whose own experience seemed to confirm them. Most working-class activists, of course, were hardly equipped to make fine theoretical distinctions – a study of police reports on a typical group in 1886 shows that 35 per cent were illiterate and a further 28 per cent nearly so.[8] In all the Socialist parties at this time, there was a wide gulf between the rank and file and the leaders who, though often achieving real popularity through their oratory or journalism, were with few exceptions professional men or intellectuals. This was one reason why many workers found the political parties less attractive than the trade unions and anarchist groups, which cultivated an 'ouvriériste' spirit hostile to bourgeois leadership.

In the 1880s, the *Parti ouvrier* began to build up working-class support, especially in the textile industries of the north, which were to remain the Guesdist stronghold. It also gained influence in the trade-union movement, which was now expanding, and which was fully legalized in 1884. Extensive strike movements reappeared in the 1880s, stimulated by the economic crisis, and gave many workers their first experience of politically oriented activity. For the first time, local trade unions began to come together in national 'federations' on a trade basis: the first was formed by the hatters in 1879, but more significant were those of the printing workers (the *Fédération du Livre*, 1881), the miners (1883), and the railwaymen (1890) – three groups which were to be among the largest and also the most moderate of the unions down to 1914. In 1886, a number of unions held a national congress at Lyons and formed the *Fédération des syndicats*, the first organization to represent unions on a permanent basis. This body was dominated by the Guesdists, who tended to treat it simply as an auxiliary of their party, taking the view that trade-union activity should be subordinated to political ends, and was useful less for its own sake than as a means of building up class consciousness. It was in reaction to the Guesdist dominance that syndicalist views began to develop, and the idea of the revolutionary general strike appeared at the end of the 1880s.

Even if their motives were political, the Guesdists gained credit by involving themselves in workers' everyday problems and by supporting strikes. A major strike led to the appearance of orators and organizers from Paris, and if successful left behind it a permanent party organization. The Guesdists also took up the new idea of strikes and demonstrations on 1 May, which began in 1890. The shooting of nine May Day demonstrators at Fourmies in 1891 led to Lafargue's trial and imprisonment for an inflammatory speech, and his subsequent election as a deputy for Lille. In Brousse's words, 'Fourmies achieved more than all the pamphlets of Lafargue, the doctrines of Karl Marx and the speeches of Guesde.'[9] At any rate, Lafargue's election marked a new interest on the part of the Guesdists in parliamentary methods, their attitude to which had previously been hostile.

The first deputy elected as a Socialist was Clovis Hugues, returned at Marseilles in 1881, and in 1886 the Socialists had formed a parliamentary group, distinguishing themselves clearly for the first time from the Radicals. The Boulanger movement helped Socialism in the long run by detaching many workers from their Radical allegiance, and had Socialist aspects of its own – a number of its leaders came from the

Blanquist party, and even Lafargue had seen possibilities in the movement at first. After the 1893 election, there were nearly fifty Socialist
deputies in Parliament, though only sixteen were connected with the
various Socialist parties, the others being on the fringes of Radicalism,
ex-Boulangists, or independents like Jaurès and Millerand. The
Socialists had now become a force to be reckoned with. They were
also making progress in local government, as the Guesdists captured
northern industrial towns like Lille and Roubaix – an experience which
proved frustrating, since the powers of town councils were limited,
and the prefects had a veto. Socialist municipalities did achieve
something in the field of public health and education, with innovations
like *cantines scolaires* which provided hot meals for poor schoolchildren.

In the 1890s, the Guesdists were the party which made most
progress, and they achieved this by adopting parliamentary methods.
The Guesdists still rejected reformism, but they began to feel that they
could achieve a Socialist majority within the near future, over-
estimating the rapidity with which Socialism could spread from its
base in the industrial working class. One symptom of the new approach
was that in order to gain peasant support Socialists began – like their
Republican predecessors in the 1870s – to study agrarian problems and
adapt their doctrines to peasant prejudices. At their Marseilles
congress in 1892, the Guesdists adopted an 'agrarian programme'
which promised that peasant proprietors would not be collectivized,
and which attracted the criticism of Engels. It was also in the 1890s that
Socialism began to appeal to some white-collar workers – notably the
primary school-teachers, with their left-wing tradition – and to intellectuals steeped in bourgeois culture. The first Socialist group among
Paris students appeared in 1891 – soon splitting into rival anarchist and
Guesdist groups[10] – and the *Ecole normale supérieure*, which trained the
elite of France's secondary and university teachers, became a centre of
Socialist influence through its celebrated librarian, Lucien Herr.

The ascendancy of the Guesdists was helped by the break-up of the
Possibilist party in 1890: a group led by Jean Allemane seceded, and
the rump led by Brousse dwindled into insignificance. Allemane was
a veteran of the Commune, and as a printing-worker one of the few
working-class party leaders. The Allemanists and the Blanquists were
the leading parties in Paris, among whose unproletarian workers
Marxism made little progress. They criticized the gradualist tactics of
Guesde, but the real difference was of temperament rather than
doctrine. Allemanists and Blanquists were faithful to the memory of
the Commune and to the individualism of the old revolutionary

tradition; they were *ouvriériste* (especially the Allemanists), resistant to the docrinaire dogmatism of Guesde, and prickly in their defence of the autonomy of local groups and the right of the individual to participate in decisions. Both parties had close links with syndicalism, and their mentality differed only in degree from that of the anarchists.

It was in the years 1892–4 that the anarchist bomb outrages were concentrated. There were anarchist groups scattered throughout France; the movement was not large, but it attracted able and independent-minded working-class militants, talented journalists (like Emile Pouget, whose *Le Père Peinard* was written in Paris workers' argot), and a number of writers and artists. Anarchists were hostile to authority in every form, and they had talked of 'propaganda by deed' since the 1870s; but they rarely went beyond talking, and the incidents of 1892–4 were not the work of regular anarchist groups but generally of young men with unhappy life-histories as social outsiders or criminals, like the celebrated Ravachol. Anarchist writers defended their deeds by arguing that the inherent injustice of bourgeois society justified any attack on it, and that individual acts of courage and defiance stiffened the revolutionary will of the working class. But most anarchists were moving away from 'propaganda by deed' to the idea of 'direct action' through strikes and union agitation, and anarchist penetration of the union movement did much to ensure the triumph of the doctrines of revolutionary syndicalism.

The Guesdist hold over the unions through the *Fédération des syndicats* (always a feeble body in any case) was challenged and broken by the *bourses du travail* movement. The *bourses du travail*, an institution peculiar to France, were originally buildings provided by town councils as a kind of labour exchange, but became trade-union centres which brought workers of different trades together and provided a focus for social, educational and propagandist activities. The first was opened in Paris in 1887; by 1892 there were fourteen, by 1901 seventy-four, by 1908, 157.[11] Even when they became politicized, municipal councils continued to subsidize them – though the Paris *bourse* was closed by the government between 1893 and 1895. The man who turned the *bourses du travail* into a movement was Fernand Pelloutier, a journalist with a passion for workers' self-improvement: the educational emphasis of the *bourses* was strong, and their appearance, and the growth of revolutionary syndicalism, may be connected with the advent of the first generation of working-class activists inspired by the earnest idealism of the Third Republic's primary schools.

Pelloutier was the champion (with Briand) of the revolutionary general strike (though the idea was first put forward by the otherwise obscure anarchist Tortelier) and in 1892 he became secretary of the new *Fédération des bourses du travail*. The growing popularity of the general strike idea and its rejection by the Guesdists led to the break-up of the old *Fédération des syndicats*, which was replaced in 1895 by the *Confédération générale du travail*, which was free of Guesdist influence. The CGT and the *Fédération des bourses* were linked in theory but rivals in practice, and until their amalgamation in 1902 the latter was much the more dynamic.

In the 1890s, therefore, the working-class movement was a growing force, but reached the maximum of confusion and division, with four Socialist parties (Guesdists, Blanquists, Allemanists and Broussists), an unorganized anarchist movement, a number of independent Socialist deputies and two trade-union bodies. Before describing the moves which led to greater unity, one may pause to consider the sociology of the movement. Why did workers turn to Socialism, and why did they choose one party rather than another? What conditions favoured the growth of trade-union organization and the use of the strike weapon? Strikes have attracted special attention from historians recently, and both Perrot in her study of the 1880s and Shorter and Tilly in their quantitative analysis of strike movements stress the links between strike activity and parallel political developments, with Shorter and Tilly giving more weight to political motives and to the strength of working-class organization and leadership, while Perrot emphasizes the spontaneity of strikes and their concern with practical economic grievances.[12]

The political behaviour of workers, like that of other classes, showed marked regional variations, and was affected by all kinds of local and personal factors. Often the conversion of an area to Socialism can be traced to the activities of one propagandist, and his opinions did much to determine the party to which the area adhered: Claude Willard, whose book on the Guesdists includes a pioneering study of the local implantation of Socialism, finds individuals decisive in forming the Guesdism of the Aube department, the Allemanism of the Ardennes, and the Blanquism of the Cher.[13] In many cases, these labels did not indicate profound differences in working-class attitudes; but there was a broad division between reformists and revolutionaries, and between the kind of disciplined, collectivist Socialism represented by the Guesdists and the individualism of Blanquists, Allemanists and anarchists.

The history of Guesdism supports the generalization that 'modern'

Map 4 Industrial France

Socialism appeals most to factory workers, whose conditions of labour promote class consciousness and the idea of collective action. The textile workers of the north were always the backbone of Guesdism – in 1899 about half the strength of the *Parti ouvrier* was in the Nord and Pas-de-Calais departments[14] – and there was also support in some of the textile centres of the region centred on Lyons; the Guesdists also made progress in industries where domestic production was giving way to the factory system, as in the Aube hosiery district and the leather and glove industries of the Isère. Willard suggests that medium-sized enterprises favoured political organization more than really large ones, and it was certainly not the case that large-scale industrial organization automatically produced a militant proletariat. This was shown by the case of mining, for the French miners did not play the leading role in the labour movement that one might expect.

Some of the most celebrated strikes of the period were indeed in the coalfields, and union organization was quite strong by French standards. But the miners' action was hampered by lack of co-operation between the different coalfields and was rather inward-looking; the miners' trade-union federation did not join the CGT until 1908, and had little sympathy with revolutionary syndicalism. Unlike most workers, the miners were numerous enough to get their own leaders elected as deputies, and this gave them an untypical faith in parliamentary action, which seemed justified by the legislation on working conditions which they obtained. In the first years of the Republic the Loire coalfield was the best organized (and was to remain politically moderate in later years); it was soon overtaken by the rapidly expanding Nord and Pas-de-Calais field, and it was there that a widespread strike led to the establishment of collective bargaining with the employers – a rarity in France – in the 'Convention of Arras' of 1891. In the same year, Emile Basly, who was to be the archetypal 'miners' M.P.', was elected as deputy for Lens. Until about 1900, Basly was to be more sympathetic to Radicalism than Socialism, and when he became a Socialist he stood on the right wing; he was also a powerful political boss who ruled with an iron hand, which led to the formation of the breakaway 'jeune syndicat' in the north led by the anarchist Broutchoux.[15]

It has sometimes been argued that workers who live in isolated communities are more likely than others to be militant and to have a high strike propensity, since isolation favours the growth of class consciousness and removes the moderating influence of a hetero-geneous community.[16] This does not seem borne out by the case of the French miners; mining settlements and other one-industry towns rather provided conditions where employer domination could be challenged only with difficulty. At Le Creusot, for example, there were no strikes between the end of the Second Empire and 1899–1900, and the Schneider company succeeded in breaking the union movement after 1900 by expelling militant workers and sponsoring the first of the 'yellow' unions;[17] just as a successful strike was often the catalyst which established labour organization in an area, so a failure could be disastrous – the miners of Anzin took no part in union activities in the north for nearly fifteen years after the failure of their strike in 1884. Mineowners were generally Catholic, and used Catholic institutions to discipline their workers; in a number of coalfields it was long the custom for employers and workers to join together in annual religious processions, and in one small centre (La Grand'Combe, in the Gard) the miners were still voting royalist in 1914.[18] Willard suggests that the organization and discipline required in mining encouraged the acceptance of a corporatist mentality by the workers, and something of the kind may also account for the moderation of the railwaymen.[19]

A division between moderates and revolutionaries appeared clearly within the trade-union movement in the 1900s, but one can accept only with caution the generalization that skilled workers were moderate while unskilled ones were revolutionary. Most unskilled workers were not unionized in any case, and the rise of syndicalism cannot be explained by an influx of unskilled workers into the union movement. It is probably true that unskilled workers were attracted by anarchism, especially if they were first-generation workers uprooted from their peasant origins, though their characteristic form of action was the violent, spontaneous strike which did not result in the formation of permanent union organization. It is true too that the best-organized skilled union, the *Fédération du Livre*, was also one of the most moderate; its leader Keufer was a working-class positivist rather than a Socialist. On the other hand, the leaders of revolutionary syndicalism tended to come from the traditional Parisian working class, and anarchism as well as the kind of Socialism represented by Blanquism and Allemanism had much appeal among artisans and skilled workers. It was perhaps natural that in France the old urban working class should take the lead in developing new forms of working-class organization, and it seems that the larger towns, with their *bourses du travail* and their Socialist newspapers, provided the best conditions for integrating new groups of workers into an older tradition of class-conscious activity. It was no coincidence that the great ports were centres of

Socialism, and even in smaller towns like Carmaux the urban milieu was an important factor stimulating working-class militancy.[20]

French Socialism was partly based on older traditions, but it also made new conquests – notably in the north, where the absence of such traditions helped the victory of Marxism. Even in 1914, however, there were many areas where the workers remained unconvinced, including the important industrial regions in Normandy and in the Catholic and nationalist east (see Map 3). Conversely, not all Socialist voters were workers, for as we have seen there was extensive peasant support in central and southern France. In the centre, there was an active agrarian trade-unionism which interacted with the Socialist ideas emanating from the towns. In the Allier, for example, the discontented *métayers* combined with the Guesdist industrial workers of Montluçon and the Blanquist miners of Commentry (who like miners in some other areas retained their links with the land) to make the department a Socialist stronghold: 34 per cent voted Socialist in 1914, the second highest proportion in France. Commentry was the first town to elect a Socialist municipality (in 1881), and its mayor Thivrier became famous as a deputy who sat in worker's costume – but it was, significantly, a peasant's blouse.[21]

In south-eastern France, on the other hand, Socialism took over the advanced Republican tradition, and appealed to peasant proprietors and artisans who had no special sense of social grievance. Its local leaders were frequently bourgeois notables of the traditional type: advocates and doctors with their roots in Radicalism and freemasonry, like Dr Ferroul, mayor of Narbonne, a prominent figure in the disturbances of 1907. Socialism became integrated into the life of the Midi, and lost much of its specifically Socialist content; the more Socialism expanded from a purely working-class base, the more pressure there was from below to act as a reformist party and play the parliamentary game.[22]

It was the experience of working together in Parliament which set the Socialist leaders on the road to unity. Whatever their party allegiance, deputies found causes in the 1890s which forced them to work together – the defence of workers on strike, opposition to the anti-anarchist *lois scélérates* (which it was feared would be used against Socialists), support for income-tax. In attacking the corruption of bourgeois society as revealed by the Panama scandal, or the way in which Republican principles were being betrayed by the 'opportuno-clerical alliance' under Méline, they could make common cause with Boulangists or Radicals. But as the Socialists came closer together, they felt the need to assert their own identity: Millerand's 'Saint-Mandé speech' to a gathering of Socialists from all parties in 1896, usually seen as the beginning of the moves towards unity, emphasized collectivism as the test of a true Socialist and as the common ground on which all could agree. Closer contacts between the parliamentary leaders followed, but this process was interrupted by the Dreyfus affair.

The Dreyfus affair posed a problem for Socialists even before the question of governmental participation arose, because it involved their attitude to bourgeois society and to the ideals for which the Republic stood. The first reaction of the Socialist deputies, expressed in a manifesto which they issued in January 1898, was to declare their neutrality in this 'bourgeois civil war'. Jaurès signed this manifesto, but before long won most other Socialist leaders round to his own view that justice, humanity and liberty were ideals which were not exclusively bourgeois, but worth defending for their own sake, and that the battle against the forces of reaction was of direct concern to working-class interests.[23] In fact, the anti-clerical and anti-militarist aspects of the affair were irresistible to Socialist leaders and voters, and the nationalist and anti-Semitic exploitation of it opened their eyes to the way in which the Right might use these emotions to divert the workers' loyalties; one by-product of the affair was that the anti-Semitic tendencies which had existed in the Socialist movement disappeared.

If all could agree on defending 'the Republic in danger', support for Millerand was a different matter. His participation in the Waldeck-Rousseau government did not lead to any very radical social reforms, and the shooting of some strikers at Chalon-sur-Saône in 1900 confirmed the distrust inspired by Galliffet's presence in the Cabinet. On the 'ministerial' issue, the Guesdists repudiated the evolution towards reformism which they had shown in the 1890s, and drew close to the Blanquists. A series of Socialist congresses in 1899–1901 intended to lay the foundations of a united party collapsed in acrimony, and the upshot was the formation by 1902 of two rival parties, the *Parti socialiste de France* (the Guesdists and Blanquists) and the *Parti socialiste français*, consisting essentially of the independent deputies led by Jaurès (cf. Appendix 2). The latter was supported by many local Socialist groups which had previously been independent or which broke with Guesdism because they disapproved of its new intransigence, and in the 1902 election it won more than twice as many seats as the PSdeF. The PSF did not really endorse participation in 'bourgeois Cabinets' – it expelled Millerand in 1904 – but it gave consistent parliamentary support to the governments of the Bloc.

The formation of the SFIO in 1905 seemed a triumph for the anti-ministerialists, since it involved repudiation of the Bloc policy; but Jaurès was ready for this in any case, since the Bloc had outlived its usefulness. The strike-breaking of Clemenceau was soon to rule out collaboration with Radicals (except in electoral alliances), and down to 1914 the SFIO attitude was one of outright opposition to virtually all governments. Meanwhile its electoral strength increased steadily: in 1906 it had 877,000 votes and fifty-four seats; in 1914, 1,400,000 votes (nearly 17 per cent of the total) and 103 seats, making it the second largest party.[24] As we have seen, its base extended beyond the working class, and its 1914 election manifesto appealed to workers, peasants, shopkeepers, artisans and 'all men of sincere conscience who suffer from the moral disorder and economic anarchy of the present society'.[25] The party had an elaborate structure including annual policy-making congresses and a permanent bureaucracy, although in practice much power was in the hands of the deputies, whom the militants strove vainly to control. The leading figures were Jaurès and Vaillant; Guesde was now a spent force, and the Guesdist wing of the party was rather ineffective.

The prestige of Jaurès and his part in the Dreyfus affair did much to attract to the SFIO the liberal intelligentsia. For many intellectuals, the Dreyfusard cause became identified with Socialism; for the younger generation, like the future SFIO leader Léon Blum, the affair was the formative experience of their lives, while it also galvanized into Socialist activity previously uncommitted figures like Anatole France and Durkheim. One symptom of this mood (though it petered out after a few years) was the *universités populaires* movement, which involved university intellectuals in working-class adult education.

The development of the SFIO into a 'national' party with support from a diversity of quarters raised the question of its position in the political system: was it on the way to becoming just another political party, or did it retain aims which could only be satisfied through revolutionary change? Unlike the German SPD, the SFIO was not a 'counter-society' which offered a whole way of life to its members and kept the working class apart from the institutions of bourgeois society; auxiliary activities like women's or youth movements were hardly developed.[26] To this extent, the SFIO was less a 'party of integration' (to use Neumann's terminology) than a 'party of representation' which acted as an electoral organization and a pressure-group in the parliamentary arena.[27] On the other hand, this definition of the party's function would have been rejected by many of its members, for the debate between 'reformists' and 'revolutionaries' continued within the SFIO after 1905 (notably at the 1908 Toulouse congress), and it is difficult to believe that party unity could have survived if a new alliance with the Radicals had been attempted, as seemed possible after the 1914 election. The Guesdist wing had little faith in concrete reforms, and many of the reforms which the party supported in its 1914 manifesto, like repeal of the three-year law or proportional representation, were not specifically Socialist. Measures which directly challenged capitalism, like nationalization, did not figure in the party's programmes because it was thought that the economic basis of society could only be changed when the Socialists captured power for themselves. The growth in the Socialist vote made it seem that this would happen in the near future by peaceful means, and this hope allowed the party for the time being to reconcile reformism with the maintenance of revolutionary aims.

The intellectual basis for this kind of compromise position was provided by Jaurès, who did much to hold the SFIO together through his political skill, the integrity and sincerity of his character, his control of L'Humanité and his oratory. Jaurès was a bourgeois intellectual of the first rank, but he earned his position in the Socialist party the hard way. A normalien and philosophy teacher, Jaurès first represented his native Tarn in Parliament in 1885, but he then sat as an Opportunist, and was defeated in 1889. His intellectual conversion to Socialism was completed by the miners' strike at Carmaux in 1892, which attracted national attention. The strike began when the company dismissed the miners' leader Calvignac after he became mayor of the town, and it demonstrated starkly the interlocking of economic and political power. The Carmaux mines had belonged to the Solages family since the eighteenth century, and the Marquis de Solages was also the deputy for Carmaux; his father-in-law, Baron Reille, was chairman of the company and a prominent Rallié deputy. The strike ended only after government mediation, and Solages then resigned his seat. Jaurès was chosen as the miners' candidate in the by-election, and returned to Parliament as a Socialist in 1893. The Solages interest continued to mobilize their influence against him, and he was defeated in 1898. His support for the miners, and also for the glassworkers of Carmaux who were involved in a major strike in 1895, gave Jaurès first-hand knowledge of working-class conditions, and his semi-rural constituency also taught him the need for peasant support.

As a thinker, Jaurès's aim was to show that Socialism was a completion and fulfilment of the principles of the French Revolution and the

Enlightenment. He accepted many Marxist ideas, but tried to graft them onto the democratic, idealist tradition, and to show (perhaps more by eloquent assertion than by rigorous logic) the compatibility of individualism and collectivism, liberty and equality. Socialism, he claimed, was simply the application of the principle of popular sovereignty in the economic field, and 'Socialism alone will give the Declaration of the Rights of Man its full meaning and realize human justice in full.'[28] Bourgeois ideals were not to be rejected, because 'the bourgeoisie, whose historical and economic function is now nearly over, has been despite everything a wonderful force for progress, and it still has in it powerful reserves of thought, initiative and energy.'[29] The moment had come, however, for the proletariat to replace the bourgeoisie as the spearhead of progress. Jaurès had a mystic faith in the proletariat ('in the proletariat the word of France is made flesh', he said, in the style of Michelet),[30] and he expected it to become 'the centre of attraction for all democratic forces',[31] taking over the moral leadership of the nation. In this way, although the working class was a minority it would become a hegemonic force without compromising its ideals and while building on what was best in the Republican inheritance. Jaurès was a reformist in that he thought peaceful evolution towards Socialism possible in France, and valued partial reforms for their own sake, but he also believed that the workers should retain their separate class consciousness and that reforms could not be simply introduced from above, but needed the active participation and revolutionary determination of the workers to carry them through. Despite his appreciation of the bourgeois liberal inheritance, it is by no means certain that Jaurès was contemplating a new Radical/Socialist alliance in 1914, for towards the end of his life he seems to have been more interested in closer links with syndicalism, in which the revolutionary will of the proletariat seemed to preserve the greatest vitality.[32]

The trade-union movement had been united since 1902, when the CGT had absorbed the *Fédération des bourses du travail*, though it was the syndicalist spirit of the latter that triumphed in the new organization. Syndicalists rejected political agitation in favour of strikes and other forms of 'direct action' (including 'sabotage', though by this they meant go-slows rather than blowing up trains). 'Revolutionary syndicalism' implied in addition that strikes should be used to develop the revolutionary potential of the workers, and that the general strike was the means by which revolution should ultimately come about. The classic statement of CGT policy was the 'charter of Amiens', a resolution passed at the 1906 congress;[33] this document 'commended' the general strike as a means of working towards the emancipation of the workers, looked forward to a future in which the *syndicat* would become 'the nucleus for production and distribution, the foundation of social reorganization', and declared the CGT independent of all 'parties and sects'. Political neutrality in fact suited the moderate unions as well as the syndicalists, for one motive of syndicalism had always been the fear that the trade-union movement would be fragmented if it was associated too closely with the quarrelling Socialist parties.

Revolutionary syndicalism was a form of anti-parliamentarism, and it expressed the *ouvriérisme* and suspicion of the bourgeoisie which were always a major element in working-class attitudes. Syndicalists would have endorsed Robert de Jouvenel's dictum that 'there is less difference between two deputies, of whom one is a revolutionary and the other not, than between two revolutionaries, of whom one is a deputy and the other not';[34] 'homme élu, homme foutu' was the more concise popular formula. But while the parties were in the hands of middle-class leaders, the trade unions, it was felt, were working-class organizations with workers as their leaders. It was indeed true that most of the CGT leaders were workers by origin, and this was one of the main differences between it and the SFIO; since the CGT forbade its officials to enter Parliament, it also meant that some of the ablest leaders of the working class stayed outside the political system.

Other anarchist attitudes which appeared in revolutionary syndicalism were belief in the moral value of action for its own sake, and romantic exaltation of violence. These were aspects seized on by Georges Sorel in his *Reflections on Violence*. Sorel stood outside the movement (though he found readers in it), and revolutionary syndicalism was always a 'state of mind' rather than a coherent social theory, but the syndicalists shared his idea that syndicalism was truer than political Socialism to the Marxist idea of class conflict, since it represented working-class action in undiluted form. Sorel's book is famous for its analysis of the general strike as a 'myth', a set of images which intuitively summed up the essence of the workers' ideal: 'the idea of the Syndicalist general strike contains within itself the whole of proletarian Socialism.'[35]

Sorel left it unclear whether he thought a general strike should be actually planned, or remain a mythical ideal. The syndicalists themselves did try to exploit strike movements and extend them to different industries, but these attempts coincided with the Clemenceau period and proved disastrous. The government succeeded in breaking up the CGT leadership, and in 1909 its secretary Griffuelhes was forced to resign. Syndicalist ideas never really recovered after this, and the CGT was in disarray in the last years before the war. The idea of over-throwing the existing order through a general strike was perhaps not as unrealistic as is sometimes suggested – Russia in 1905 was there as an example – but there was no revolutionary situation which made the mass of workers likely to support such a movement, and the key unions like the miners and railwaymen were among those where syndicalist ideas were weak. The degree of unionization in France was in any case low: in 1906, there were 7–8 million industrial workers, but only 800,000 or so belonged to unions, and of these only 200,000 were affiliated to the CGT – by 1912, it is true, the CGT members had risen to nearly 700,000.[36] Compared with British trade unions, the French ones were poorly organized and lacked the funds to finance sustained action – the syndicalist emphasis on short but menacing strikes has indeed sometimes been explained as a rationalization of weakness.

One reason for the weakness of trade unions was the almost unbroken hostility of employers, who refused to accept them as legitimate spokesmen. The atmosphere of French business was autocratic, and employers were determined to preserve the 'principle of authority', which they did by sacking militants, sponsoring company unions, hiring blacklegs and organizing bodies for mutual aid in strikes. Collective bargaining had made little progress by 1914, being more or less confined to the printing trade (thanks to the powerful *Fédération du Livre*) and to mining, though the northern coalowners had accepted it very reluctantly. On the other hand, government attitudes in labour disputes were less inflexible than the occasional bloody incidents suggested. Local officials often acted as arbiters, and in major disputes the dependence of employers on the use of troops allowed the government to bring pressure on them to settle.[37] Sometimes mediation came from the highest level, as when Waldeck-Rousseau intervened at Le Creusot in 1899. Despite this, strikes were still seen in 1914 as a challenge to authority rather than a normal incident of disputes, and trade unions were not accepted as legitimate and respectable bodies or integrated into the machinery of bourgeois society.

One reason why they seemed beyond the pale was the strong anti-militarism which was a part of revolutionary syndicalism. Syndicalist theorists justified anti-militarism precisely because it antagonized the bourgeoisie and expressed the essential nature of Socialism as 'the practical negation of everything which belongs to the bourgeois world'.[38] It was an old anarchist theme – a *Ligue des Antipatriotes* had appeared in the 1880s to combat Déroulède's organization[39] – and was naturally intensified by the use of troops in strikes and by the Dreyfus affair. Anti-militarism was also strong in the SFIO, where Gustave Hervé led an extreme anti-militarist faction, and among school-teachers, where it took a more humanitarian and internationalist form.[40]

Anti-militarism took on a new significance as international tensions increased after 1905. The Socialists saw the danger of war arising from imperialist rivalries at an early stage, and Jaurès became increasingly preoccupied by the problem. The SFIO was, of course, a member of the Second International and the Socialists put their faith in collaboration between the workers of different countries to bring pressure for negotiations and arbitration in a war crisis. The resolution on the subject passed by the SFIO at Limoges in 1906 did not rule out, however, resort to insurrection or the general strike, and it was on the latter that the CGT counted to paralyse mobilization. The campaign against the three-year law tended to bring the SFIO and the CGT together, and in the crisis of July 1914 they co-operated for the first time in organizing demonstrations. Despite these, and despite the desperate efforts of Jaurès to keep open the links with Germany through the International, syndicalists and Socialists alike supported the war when it came. The government did not have to use 'Carnet B', the list which had been prepared of syndicalists and anarchists who were to be arrested on the outbreak of war, and the working class were included in the 'sacred union'. Vaillant shook hands in the Chamber with de Mun, and Guesde ended his career not as the French Lenin but as a minister under Briand.

This reversal of policy has attracted much attention from historians. One reason for it was simply that the leaders were helpless when confronted with the tide of popular patriotism which swept away their followers. Another, suggested by Kriegel and Becker, is that the situation in 1914 was not that previously envisaged by the Left: France appeared not as an imperialist power sharing the guilt for the outbreak of war, but as a peace-loving nation whose efforts were frustrated by the aggressiveness of Germany and Austria. But beyond this, the war raised in the most direct way the question of the working class's integration into French society. Because a man was a worker, was he any less a Frenchman? And in fighting for France, was he not also defending those values of democracy and justice for which the working-class movement itself stood? The answer was given by the CGT secretary, Léon Jouhaux, in his speech at the funeral of Jaurès:[41]

Forced reluctantly into war, we rise to repel the invader, and to safeguard the patrimony of civilization and generous ideology which history has bequeathed to us. . . . Our wish was always to enlarge the rights of the people, and widen the field of liberty. It is in harmony with that wish that we reply 'present' to the mobilization order.

CHAPTER 9

France and the world

French external policy in the first inter-war period of 1871–1914 was dominated by the problem of Germany, for even when the immediate consequences of defeat had passed the growing demographic and industrial imbalance between the two countries had worrying military implications. The search for allies was an obvious aim of foreign policy, and the Russian alliance of 1892 and the entente with Britain in 1904 gave the French some security against the German power block; but France's role in continental affairs remained essentially passive. Outside Europe, France retained her freedom of action, and between the 1880s and 1914 turned herself into the second colonial Power. For many Frenchmen, ten million square kilometres of colonies could not compensate for the loss of Alsace-Lorraine, but the emergence of France as a 'World Power' was nevertheless one of the major achievements of the Third Republic.

France's humiliation in 1870–1 obscured some of the underlying strengths of her position in Europe and the world. Being relatively self-sufficient economically, France did not develop a large export trade, but her growing wealth under the Second Empire had made her a leading exporter of capital and of entrepreneurial skills, producing a large income from foreign investments. French engineers and bankers had built many of the railways of Europe, and the Suez Canal, opened in 1869, was their latest triumph. This experience was a valuable foreign-policy asset, as was the French money market's efficiency at channelling the savings of small investors into overseas funds. Access to the Paris *bourse* was a privilege which the government conceded sparingly, and it could be used at times, as in Turkey and the Balkans before 1914, to win influence at the expense of Germany. France also enjoyed a less tangible intellectual and cultural influence in many parts of the world, and sent out a high proportion of all Catholic missionaries (partly because of the persecution of religious orders at home). Missionary expansion often preceded or accompanied

colonial rule, and Republican politicians were careful to follow
Gambetta's dictum that 'anti-clericalism is not for export' by pre-
serving missionary orders from the various purges and by asserting
France's traditional role as the protector of Christians in the Turkish
Empire.

The Church was thus one of the many interests involved in foreign
and colonial policy, and its missionary role was one reason why (after
initial opposition) colonial expansion became a cause supported by the
Right. The economic interests – investors, banks, exporters, arms firms
– were no doubt even more powerful, and their role is currently
attracting historical study as part of the general debate about the economic motives of imperialism. As we have seen, parliamentary control
over foreign and colonial policy was weak, and this made it easier for
business interests and pressure-groups like the colonial party to get
their own policies adopted by the government. The interest of public
opinion in this field was rather desultory, and depended on the guidance of newspapers which were often controlled by financiers with
foreign interests or subsidized directly by foreign powers. Nevertheless, public opinion was a force to be reckoned with, for the psychological effects of defeat were deep if normally dormant, and dangerous
outbursts of xenophobia could appear, as at the time of the Boulanger
movement, the Fashoda incident in 1898 or the two Moroccan crises.
It could also react the other way if it seemed that selfish minorities
threatened to drag France into war, as with the popular rejection of
Ferry's colonial policies in 1885. This is a field, however, in which it is
particularly difficult to assess the real feeling behind the hysteria of the
Press.

Between a capricious public opinion, the demands of private interests, and a usually passive but ultimately powerful Parliament, the
officials of the foreign ministry trod a delicate path. They were more
likely than most ministries to have a minister who stayed for several
years, but were usually successful in imposing their own conception of
the permanent interests of France as something to be set above the
fluctuations of politics, and like most of the professional diplomats of
the age they were guided primarily by ideas of prestige, military
strength and Great-Power interest, and subordinated economic considerations to these. The diplomatic service remained something of a
haven for aristocrats (even in 1898, half the ambassadors were noble),[1]
but recruitment under the Republic favoured the *grande bourgeoisie*, and
it was this class which provided the celebrated and influential ambassadors of the period like Paul Cambon (at London, 1898–1920), his

brother Jules (at Berlin, 1907–14) and Camille Barrère (at Rome, 1897–1924).

As seen from the Quai d'Orsay, French policy operated in three spheres – the continental, the Mediterranean and the colonial. In Europe, the problem was that posed by Germany and her ally Austria. The first priority was defence of the eastern frontier, the second to find an ally; but there was not much hope of the latter until the 1890s. While Bismarck was in office he was able to isolate France and keep Russia in the German orbit, and there was genuine fear in France that war might be renewed. After 1890, German attitudes fluctuated, sometimes seeming friendly and sometimes menacing, but the Alsace-Lorraine question stood in the way of any real détente. The lost provinces were at the centre of French patriotic feeling for a generation after 1871, and the hope of regaining them was never renounced. But governments generally obeyed Gambetta's injunction to 'think of it always, speak of it never' and to rely on 'immanent justice' to right the wrong in the future. There were no plans to regain Alsace-Lorraine by either diplomatic or military means, and the French were careful to give no overt support to the pro-French elements in the provinces.

French interests in the Mediterranean centred on Algeria, with its European population and its highly developed trade with France, the need to protect which (and the trade of Marseilles with the East via Suez) was the leading task of the French navy. Algeria was a natural base for the extension of control over the native regimes in Tunisia and Morocco, and by 1914 North Africa had become the heart of the French empire. This expansion brought unfriendly relations with Italy, whose own ambitions it frustrated, and who might otherwise have been a useful ally. The French annexation of Tunisia in 1881 led Italy to join Germany and Austria in the Triple Alliance in 1882, and the 'Mediterranean agreements' of 1887 aligned her with France's maritime rival Britain; there followed a ruinous tariff war between France and Italy lasting from 1888 to 1898. Britain was now a rival because of her establishment of control over Egypt in 1882, which was seen as excluding legitimate French financial and cultural interests, and was much resented. France continued, however, to co-operate with Britain in the general policy of propping up the Turkish Empire, and the Franco-Russian alliance did not lead her to support Russian claims to the Straits; in the years before 1914, the main cause for alarm in this area was the growing economic and political influence of Germany.

Britain was also the main rival, of course, in the colonial sphere. In 1870, France's overseas empire consisted of a scattering of islands, and of trading settlements and military posts in West Africa and Indo-China. There had been some expansion outwards from the latter under the Second Empire, but this was not resumed until the 1880s. By 1900, France was indubitably a World Power: all her possessions in West and Central Africa had been linked into a vast if not very populous territory, and direct or indirect rule was established over the whole of Indo-China. Much of this expansion was in territory not coveted by other Powers – there was no clash with German ambitions, for example, until the Morocco question. But there were areas (West Africa, the Sudan, Siam) where France posed a direct challenge to Britain; throughout the 1890s, Britain seemed the main enemy rather than Germany, and the alliance with Russia had strong anti-British overtones. As the Fashoda crisis in 1898 showed, colonial expansion could be a dangerous game, but on the whole French and British world ambitions were complementary, and unlike Germany France did not alarm the British by threatening to replace Britain as a world trading power or by building up a great battle-fleet. The Franco-British entente of 1904 liquidated the remaining colonial disputes, and Britain's entente with Russia in 1907 created the Triple Entente, centred on France. To have provided security for France through this alliance system, to have seized every opportunity that offered itself for overseas expansion, and to have restored France to the first rank of World Powers, all without seriously risking war or disturbing the European balance of power, was a remarkable work of skill and determination on the part of those who directed French policy.

In the 1870s, ambitions had necessarily been modest, and France pursued a policy of 'contemplation' (*recueillement*). The more zealous Catholics, indeed, wanted France to intervene to restore the temporal power of the Pope, but this demand was firmly resisted by the Orleanist Decazes, foreign minister between 1873 and 1877. The danger of such a policy, especially at a time when Bismarck was in conflict with the Church, only increased the unpopularity of the Right. The National Assembly's most significant contribution to France's national revival was the law of 1872 which moved towards the Prussian system of universal military service. The traditional French system was selective service by drawing lots: all were liable to be drawn, but those who drew an unlucky number had been able to buy substitutes. This produced a long-service and virtually professional army with few trained reserves, and was socially unjust because only the poor were forced to serve. The Republicans demanded short but universal service as the only democratic system, but the generals, supported by Thiers, claimed that only long service could produce trained and disciplined men. The law of 1872 was a compromise: the annual 'contingent' was divided by lot into two parts, one serving for five years and the other for only a few months. Substitution was abolished, but inequalities remained through various exemptions, which being based on education mainly favoured the middle class. About 30 per cent escaped service; the Republicans were especially irritated by the exemption of seminarists, and continued to campaign for a more democratic system.[2] But the law of 1872 succeeded in creating numerical equivalence between the French and German armies.[3] At the same time, a general staff on Prussian lines began to evolve, and the construction began of a massive line of fortifications along the eastern frontier designed by General Séré de Rivière. These moves were enough to alarm Bismarck; the 'war-in-sight crisis' of 1875 was set off by a modification of the French military system, and seems to have been intended to force the French to abandon it. In fact, the sympathy shown by other Powers during this war scare increased French confidence, and France's participation in the Congress of Berlin in 1878 marked the re-establishment of her European status.

When the Republicans took over power, they chose to flex their muscles in the colonial rather than the continental field, and it is with Ferry that the beginnings of colonial expansion are associated. In his first ministry, he established the French protectorate over Tunisia (1881); in his second, he began a war in Madagascar which led on to a virtual protectorate in 1885, and extended French power in Indo-China from its base in Cochin-China to Cambodia, Annam and Tonkin, which involved a war with China successfully concluded in 1885. The temporary reverse at Lang Son, however, brought Ferry's political career to an end, and showed that the colonial cause was still far from popular. Conservatives condemned it as wasteful and dangerous, but the strongest opposition came from Clemenceau and the Left. Colonial expeditions were unpopular because they meant higher taxes and the death of conscript soldiers (a problem later avoided by creating a 'colonial army' of native troops and French volunteers). Ferry was also attacked for bypassing and deceiving Parliament: his technique, pioneered in the capture of Tunis and to be imitated later during the acquisition of Morocco, was to start with police operations or 'punitive' campaigns, and to appeal to the Chamber for credits only when things had gone so far that French prestige and honour would suffer from withdrawal.

The real charge against Ferry was the patriotic one that he was diverting French attention from the blue line of the Vosges and the task of *revanche*. He was accused of being a dupe of Bismarck, who was encouraging colonial adventures in order to weaken France and embroil her with potential allies like Britain and Italy. It was true that Bismarck was prepared to give France a free hand in the colonial field, and the French statesmen knew this. But Ferry was hardly lacking in patriotism, and he defended his policies vigorously in speeches and in a book published after he left office. Their significance lies in the stress put on economic motives for expansion, although this may not reflect the real balance of motives in Ferry's mind – when colonies were attacked for their cost, it was natural to emphasize the return they could bring.

Ferry's arguments gave pride of place to French industry's need for new and secure outlets for its products. Like others at the time, Ferry feared that the growth of protectionism in Europe would squeeze France out of her traditional markets, and create a crisis of overproduction with grave social consequences. 'Colonial policy is the daughter of industrial policy . . . . The protective system is a steam engine without a safety-valve, if it does not have a sound and serious colonial policy as its corrective and auxiliary.'[4] It is easy to show that these fears were misplaced, and to demonstrate that France's colonies proved disappointing from an economic point of view – by 1914 they accounted for only 11 per cent of France's exports, 9 per cent of her imports and 9 per cent of her foreign investment;[5] but that does not prove that the economic motive was not a real one at the time.

It seems agreed, however, that Ferry's own initiatives were taken for political reasons rather than under pressure from economic interests. In Tunisia, the ruler was entangled in debts to French bondholders, and French companies competed with Italian ones for railway concessions, but the decisive motives were the need to pre-empt action by Italy and the desire to assert French prestige. The expedition went ahead when Gambetta was converted to support for it; 'France regains her rank as a great power', he wrote to Ferry, congratulating him on its success.[6] This theme was taken up by Ferry, speaking in 1885: colonization was the great European enterprise of the age, and if France stood aside while other countries acted she would be 'abdicating' her position and would fall to the third or fourth rank among Powers.[7] As the colonial propagandist Leroy-Beaulieu wrote in 1882, colonization 'is the only great enterprise which destiny permits us. . . . Colonization is a question of life or death for France.'[8] Ferry and the colonialists were well aware that colonies were in a sense a 'compensation', both material and psychological, for the loss of Alsace-Lorraine, though it was an idea not to be publicly expressed. Brunschwig, indeed, who has argued against the economic interpretation of colonialism, sees the fundamental cause of French colonial expansion in nationalist reaction to France's defeat.[9] Despite Ferry's unpopularity, the conquests which he made were retained, and by 1900 France's empire was generally regarded as a source of pride and justified by reference to its 'civilizing mission'. The Radicals had forgotten their opposition to the empire, and were among those who profited from it as colonial governors or businessmen.[10] The Right too had come to identify the empire with the values which it defended – it was, after all, the scene where the Church and the army were contributing most to France's glory – although the empire was never at the centre of French national feeling as it was of British.

In 1885, the feeling that the Opportunists were failing to tend the flame of *revanche* was part of the general disillusion with their rule which led to the Boulanger crisis, in which the revival of anti-German feeling was a significant element. Two incidents had their place in the episode: in January 1887, Bismarck named Boulanger as the main obstacle to friendly relations with France, which greatly increased the general's popularity; and in April 1887 there was the Schnaebelé affair, when a French police agent was arrested on the frontier – the most serious war scare since 1875. These incidents were not unconnected with the Reichstag election and Bismarck's desire to secure the passing of a new army law. In France, the war scare contributed to the military reform of 1889, which abolished exemptions from service (even for the *curés*) and the division of the contingent by lot; service was now for one year or for three, the main criterion for short service being educational, so that the middle class were still privileged. This law was the work of Freycinet, who also carried out some important improvements in the army's command structure.[11]

The dismissal of Bismarck did much to relieve French fears of Germany, and opened the way for the Franco-Russian alliance. This alliance had always made geopolitical sense, but went against the inclinations both of the French Left, who were hostile to autocracy, and of Alexander III, who detested Republics and feared that chauvinist agitation of the Boulanger type might drag Russia into a Franco-German war. On the French side, the main proponents of the alliance were revanchist journalists like Juliette Adam (former mentor of Gambetta), the military, who could see the advantage of forcing Germany to fight on two fronts, and financiers who saw Russia as a fruitful field for investment – the first Russian loan was raised in Paris in 1888. The downfall of Boulanger and the stable government of Freycinet in 1890–2 reassured Alexander III, and a move towards closer relations began. In 1891, a French naval squadron visited Kronstadt, and an informal political entente followed. In 1892, the military convention which was the kernel of the alliance was signed for the French by General Boisdeffre. Under its terms, which were of course secret, each country would help the other if attacked by Germany, with or without her Triple Alliance partners, and each would mobilize in any case as soon as any of the Triple Alliance powers did so; the convention was to last as long as the Triple Alliance itself.[12] The alliance was finally ratified by an exchange of letters in December–January 1893–4.

The alliance gave France both military and emotional security – the importance of the latter was shown by the scenes when Russian sailors visited Toulon in 1893, and during the subsequent State visits of Nicholas II. The Republicans swallowed their objections to tyranny, and criticism of Russia became an unpatriotic act. The middle class demonstrated their enthusiasm in a practical way by investing in Russian State and railway bonds. By 1914, a quarter of all French foreign investment was in Russia, and was to be lost in 1917. The French government tried to tie these loans to the purchase of French arms (Schneider was now becoming one of the great European arms firms, renowned for the quality of its armour plate) and to the construction of strategic railways. After Fashoda, for example, one loan was earmarked for the Orenburg–Tashkent railway, to threaten the British in India, and later the French encouraged railway-building which would speed up mobilization against Germany. French firms came to play a large part in the industrialization of Russia, and recent research has stressed that French investment was 'entrepreneurial' as well as 'rentier' in character.[13]

In the 1890s, the implications of the alliance seemed as much anti-British as anti-German, as France's colonial expansion brought her into conflict with Britain in several parts of the world. This rivalry was embittered by the Egyptian question. France had traditionally co-operated with Britain in expanding European interests in Egypt and exploiting its rulers' indebtedness, but in the crisis of 1882 caused by nationalist agitation she had refused to join Britain in the bombardment of Alexandria and the subsequent military occupation. Gambetta had been willing to participate, but neither his successor Freycinet nor Parliament were prepared to take the risk of acting against Bismarck's disapproval. Once British rule was established, however, it was resented by the French, and the Quai d'Orsay continued until 1904 to complain that French interests in Egypt were being unfairly treated, and to demand the end of the British occupation.

Conflict also arose in Asia, as the French extended their rule westwards from Indo-China over Laos, and cast eyes on Siam, which Britain wished to preserve as an independent buffer State. In 1893, France forced various concessions on Siam through gunboat diplomacy, causing a confrontation with Britain which was not resolved until 1896. Other French advances in this period were in Madagascar, where determination to turn the protectorate into a colony led to serious fighting in 1895–6 and to guerrilla resistance which was only gradually suppressed by General Galliéni, and in West Africa, where – also against serious local resistance – the army pushed the frontier eastwards from Senegal, linked the French coastal settlements with the interior, established a Saharan frontier with Algeria, and so by the mid-1890s created a single West African domain. The greatest challenge to Britain, however, came from the Congo, where the French colony had been established by the explorer Brazza in 1879–82. As the French pushed north towards Lake Chad, the colonial party conceived the idea of beating the British to control of the upper Nile, and establishing a barrier across Africa from east to west. The *Comité de l'Afrique française* was very active in sponsoring and gaining official approval for the Marchand expedition, which reached Fashoda from the Congo in July 1898; Kitchener appeared soon afterwards, and demanded its withdrawal. Despite strong nationalist agitation and anti-British feeling, the French government had no choice but to back down, and Britain and France shared the Sudan between them. French diplomatic preparation for the crisis had been inadequate: the idea was to force an international conference on Britain which would reopen the Egyptian question, but support was not forthcoming even from Russia.

The foreign minister at the time of Fashoda was Delcassé, who had just succeeded the more cautious Hanotaux; he was to stay in office until 1905 and do more than most ministers to bring about a reorientation of policy. Delcassé is best remembered as the architect of the *entente cordiale*, but he was not originally pro-British – he was a leading member of the colonial party, and had encouraged the idea of a challenge on the Nile when himself colonial minister. But the lesson of Fashoda for the colonial party was that there was little future in challenging Britain, and the idea arose of a bargain involving Egypt and Morocco. Delcassé's policies were directed towards a French takeover of Morocco and to strengthening France's position against Germany.

In 1899, he secured a revision of the Franco-Russian alliance which tied it less narrowly to the Triple Alliance, and in 1902 Italy gave a secret assurance that her membership of the Triple Alliance was not directed against France. Support for French action in Morocco was promised by Italy in 1900 (in return for a free hand in Libya) and by Spain in 1904. The entente with Britain was a late development, and was not helped by the pro-Boer attitude of French opinion in the Boer war. But the visit to Paris in 1903 of Edward VII (whose influence on policy the French were inclined to overestimate) paved the way for the Franco-British entente of 1904. This was not an alliance, but a settlement of old disputes, and Britain promised support over Morocco in return for French acceptance of the British presence in Egypt.

Rival French financial groups were already active in Morocco, Eugène Etienne formed a special *Comité du Maroc* to supervise the operation, and General Lyautey began a policy of 'peaceful penetration' by military incursions across the Algerian frontier. These initiatives sometimes had to be restrained by Delcassé, and in general the pressure of economic interests was subordinated to political aims. Delcassé did not make any attempt to conciliate German interests, and believed that his diplomatic preparations would allow France to defy German opposition. In March 1905, the German intervention came, with William II's visit to Tangier. In the subsequent crisis, France was forced to agree to an international conference, and the prime minister Rouvier dismissed Delcassé. This might seem a humiliation, but opinion was generally against Delcassé, who was felt to have taken unnecessary risks and subordinated French policy to the interests of the colonial clique. The Moroccan affair had come to a head at a time of weakness for France, with the army demoralized after the Dreyfus affair and the 'affaire des fiches', and Russia in chaos; when the Tsar met William II at Björkö in July 1905 it seemed that the alliance itself might be crumbling. In the event, however, the Algeciras conference was a success for France: thanks to the support of her allies, she gained the essential footholds in Morocco (control of the ports and finances), and the German design of intimidating France into abandoning the *entente cordiale* failed.

The first Moroccan crisis was notable for the lack of bellicose feelings in France. The Left was now in power, and although the anti-militarism of Socialists and syndicalists had little influence at government level, the Radicals also had a strong internationalist wing, as was shown by the leading role of Léon Bourgeois in the Hague conferences

of 1899 and 1907. The Radicals were responsible for the army law of
1905, which reduced service to two years and for the first time made it
the same length for all conscripts – a reduction which was opposed by
the military, but was undoubtedly popular. More radical military ideas
also appeared on the Left, and in his *L'Armée nouvelle* of 1911 Jaurès
proposed a citizen militia on Swiss lines: one of his aims was to break
down the barrier between the officer class and the rest of the nation –
officers were to be educated at the universities instead of at special
schools – but he also argued that the abolition of standing armies and
general staffs would make aggressive war impossible.

It was also Jaurès who led the Left's attack on the Moroccan enterprise, which he denounced as a threat to European peace, and a bad
example to other Powers. Until then the colonial question had been
largely ignored by Socialists, but colonialism was now attacked both
on humanitarian grounds and as a menacing extension of capitalist
exploitation. The anti-colonial case was strengthened by the un-
savoury colonial scandals which surfaced from time to time, like the
N'Goko Sangha affair, in which a company with a concession in
the Congo tried to obtain a huge indemnity from the French government for damage supposedly caused by German incursions.

Morocco remained a potential flashpoint, for the French were
determined to establish full control of the country by exploiting tribal
dissensions and internal disorder, while Germany refused to drop her
interest in the question, despite an agreement on joint commercial
exploitation in 1909. In 1911, the second crisis began when the French
sent an expedition to Fez which was obviously the prelude to a takeover, and the German gunboat *Panther* appeared at Agadir. At the end
of the lengthy negotiations which followed, Germany recognized the
French protectorate over Morocco (formally established in 1912) in
return for the cession of part of the French Congo, a sacrifice imposed
against significant French opposition by the pacific Caillaux.

Now that Germany had been 'compensated', it might seem that
relations could return to normal. In fact, the 1911 crisis led to a period
of intensified national feeling in France, in which a large segment of
opinion became convinced that Germany was preparing war. The
election of Poincaré as president and the passage of the three-year law
were among the consequences of this new mood, and they showed also
that Franco-German relations had become a major question in domestic politics, with Poincaré and Clemenceau among the hard-liners and
Caillaux and Jaurès at the head of the conciliators. The 1914 election
was a victory for the latter, and if international tension had relaxed it is

unlikely that the three-year law would have lasted long. But it was impossible for France to avoid involvement in the crisis of 1914, and once Russia was at war with Germany the provisions of the 1892 convention came into force (though it was concealed from French opinion that Russia had mobilized first). Because of the requirements of the Schlieffen plan, Germany declared war on France rather than vice versa, so that no debate on the issue was held in the French Parliament. The mood of patriotic exaltation in which the 'sacred union' was formed does not suggest that any force in France could have resisted the tide of war.

Historical debate over the origins of the First World War has recently revived, and the way in which German policy and German domestic tensions pointed to war has become clear. Nobody would now claim, as did German propagandists between the wars, that French 'revanchism' was a cause of war. The extreme nationalism of the *Action française* movement, which was in any case directed against other Frenchmen as much as against Germany, was not representative of opinion as a whole, and had no influence in governing circles. The French political system, for all its faults, placed power in the hands of moderate and responsible men, who were prepared to ignore pressure-groups like the colonial party and to sacrifice their colleagues (like Delcassé in 1905) if a real danger of war appeared, just as in the last resort it was Parliament and the civilians who controlled France's military plans. Nevertheless, the mood did change in France in the years before the war, and her policies raise a number of interesting questions.

France was a formidable military Power, and one historian speaks of the 'aggressive confidence of the French General Staff' in these years.[14] Before the three-year law, the French had an active army of 524,000 compared with Germany's 645,000.[15] But this near-equality was maintained only through considerable sacrifices: the proportion of the budget spent on the armed forces rose from a quarter in 1872 to 36 per cent in 1913, and manpower resources were stretched to the limit, since France called up 83 per cent of those liable for military service, while Germany could get by with 53 per cent.[16] The population question was causing great concern on the eve of the war, and the French were looking to the empire to compensate for their own inferiority – conscription was extended to the native population of Algeria in 1912. The additional strain of the three-year law was therefore hardly welcomed in France, and was accepted only because of the German army laws of 1912 and 1913, which raised the German forces to over 800,000;

France was able to keep up only by lowering the recruiting age, so that two 'classes' of conscripts were called up in 1913.

The French generals also wanted longer service because only well-trained soldiers were suited to the aggressive tactical doctrine, associated with Colonel Grandmaison, which was now accepted as orthodoxy. This stressed the importance of taking the initiative in warfare, and the need to maintain high morale by cultivating the offensive spirit and putting the emphasis on attack – an idea that was to prove disastrous in the conditions of trench warfare. The appointment of Joffre as Chief of the General Staff in 1911 was a victory for the offensive school, and the war plan prepared by Joffre which was in force in 1914 ('Plan XVII') included provision for a French offensive in Lorraine, to provoke a decisive battle at an early stage. Joffre's predecessor Michel had had a more defensive plan, and had also made more provision for a German attack through Belgium – though the French had failed to find out about the Schlieffen plan. But even Joffre's plan was conceived within a fundamentally defensive strategy: all French war plans were concerned with how to respond to a German attack, and there was no thought of invading Germany. An additional point about Joffre's appointment was that it coincided with a reform of the command structure which for the first time gave the peacetime army a single commander, so that Joffre had unprecedented power: this was a sign that the army's prestige had recovered from the Dreyfus affair, and that the politicians were prepared to trust it to devise its policies autonomously.[17]

French naval power was a good deal less impressive, for public opinion took little interest in it, and Germany's naval expansion did not pose a direct threat to France. In the 1870s, France was the second naval Power, but in 1914 she had only two Dreadnoughts of the most modern class. This was partly because energies were diverted instead into building torpedo-boats and submarines, an emphasis which went back to the doctrines of Admiral Aube and the 'jeune école' in the 1880s. Aube had argued that France's need was not to challenge Britain directly, but to be able to break a British blockade and raid commerce with cruisers. The inability of the navy to protect France from Britain had, however, become apparent at the time of Fashoda, and the navy became a byword for neglect and maladministration; a series of explosions and sinkings in the 1900s gave rise to several parliamentary enquiries, and the navy reached its nadir under Combes's naval minister, the sectarian Radical Camille Pelletan, who offended the officer corps by fraternizing with the dockyard workers and naming

battleships *Justice* and *Vérité* to underline the triumph of the Dreyfusards. Matters only really improved when Delcassé returned to office
as minister of marine, and initiated a large-scale building programme
in 1912.

The *entente cordiale* allowed the French navy to concentrate its efforts
in the Mediterranean, and this arrangement was formalized in the
Franco-British naval agreement of 1913. On the military side, regular
staff talks had been taking place since 1906, and it was agreed that in
the event of war Britain would send an expeditionary force to the
continent (though this was given only marginal significance in the
French military plans). Britain was not formally committed, of course,
to aiding France if war came; the veiled assurances of Grey's letter to
Cambon in November 1912 were the most that could be extracted, but
the assumption that Britain would in fact intervene was one of the
bases of French policy-making.

One of the arguments against the 'alliance system' is that it
encouraged rash actions inspired by overconfidence – France was
bolder in Morocco, for example, than she could have been without
British support. The main charge made against France by 'revisionist'
historians after the First World War was that French support encouraged Russia's ambitions in the Balkans, and that under the influence of Poincaré Russia was given *carte blanche* in much the same way as
Austria was by Germany. Poincaré certainly worked to strengthen the
Franco-Russian alliance, and visited St Petersburg as prime minister
in 1912 and as president; he and Viviani were there in July 1914, and
the advice they then gave cannot be known. Poincaré felt unable to
restrain Russia's forward policy in the Balkans (as France had restrained
Russia during the 1908–9 Bosnian crisis), but it is probably going too
far to accuse him of encouraging it or of wanting a general war. He
felt obliged to support Russia because the alliance was France's chief
defence against the growing German menace, and like other European
statesmen he acted on the assumption that peace was preserved by the
balance of power, so that to weaken the alliance would be catastrophic.
In critical situations, this meant accepting the risk of war – in Poincaré's
own words, 'France must give the impression of a Nation which does
not want war, but does not fear it.'[18] It seems fair also to say that
Poincaré did nothing positively to avert war, and that he allowed
himself to hope that a war would be short and successful and would
lead at last to the return of Alsace and Lorraine.[19]

The case against Poincaré was put most strongly in the memoirs of
the 'pacifist' Caillaux, who was imprisoned during the war for his

supposedly pro-German tendencies. Several historians have pointed out the contrast between the traditional nationalism of Poincaré and Clemenceau, who saw Germany as the hereditary enemy waiting her chance to strike again, and the capitalist internationalism of Caillaux, an international banker with close German connections, who looked forward to a Europe in which frontiers would disappear through economic co-operation.[20] In the style of Norman Angell's *The Great Illusion*, Caillaux argued that war did not pay, and that it would fatally damage European civilization.[21]

The tendencies represented by Caillaux were powerful ones, and German capital had already penetrated to a considerable extent in France itself, especially through German ownership of French iron-ore resources. Both Socialists and extreme nationalists attacked this German influence, and in the years after 1911 the campaigns against German firms and German goods were significant enough to force the government into action.[22] Outside France, too, French and German capital interpenetrated. Krupp and Schneider both participated in the Ouenza mining company, formed to exploit the orefields of Algeria, and French and German companies frequently formed consortia in both Morocco and the Balkans; often it was only political pressure from the Quai d'Orsay which forced banks and industrial companies into breaking these links and acting more nationalistically.[23] This was especially the case in the Balkans, where after about 1910 French and German companies competed fiercely to supply arms and loans to the warring nations, and to build up rival spheres of influence. The power of French capital was used in the service of the Franco-Russian alliance, and France scored some notable successes, becoming the chief supplier of Serbia and Greece, and challenging Germany strongly in Bulgaria. Even in Turkey itself, France secured an important agreement in 1914 which put German interests on the defensive.[24]

If imperialist rivalries are to be seen as the cause of the war, it is in the Balkans that they must be sought, for it was the only field where French and German economic interests were in conflict in 1914. It was also a field where the French were successfully challenging Germany, so that the Germans might complain of 'encirclement'. These complaints, however, had little foundation. In her foreign and colonial policy since 1871, France had done no more than exercise the rights considered legitimate for any great power. If she had 'encircled' Germany with the Franco-Russian alliance, it was because she felt threatened by the German-dominated power block in central Europe, and if she had prepared for war against Germany in the years before

1914 it was because of the deep mistrust aroused by that country's policies. What was new about the last years was perhaps that France had a new-found confidence which made her prepared to confront Germany rather than back down before threats. But as in other countries, the sense of confidence and the sense of insecurity existed uneasily together, and French statesmen were no more able than others to escape from the situation created by the independent pursuit of national interests.

Conclusion

It is difficult to assess the strengths and weaknesses of the Third Republic in this period without being influenced by the events of the inter-war period and the collapse of the regime in 1940. But as Siegfried pointed out, if the Third Republic had ended in 1918 it would have been considered a glorious episode in French history.[1] The First World War was to have profound effects on France, both material and psychological – especially perhaps in destroying her self-confidence and receptiveness to change – and it is far from clear that the weaknesses which appeared later were implicit in the situation in 1914. Some of them, however, were undoubtedly latent, and some features of the political system which were tolerable before 1914 were to prove deficient in the harsher economic and international climate of the inter-war years.

One of these was the Republic's 'ministerial instability'. Although this was offset by certain elements of continuity – the 'musical chairs' aspect of Cabinet changes, and the power of the bureaucracy – it did work against effective government and political initiatives. Contemporaries often sought a remedy in different constitutional or electoral arrangements, but it seems clear to the historian that the fundamental cause of instability was the absence of a strong party system. Government was most stable during the period of the Bloc, but centre-based coalitions returned in the years before 1914, and there was no indication that France was moving towards a two-party system. The intersection of different sets of values made this unlikely, and in any case one can hardly claim that such a system is a necessary adjunct of a democracy. The British observer Bodley, who thought that only plebiscitary government would work in France because of the strength of the centralized State, saw the failure of the French to develop a party system as 'a sure sign of their incapacity for parliamentary government',[2] though in fact by 1914 party organization was growing.

The strength of ideological division was arguably another weakness of the Third Republic. As has frequently been pointed out, there has never been complete consensus about the form of government in modern France, and throughout the life of the Third Republic there were those on both wings of politics who stood outside the system. But by 1914, it would seem that consensus was more general than it ever had been before, or than it was to be after the war, with the rise of Communism and the growth of the nationalist and near-fascist Right. The nucleus of an anti-parliamentary Right existed in 1914, but the progressive *ralliement* of the traditional Right had left only a handful opposed to the Republic itself, and even they accepted constitutional methods. On the Left, the rejection of 'bourgeois' democracy by Socialists and revolutionary syndicalists seemed more extensive, but it is questionable how far a genuine revolutionary impulse survived. Revolutionary syndicalism seems to have been on the decline after 1910, and the success of the SFIO in the 1914 election would probably have led it further along the parliamentary path. The crisis of 1914 revealed the underlying national unity of France, as patriotism overcame the doubts of the Right about democracy and loyalty to democratic ideals overcame the doubts of the Left about bourgeois society. France's experience in the First World War was on the whole to vindicate the democratic system, and to show that popular attachment to the Republic was deep. Despite the occasional dismaying scandals and the disillusion with parliamentarism, most Frenchmen in 1914 seem to have approved of the regime under which they lived and of the leadership which it provided – something which could not be said of all European countries.

It is in any case easy for historians to exaggerate the extent of ideological conflict at this time – especially perhaps if they are not French, so that it is difficult for them to appreciate the instinctive values and experiences which all Frenchmen shared, or if they write the kind of intellectual or literary history which divorces ideas from the men who held them. This is not to deny that the conflict of ideals was real. Indeed, it gave the politics of the Third Republic much of their dignity and interest. Politics were often selfish and sordid, but all parties retained an essentially ethical approach to political life, and acted in the name of democracy, religious faith, patriotism or social justice. Parliamentary debates, in this age of great orators, often reached a remarkably high level of seriousness and generality.

Parliament remained at the centre of the political system. From a functional point of view, it was quite efficient at acting as a forum for interests and distributing benefits, although it has been argued that the weakness of its interest articulation and aggregation structures (i.e.

pressure-groups and parties) was one reason for French 'immobilism'.[3] Another weakness was that those who did not share fully in power could not play the parliamentary game: the permanent exclusion from power of the Right meant that satisfaction could not be gained for the legitimate interests which it represented, notably the Church, and the paucity of social reforms showed the ineffectiveness of working-class pressures. The Left, however, remained outside more through its own cultivation of class separatism than through exclusion, for many Republican leaders were only too anxious to absorb Socialists into the system and let them taste the fruits of power. One of the unanswerable questions about France in 1914 is whether the Socialist party could have been integrated into the system, and whether Socialism could have come about without revolution through a Jaurèsian synthesis of the liberal and Socialist ideals of democracy. The existence of a powerful Radical party whose ideas and supporters overlapped with those of the Socialists was an element which favoured this, and it was a virtue of the parliamentary system that it was flexible enough to accommodate shifts in the balance of social power – as it had allowed the reluctant but peaceful yielding of power by the notables in the 1870s.

One thing which kept conflict within tolerable limits was that France did not have to cope at the same time with all the problems which confront modern societies.[4] The upheavals following the Revolution had already modernized society in certain crucial ways, so that the stresses of industrialization could be absorbed without excessive disruption, while the question of formal popular participation in government through universal suffrage was resolved before 1870. There remained two main forms of conflict – that between the secular and religious ideals, involving rival systems of moral and social values, and class-based conflict over the distribution of the national wealth. The latter gradually became more important than the former, and historians like Thomson have seen 1905 as the 'watershed' of the Republic: with the liquidation of the religious question by the Separation of Church and State, 'dynastic, ecclesiastical and militarist issues were replaced by social and economic issues.'[5] This is perhaps too simple – social issues were hardly unknown in the decades which began with the Commune, while the old questions of power and democracy remained essential ones down to 1940.

Thomson's basic point, however, with which most historians would agree, was that the rise of a more socially polarized society, and the substitution of a wage-earning proletariat for the peasants as the 'masses', disrupted the social balance which had made the Third

Republic a success in its early years. In the classic period of the Republic, the political system was in harmony with the underlying social
structure; an individualist form of democracy reflected the significance
of property and economic independence. A more jaundiced view is that
the Republic represented above all the more old-fashioned and ineffi-
cient elements in French society, and that its 'immobilism' and inherent
preference for weak government were suited only to a rigid and stagnant 'stalemate society'.[6] But this is perhaps to apply an image of
France which became current under the Fourth Republic wrongly to
the years before 1914. During the 'belle époque', France was by contemporary European standards an open society with high social
mobility, in which the barriers to talent were low; the ideals of the
Republicans and the educational system which they promoted were
designed to encourage this openness, and surely deserve some of the
credit for the brilliant achievements which are found in this period in
so many fields.

The founders of the Republic had a very clear vision of what they
wanted to achieve, and the cohesion and nature of the political elite
remained one of the strengths of French democracy. Unlike their
counterparts in Spain or Italy, the leaders of the liberal middle class
succeeded in grouping the major forces in the country around them.
Capturing the support of the peasantry was vital, and was achieved in
the 1870s by skilful and tireless propaganda, but also significant were
the appeal of Radicalism to the lower middle class and the way in
which workers, even when they began to vote Socialist, saw Socialism
as complementing and fulfilling Republicanism rather than replacing
it. Some of this success was due to the deliberate programme of
political socialization undertaken in the schools; more, perhaps, to a
political culture in which the seeds of democracy were already planted
by the nation's historical experience.

The advent of the Republic had involved a limited social revolution
– the 'end of the notables' – and as a result France stood out among
continental countries for her bourgeois political leadership and for the
powerlessness of aristocracies and military cliques. Both the Republicans of the 1880s and the Radicals of the 1900s showed a remarkable
toughmindedness in keeping out of power those whom they identified
as reactionaries, even when – as in the case of the Church – this led
them into intolerant and vindictive measures. The old agrarian and
upper-bourgeois elites had the consolation of retaining economic
power and the ability to stop or delay social reforms by informal
pressure, but they were unable to manipulate the political system them-

selves. The danger of democracy being overthrown from above was in any case lessened by the fact that a regime with the Third Republic's reverence for property and the small property-owner guaranteed a clear field for the operation of capitalism, and posed no threat to business interests. The Republic could survive because, as Seignobos said, its constitution proved 'solid, supple and ingenious, strong enough both to reassure the bourgeoisie and to adapt itself to the growth of democracy'.[7]

Political evolution

This appendix sets out some essential data in concise form: for each of four periods, it gives election results, describes the principal groups within the Chamber, and shows which of these the different governments relied on for support.

The lack of organized parties makes French electoral statistics uncertain, and there is no standard compilation; authorities often give very different figures. For the distribution of seats, I have relied for the sake of consistency on a traditional source, making minor modifications: from 1876 to 1902, the annual *L'Année politique*, and from 1906 G. Bonnefous, *Histoire politique de la Troisième République*, vol. 1 (2nd ed., 1965). Voting figures come from *L'Année politique*, P. Campbell, *French Electoral Systems and Elections since 1789* (2nd ed., 1965) or (from 1902) M. Duverger, *Constitutions et documents politiques* (1957), pp. 234–5.

The history of parliamentary groups is very confusing, as their names often differed from those of parties, and until 1910 a deputy could join more than one (*double appartenance*), or none at all. The best guide is the list by A. Bomier-Landowski in F. Goguel and G. Dupeux, *Sociologie électorale. Esquisse d'un bilan* (1951).

Governments are mentioned in chronological order, with the date of their assuming office (as with Presidents of the Republic). A complete list is thus provided. 2 FERRY means Ferry's second government, and so on.

I. 1871–1879

A. ELECTIONS

1871 (February)
Voting by list, with one ballot.
The results are often summarized as 400 Monarchists, 200 Republicans,

but the following approximate figures are given by Gouault (*Comment la France est devenue républicaine* (1954), p. 73):

Legitimists	180
Orleanists	214
Bonapartists	20
Centre Left	80
Moderate Republicans	110
Extreme Left	40

The composition of the National Assembly changed considerably through by-elections.

1876 (February–March)

Voting in single-member constituencies with two ballots – as for all subsequent elections except 1885.
Republican victory. About 153 Conservatives, 340 Republicans and 22 *Constitutionnels* in the centre:

Extreme Right	24
Right and Centre Right	54
Bonapartists	75
Constitutionnels	22
Centre Left	48
Moderate Republicans	193
Extreme Left	98

Breakdown of votes (following the *Année politique*):

Conservatives	3,202,000
Republicans	4,028,000

1877 (October)

The election following the *Seize Mai* crisis; the Republicans returned with a slightly reduced majority. There were usually only two candidates at the first ballot, and the result was Conservatives 207, Republicans 321. The Conservatives divided as follows:

Legitimists	44
Orleanists	11
Bonapartists	104
Uncertain	48

Breakdown of votes:

Conservatives	3,577,000
Republicans	4,367,000

B. PARLIAMENTARY GROUPS

Parliamentary groups were fairly distinct in this period because the question of the regime was paramount. The Legitimists were generally known simply as the Right; an Extreme Right (the *'chevau-légers'*), rejecting fusion with the Orleanist line, existed during the National Assembly but not after 1876.

The Centre Right comprised the Orleanists, but tended to fragment into smaller groups, and ceased to exist as such after 1877. Those left joined either the Right proper, or the *Constitutionnel* group, formed in 1875 by Orleanists who accepted the Republican constitution once it was voted (this group was dissolved in 1878).

The Bonapartist *Appel au peuple* group existed from 1872.

The Republicans at first formed three main tendencies: the Centre Left (ex-Orleanists and ultra-moderates), the *Gauche républicaine*, and the Extreme Left. In the National Assembly, the Extreme Left was led by Gambetta, and also called the *Union républicaine*, but in 1876 Gambetta set up the *Union républicaine* as a distinct group closer to the *Gauche républicaine* (led by Ferry). In the 1877 legislature, about 130 deputies belonged to each of these two groups, 30 to the Centre Left, 35 to the Extreme Left.

C. GOVERNMENTS

The GOVERNMENT OF NATIONAL DEFENCE (4 September 1870) demitted office when the National Assembly met. The Assembly appointed THIERS as 'chef du pouvoir exécutif' (17 February 1871); he became President of the Republic 31 August 1871. MACMAHON became President 24 May 1873.

The governments appointed by Thiers – 1 DUFAURE (19 February 1871), 2 DUFAURE (18 May 1873) – were based on the 'conjonction des centres' (Centre Left and Centre Right). But MacMahon's 'moral order' governments – 1 BROGLIE (25 May 1873), 2 BROGLIE (26 November 1873), CISSEY (22 May 1874) – excluded the Centre Left, and 1 BROGLIE included Legitimist ministers. This proved unworkable – the BUFFET ministry (10 March 1875) was a return to the 'conjonction des centres', and after the 1876 election MacMahon was forced to base governments on the Centre Left: 3 DUFAURE (23 February 1876), 4 DUFAURE (9

March 1876), SIMON (12 December 1876). 3 BROGLIE (17 May 1877) was formed after the *Seize Mai* crisis, and the ROCHEBOUËT government (23 November 1877), a non-parliamentary ministry of officials, was MacMahon's last attempt to resist the verdict of the electorate. 5 DUFAURE (13 December 1877) was based on the Centre Left, but included Freycinet from the *Gauche républicaine*.

II. 1879–89

A. ELECTIONS

1881 (August–September)

The Right lost heavily: 90 Conservatives, 457 Republicans. The abstention rate was higher in this election than in any other down to 1914. Breakdown of seats:

Royalists	45
Bonapartists	45
Centre Left	39
Gauche républicaine	168
Union républicaine	204
Extreme Left	46

Breakdown of votes:

Conservatives	1,789,000
Republicans	5,128,000

1885 (October)

Voting by list, with two ballots.
The Right recovered ground, generally putting forward a single list, while Republicans and Radicals had separate lists at the first ballot. The result was 201 Conservatives, 383 Republicans, but there are no reliable figures for the tendencies within each block. Breakdown of votes:

Conservatives	3,541,000
Republicans	4,327,000

B. PARLIAMENTARY GROUPS

The period was dominated by the Opportunist majority, flanked on either side by the Right and the Radicals. But each tendency was further subdivided.

The Legitimist Right remained distinct from the Bonapartist *Appel au peuple* group, but after 1885 the two formed the *Union des Droites* to co-ordinate their action.

The Opportunists were divided between the *Gauche républicaine* (renamed *Union démocratique* in 1883) and the *Union républicaine* until 1885, when they fused to form the *Union des Gauches*. The Centre Left survived in 1881–5, but was eliminated by the 1885 election.

The Radicals were divided between the moderate *Gauche radicale* and the Radical-Socialists, still also called by the old name of Extreme Left.

Some Socialists were elected on Republican lists in 1885, and formed a *groupe ouvrier* in 1886.

C. GOVERNMENTS

Presidents: GRÉVY (30 January 1879; re-elected for second term, 28 December 1885); CARNOT (3 December 1887).

The first government appointed by Grévy – WADDINGTON (4 February 1879) – was the last in which the Centre Left was important. Subsequent governments were based on the Opportunist majority, but the rivalry between Ferry's and Gambetta's groups was a source of instability. 1 FREYCINET (28 December 1879) and 1 FERRY (23 September 1880) were based on the *Gauche républicaine*, while GAMBETTA'S government of 14 November 1881 ('le grand ministère') relied rather narrowly on his own supporters. 2 FREYCINET (30 January 1882) was consciously anti-Gambettist, but the succeeding governments – DUCLERC (7 August 1882), FALLIÈRES (29 January 1883), 2 FERRY (21 February 1883) – marked a reconciliation between the two factions, especially after Gambetta's death in December 1882.

The Radicals were hostile to Ferry, but his fall in 1885 forced the 1 BRISSON government (6 April 1885) to inaugurate a policy of reliance on Radical support ('concentration républicaine'). This became more necessary after the 1885 election deprived the Opportunists of their overall majority, and was continued by 3 FREYCINET (7 January 1886) and GOBLET (11 December 1886). The 1 ROUVIER government (30 May 1887) was an exception: formed when the Radical–Opportunist alliance broke down over the question of Boulanger's continuance in the Cabinet, it was formed exclusively of Opportunists and depended on the tacit support of the Right – an anticipation of the Méline period. 1 TIRARD (12 December 1887) returned to 'concentration républicaine', and FLOQUET (3 April 1888) was especially Left-leaning.

III. 1889–99

A. ELECTIONS

1889 (September–October)

The following figures are given by Mayeur (*Les Débuts de la Troisième République 1871–1898* (1973), p. 178:

	Votes	Seats
Conservatives	2,914,985	168
Boulangists	709,223	42
Republicans	4,333,239	366

The Republicans were divided approximately as follows:

Centre Left	40
Moderates	210
Radicals and Socialists	100

1893 (August–September)

Right	58
Ralliés	35
Moderates	311
Radicals	122
Socialists	49

Of the Socialists elected, only 16 were representatives of Socialist parties – 5 Guesdists, 5 Allemanists, 4 Blanquists, 2 Broussists (Mayeur, op. cit., p. 210).

Breakdown of votes (from Campbell):

Right and *Ralliés*	1,636,000
Moderates	3,188,000
Radicals	1,616,000
Socialists	598,000

1898 (May)

Right	44
Ralliés	38
Nationalists	15
Moderates	254
Radicals	104
Radical-Socialists	74
Socialists	57

Breakdown of votes (from Campbell):

Right and *Palliés*	1,544,000
Moderates	3,248,000
Radicals and Radical-Socialists	2,148,000
Socialists	888,000

B. PARLIAMENTARY GROUPS

The divisions between deputies were often unclear in this period, and the line between moderate Republicans and Radicals was especially fluid.

On the Right, the main development was the emergence of the *Palliés*. Jacques Piou founded the *Droite constitutionnelle* in 1890; in 1894, it became first the *Droite républicaine*, then the Independent Republican group. The Boulangists (or 'revisionists') elected in 1889 had ceased to form a distinct group by 1893.

The term Opportunist fell out of use, and the majority called themselves moderates or *Républicains de gouvernement*. In 1889 the ultra-moderate Centre Left (or *Union libérale*) reappeared, but did not remain distinct for long. At this time, the term Progressist had a left-wing implication: the *Union progressiste* was formed during the 1893 legislature by members of the moderate majority who favoured co-operation with the Radicals.

The Radicals remained divided into two tendencies. The moderate *Gauche radicale* was renamed first *Gauche progressiste* and then *Gauche démocratique*. The Radical-Socialists and Socialists were both now established groups.

C. GOVERNMENTS

Presidents: CASIMIR-PERIER (27 June 1894); FAURE (17 January 1895).

The first governments of the period – 2 TIRARD (22 February 1889), 4 FREYCINET (17 March 1890), LOUBET (27 February 1892), 1 RIBOT (6 December 1892), 2 RIBOT (11 January 1893) – continued the practice of including some Radical ministers, instability being caused partly by the Panama scandal. 1 DUPUY (4 April 1893) was a government of the same type, but Dupuy believed in moderate rule without Radical support, and the increased moderate majority in the 1893 election opened the way to this. CASIMIR-PERIER (3 December 1893), 2 DUPUY (30 May 1894) and 3 DUPUY (1 July 1894) took a strong anti-socialist line, and looked for *Rallié* support. After Casimir-Perier's resignation as President, 3 RIBOT (17 January 1895) attempted to revive 'concentration', but the gulf between moderates and Radicals was now too wide. The BOURGEOIS Cabinet (1 November 1895) was 'homogeneous' (sharing no ministers with those preceding and following it), and the first government based on Radicals alone. The tendency to polarization seemed confirmed by the MÉLINE government (29 April 1896), which was hostile to the Radicals and relied on conservative votes. But Méline resigned when the government lost ground in the 1898 election. The succeeding governments – 2 BRISSON (28 June 1898), 4 DUPUY (1 November 1898), 5 DUPUY (18 February 1899) – returned to reliance on the Radicals, but were weakened by the impact of the Dreyfus affair.

IV. 1899–1914

A. ELECTIONS

1902 (April–May)

Figures given for this election vary considerably. Those issued officially at the time show the government parties winning about 370 seats and the opposition 220, divided as follows:

Right and *Ralliés* (*Action libérale*)	50
Nationalists	59
Progressists	111
Pro-government moderates	99
Radicals	129
Radical-Socialists	90
Socialists	48

The figures for votes are unhelpful because they count Progressists and pro-government moderates together, but are in summary:

Right and Nationalists	2,768,000
Moderate Republicans	2,501,000
Radicals and Radical-Socialists	2,267,000
Socialists	875,000

1906 (May)

This showed further gains for the Left:

Right and *Action libérale*	78
Nationalists	30
Progressists	66
Républicains de gauche	90
Radicals	115
Radical-Socialists	132
Independent Socialists	20
SFIO Socialists	54

Breakdown of votes:

Right, Nationalists, Progressists	3,809,000
Républicains de gauche, Radicals, Radical-Socialists	3,910,000
Socialists, Independent Socialists	1,082,000

1910 (April–May)

Right and *Action libérale*	71
Nationalists	17
Progressists	60
Républicains de gauche	93
Radicals and Radical-Socialists	252
Independent Socialists	30
SFIO Socialists	74

Breakdown of votes:

Right, Nationalists, Progressists	1,755,000
Républicains de gauche, Radicals, Radical-Socialists	5,100,000
Socialists, Independent Socialists	1,455,000

1914 (April–May)

The following list is based on the groups joined by deputies after the election (taken from Bomier-Landowski). The *Fédération républicaine* were the successors of the Progressists; the *Fédération des Gauches* consisted of Briand and his followers; the *Gauche radicale* were self-styled Radicals outside the official Radical party. (These examples show how the word *gauche* was abused.)

Note that the Radicals and Socialists, with 298 seats, almost had an absolute majority (there were 602 seats).

Right and *Action libérale*	84
Fédération républicaine	37
Républicains de gauche and *Gauche démocratique*	88
Fédération des Gauches	23
Gauche radicale	66
Radical party group	172
Independent Socialists	23
SFIO Socialists	103

Breakdown of votes (the fragmentation of the centre makes these figures somewhat meaningless):

Right and Progressists	1,297,000
All centre parties	3,807,000
Radical party	1,530,000
Independent Socialists	326,000
SFIO	1,413,000

B. PARLIAMENTARY GROUPS

The formation of Waldeck-Rousseau's government finally split the moderate Republicans between the Progressists, who became part of the Right, and the *Républicains de gauche*, who supported the Bloc. After 1910, the return to centrist politics made the boundaries fluid again.

The *Ralliés* renamed their group *Action libérale*, and in 1902 formed a political party with this name (or *Action libérale populaire*). The *Fédération républicaine* (1903) was the electoral organization of the Progressists, and their group's name from 1914. A *Union républicaine* group appeared intermittently, comprising Progressists who favoured co-operation with the Centre. A Nationalist group existed from 1902 to 1910; after 1910 traditional royalists formed the 'groupe des Droites'.

The nomenclature of the *Républicains de gauche* is particularly confusing. Their electoral organization was the *Alliance démocratique* (or *Alliance républicaine démocratique*). Their parliamentary group at first continued with the name *Union progressiste*, then became the *Union démocratique* in 1902. In 1905, a breakaway group was formed called the *Gauche démocratique* (not to be confused with the former Radical group of the same name). In 1910 the *Union démocratique* disappeared, leaving the *Gauche démocratique* as the main group, though in 1914 a separate group of *Républicains de gauche* appeared alongside it.

The *Fédération des Gauches* was formed by Briand and his followers for the 1914 election.

Despite the creation of the Radical party in 1901, two Radical groups continued in Parliament. The more moderate *Gauche démocratique* was renamed *Gauche radicale* after 1902. In 1914, however, a single Radical party group was formed, and the name *Gauche radicale* was taken over by those who refused to accept its discipline.

There were two Socialist groups until the formation of the SFIO in 1905. The Independent Socialists (or *Républicains socialistes*) were those who refused to join it, or were expelled.

In 1910, the Chamber officially recognized groups, and all deputies had to belong to one, and only one. The group strengths at that time were (from Bomier-Landowski):

Independents	20
Groupe des Droites	19
Action libérale	34
Progressists	75
Gauche démocratique	72
Gauche radicale	113
Radical-Socialists	150
Groupe républicain socialiste	31
SFIO	75

The main subsequent changes were that the Independent group was renamed 'group for deputies who are not members of a group', and the re-forming of the *Union républicaine* group (dissident Progressists) in 1911.

C. GOVERNMENTS

Presidents: LOUBET (18 February 1899); FALLIÈRES (18 February 1906); POINCARÉ (18 February 1913).

The governments of WALDECK-ROUSSEAU (22 June 1899) and COMBES (7 June 1902) rested on the support of the Bloc – *Républicains de gauche*, Radicals, Radical-Socialists and 'ministerial' Socialists. Socialist withdrawal left two alternatives: reliance on the Radicals alone, or a policy of 'concentration' appealing to the moderates as well; thus 'concentration', which in the 1880s referred to left-of-centre governments, now referred to right-of-centre ones. 2 ROUVIER (24 January 1905), 3 ROUVIER (18 February 1906) and SARRIEN (14 March 1906 – this Cabinet was dominated by Clemenceau) were governments of 'concentration'; CLEMENCEAU's government (25 October 1906) rested more on his personality than on firm Radical support. 1 BRIAND (24

July 1909) returned to 'concentration', but 2 BRIAND (3 November 1910) made more concessions to the Radicals, and the governments of MONIS (2 March 1911) and CAILLAUX (27 June 1911) were primarily Radical. However, the governments of POINCARÉ (14 January 1912), 3 BRIAND (21 January 1913), 4 BRIAND (18 February 1913), and BARTHOU (22 March 1913) stood for a policy of 'appeasement' and national consensus, appealing increasingly to the Right on nationalist issues; Barthou's Cabinet included a Progressist minister, the first since 1898. DOUMERGUE (9 December 1913) marked a return to a Radical orientation. Poincaré's appointment of 4 RIBOT after the 1914 election (9 June 1914) was repudiated by the Chamber, and the VIVIANI government of 13 June 1914 was centred on Radical-Socialist and Independent Socialist support.

Socialist and trade-union organizations

The first *Congrès ouvrier* was held in Paris in 1876, and further congresses at Lyons 1878, Marseilles 1879 and Le Havre 1880. The Marseilles congress set up the *Fédération du parti des travailleurs socialistes de France*. In 1882, however, this party split: the Guesdists left its congress at Saint-Étienne, held a rival meeting at Roanne, and formed the *Parti ouvrier* (later *Parti ouvrier français*). The remainder – the Possibilists or Broussists – renamed their party first *Parti ouvrier socialiste révolutionnaire*, then in 1883 *Fédération des travailleurs socialistes français*.

At the Châtellerault congress in 1890, the Allemanists broke with the FTSF and formed a new *Parti ouvrier socialiste révolutionnaire*. A split within the Allemanist POSR produced the *Alliance communiste* in 1896, a group close to the Blanquists. The latter had formed the *Comité révolutionnaire central* in 1881, renamed *Parti socialiste révolutionnaire* in 1898.

Moves towards Socialist unity began in 1898 with the formation of a *comité de vigilance* (later *comité d'entente*) bringing the parties together. There followed two general congresses named after the halls in Paris where they were held: Japy, 1899, and Wagram, 1900. Japy set up a *comité général* to prepare the way for a united party, but at Wagram the Guesdists walked out. At a third general congress, at Lyons in 1901, the Blanquists and *Alliance communiste* left, and joined the Guesdists in the *Unité socialiste révolutionnaire*, which became the *Parti socialiste de France* in 1902. The more moderate *Parti socialiste français* was also formed in 1902, and included the remains of the Broussist FTSF.

The *Section française de l'Internationale ouvrière*, formed in 1905, incorporated the PSdeF, the PSF and the Allemanist POSR, which had retained its independence. In 1914 Allemane was to lead a small breakaway *Parti ouvrier*. The *Parti républicain socialiste* was formed by the 'independents' outside the SFIO in 1911; the *Fédération communiste révolutionnaire anarchiste* of 1913 was the first national anarchist organization.

The earliest separate trade-union organization was the *Fédération des syndicats* (or *Fédération nationale des syndicats*), formed by the Guesdists in 1886; the *Fédération des bourses du travail* held its inaugural congress at Saint-Étienne in 1892. The two organizations held joint congresses at Paris in 1893 and Nantes in 1894: at the latter, the majority of the *Fédération des syndicats* voted for the general strike and agreed to join the *bourses du travail* in the *Confédération générale du travail*, inaugurated in 1895; the *Fédération des syndicats* survived as a Guesdist rump until 1898.

Though connected with the CGT, the *Fédération des bourses du travail* remained independent. Trade-union groups affiliated both 'horizontally' to their local *bourse* and 'vertically' to one of the trade *fédérations* which were the constituents of the CGT. The FBT was merged into the CGT in 1902, but even then retained a certain autonomy until 1912.

Political geography of Paris

Ministries and other institutions were often referred to by their location – e.g. Quai d'Orsay for the foreign ministry. It may be useful to have a list of these expressions.

Elysée	Palace of President of the Republic
Luxembourg	Senate
Palais-Bourbon	Chamber of deputies
Pavillon de Flore	Ministry of colonies
Place Beauvau	Ministry of the interior
Place Vendôme	Ministry of justice
Rue Cadet	Headquarters of the Grand Orient, the main order of French freemasonry
Rue de Bellechasse	*Administration des cultes* (responsible for Church–State relations)
Rue de Grenelle	Ministry of education
Rue de Rivoli	Ministry of finance
Rue de Valois	Headquarters (in the 1900s) of the Radical party
Rue des Saussaies	*Sûreté* (police section of ministry of the interior)
Rue Royale	Ministry of marine
Rue Saint-Dominique	Ministry of war

The prime minister (*président du conseil*) did not have a separate residence, as he always held a ministerial portfolio.

Notes

CHAPTER 1: THE EVOLUTION OF THE REPUBLIC 1870-1914

1 J. Gouault, *Comment la France est devenue républicaine. Les élections générales et partielles à l'Assemblée nationale 1870-1875* (1954), p. 116.

2 C. Seignobos, *Le Déclin de l'Empire et l'établissement de la 3e République (1859-1875)* (1921), p. 361.

3 C. de Freycinet, *Souvenirs 1878-1893* (1913), p. 66.

4 J. B. Duroselle, *L'Europe de 1815 à nos jours. Vie politique et relations internationales* (1964), pp. 284-92.

5 P. Sorlin, *Waldeck-Rousseau* (1966), pp. 482-5.

6 E. Combes, *Mon ministère. Mémoires 1902-1905* (1956), p. 69.

7 M. Rebérioux, *La République radicale? 1898-1914* (1975), pp. 117, 134.

8 J. Julliard, *Clemenceau briseur de grèves. L'affaire de Draveil-Villeneuve-Saint-Georges* (1965), *passim*.

9 H. Goldberg, *Life of Jean Jaurès* (1962), pp. 248-9.

CHAPTER 2: THE SOCIAL FOUNDATIONS

1 *Selections from the Prison Notebooks of Antonio Gramsci* (1971), p. 180.

2 Laboulaye, quoted in J. E. C. Bodley, *France* (new ed., 1899), p. 45.

3 J. H. Clapham, *The Economic Development of France and Germany, 1815-1914* (4th ed., 1936), pp. 238, 285; J. M. Mayeur, *Les Débuts de la Troisième République 1871-1898* (1973), p. 64.

4 M. Rebérioux, *La République radicale? 1898-1914* (1975), p. 197.

5 G. Dupeux, *La Société française 1789-1960* (1964), p. 20.

6 Ibid., p. 168.

7 A. Daumard, 'L'évolution des structures sociales en France à l'époque de l'industrialisation (1815-1914)', *Revue historique*, ccxlvii (1972), p. 330.

8 Ibid., p. 326 n.

9 Dupeux, op. cit., p. 169.

10 J. C. Toutain, *La Population de la France de 1700 à 1959* (1963), Table 80 (figures based differently from Dupeux's).

11 L. Halévy, quoted in J. Dubois, *Le Vocabulaire politique et social en France de 1869 à 1872* (1962), p. 247; cf. pp. 13f.

12 M. Augé-Laribé, *La Politique agricole de la France de 1880 à 1940* (1950), p. 89.

13 T. Zeldin, *France 1848-1945*, vol. 1 (1973), p. 405.

14 J. Kayser, *Les Grandes Batailles du radicalisme. Des origines aux portes du pouvoir, 1820–1901* (1962), p. 249 n.

15 G. Dupeux, *Aspects de l'histoire sociale et politique du Loir-et-Cher, 1848–1914* (1962), pp. 288–9. Cf. P. Barral, *Les Agrariens français de Méline à Pisani* (1968), pp. 71–2.

16 C. A. Michalet, *Les Placements des épargnants français de 1815 à nos jours* (1968), p. 109.

17 Bodley, op. cit., pp. 241–5; P. Barral, *Les Perier dans l'Isère au XIXe siècle* (1964), p. 164.

18 Mayeur, op. cit., pp. 85f.

19 P. Barral, *Les Fondateurs de la Troisième République* (1968), pp. 228–34.

20 K. Marx and F. Engels, *Selected Works* (1962), vol. 1, p. 334.

21 Barral, *Les Agrariens français*, p. 26. Cf. P. Houée, *Les Etapes du développement rural* (1972), vol. 1, p. 50; Mayeur, op. cit., pp. 73f.

22 G. Chapman, *The Third Republic of France. The First Phase, 1871–1894* (1962), pp. 88–90.

23 Clapham, op. cit., pp. 161, 163.

24 Zeldin, op. cit., vol. 1, p. 151.

25 Augé-Laribé, op. cit., p. 100.

CHAPTER 3: THE MAP OF OPINION

1 C. Seignobos, *L'Evolution de la 3e République (1875–1914)* (1921), p. 288.

2 M. Duverger, *Political Parties* (3rd ed., 1964), p. 231.

3 F. Goguel, *La Politique des partis sous la IIIe République* (4th ed., 1958), p. 28.

4 G. Dupeux, *Aspects de l'histoire sociale et politique du Loir-et-Cher, 1848–1914* (1962), pp. 611–14.

5 P. Barral, *Le Département de l'Isère sous la Troisième République, 1870–1940. Histoire sociale et politique* (1962), pp. 548f.

6 H. Carel, in *Recherches sur les forces politiques de la France de l'Est depuis 1787* (1966), p. 248.

7 A. Siegfried, *Géographie électorale de l'Ardèche sous la IIIe République* (1949), p. 57.

8 P. Bois, *Paysans de l'Ouest. Des structures économiques et sociales aux options politiques depuis l'époque révolutionnaire dans la Sarthe* (1960), p. 152; cf. p. 94.

9 R. Arambourou, in F. Goguel (ed.), *Nouvelles études de sociologie électorale* (1954), pp. 81–131.

10 A. Siegfried, *Tableau politique de la France de l'Ouest sous la Troisième République* (1913), p. 364; Bois, op. cit., pp. 26–8.

11 M. Agulhon, *La République au village. (Les populations du Var de la Révolution à la Seconde République)* (1970), p. 14.

12 M. Larkin, *Church and State after the Dreyfus Affair. The Separation Issue in France* (1974), p. 7.

13 J. Gadille, *La Pensée et l'action politiques des évêques français au début de la IIIe République 1870–1883* (1967), vol. 1, p. 152.

14 J. M. Mayeur, *Un Prêtre démocrate, l'abbé Lemire, 1853–1928* (1968), pp. 98–9; C. Willard, *Le Mouvement socialiste en France (1893–1905): Les guesdistes* (1965), p. 235.

15 Siegfried, *Géographie électorale de l'Ardèche*, p. 113.

16 Siegfried, *Tableau politique*, p. 402.

17 T. Zeldin, *France 1848-1945*, vol. 1 (1973), pp. 116, 535.

18 Siegfried, *Tableau politique*, pp. 473, 492, 495, 498.

19 A. Siegfried, *Tableau des partis en France* (1930), pp. 157f.

20 P. Barral, *Les Agrariens français de Méline à Pisani* (1968), pp. 41f.

21 J. Meyer, in J. Delumeau (ed.), *Histoire de la Bretagne* (1969), pp. 433-4; M. Denis, *L'Eglise et la République en Mayenne, 1896-1906* (1967), pp. 129, 153.

22 Cf. P. Bernard, *Economie et sociologie de la Seine-et-Marne, 1850-1950* (1953), p. 249.

23 F. Goguel, *Géographie des élections françaises sous la Troisième et la Quatrième République* (1970), p. 167.

24 M. Bordes, 'L'évolution politique du Gers sous la IIIe République', *L'Information historique*, xxiii (1961), pp. 19-22; J. Rothney, *Bonapartism after Sedan* (1969), pp. 171f.

25 D. R. Watson, in D. Shapiro (ed.), *The Right in France, 1890-1919. Three Studies* (1962), pp. 49-84.

26 F. P. Codaccioni, in L. Trénard (ed.), *Histoire des Pays-Bas français* (1972), pp. 447-8.

CHAPTER 4: ELECTIONS, DEPUTIES AND PARTIES

1 M. Agulhon, *La République au village. (Les populations du Var de la Révolution à la Seconde République)* (1970), pp. 480-1.

2 J. Bécarud, 'Noblesse et représentation parlementaire, Les députés nobles de 1871 à 1968', *Revue française de science politique*, xxiii (1973), pp. 976-8.

3 R. Trempé, *Les Mineurs de Carmaux 1848-1914* (1971), pp. 865f., 880f.; J. A. Roy, *Histoire de la famille Schneider et du Creusot* (1962), pp. 71-3, 86; P. Bernard, *Economie et sociologie de la Seine-et-Marne, 1850-1950* (1953), pp. 222-3.

4 J. Bousquet-Mélou, *Louis Barthou et la circonscription d'Oloron (1889-1914)* (1972), pp. 206-8.

5 E. Combes, *Mon ministère. Mémoires 1902-1905* (1956), p. 235.

6 D. Ligou, *Frédéric Desmons et la franc-maçonnerie sous la 3e République* (1966), p. 217.

7 P. Barral, *Les Agrariens français de Méline à Pisani* (1968), pp. 105f.

8 R. Thabault, *Mon village* (1945), pp. 126-8, 185f., 195.

9 P. Barral, *Le Département de l'Isère sous la Troisième République, 1870-1940. Histoire sociale et politique* (1962), pp. 323f.

10 Y. H. Gaudemet, *Les Juristes et la vie politique de la IIIe République* (1970), pp. 15, 18-19, 22, 25, 100.

11 J. E. C. Bodley, *France* (new ed., 1899), pp. 385-91.

12 M. Dogan, 'Les filières de la carrière politique en France', *Revue française de sociologie*, viii (1967), pp. 469, 474f. Cf. R. Priouret, *La République des députés* (1959), p. 186.

13 C. Marie, *L'Evolution du comportement politique dans une ville en expansion. Grenoble 1871-1965* (1966), pp. 35-7.

14 Cf. G. Dupeux, *Aspects de l'histoire sociale et politique du Loir-et-Cher, 1848-1914* (1962), pp. 581f.

15 J. Caillaux, *Mes mémoires* (1942-7), vol. 2, p. 91.

16 J. P. Charnay, *Les Scrutins politiques en France de 1815 à 1962. Contestations et invalidations* (1964), pp. 82, 253.
17 J. P. T. Bury, *Gambetta and the Making of the Third Republic* (1973), pp. 414-17.
18 J. Kayser, *Les Grandes Batailles du radicalisme. Des origines aux portes du pouvoir, 1820-1901* (1962), pp. 114-15, 136.
19 Dupeux, op. cit., pp. 481-2.
20 M. Larkin, *Church and State after the Dreyfus Affair. The Separation Issue in France* (1974), p. 94.
21 M. Rebérioux, *La République radicale? 1898-1914* (1975), pp. 42f.
22 Kayser, op. cit., p. 310.
23 M. Duverger, *Political Parties* (3rd ed., 1964), pp. 63f.; *From Max Weber: Essays in Sociology* (1948), pp. 101-2, 113.
24 Duverger, op. cit., pp. xxivf.
25 R. Michels, *Political Parties* (1915), p. 180.
26 A. Siegfried, *De la IIIe à la IVe République* (1956), pp. 40-1.
27 Bousquet-Mélou, op. cit., p. 91.

CHAPTER 5: PARLIAMENTARY POLITICS

1 J. J. Chevallier, *Histoire des institutions politiques de la France de 1789 à nos jours* (1952), pp. 361f.
2 P. Barral, *Les Fondateurs de la Troisième République* (1968), pp. 301-6.
3 J. E. C. Bodley, *France* (new ed., 1899), p. 314.
4 T. Zeldin, *France 1848-1945*, vol. 1 (1973), pp. 347-50.
5 Cf. A. Bomier-Landowski, in F. Goguel and G. Dupeux, *Sociologie électorale. Esquisse d'un bilan. Guide de recherches* (1951), pp. 75f.
6 A. Soulier, *L'Instabilité ministérielle sous la Troisième République (1871-1938)* (1939), p. 479.
7 J. Ollé-Laprune, *La Stabilité des ministres sous la Troisième République 1879-1940* (1962), pp. 13, 21-2.
8 Soulier, op. cit., p. 407. Cf. M. Duverger, *Political Parties.* (3rd ed., 1964), p. 336.
9 J. M. Mayeur, *Les Débuts de la Troisième République 1871-1898* (1973), pp. 211-17.
10 Soulier, op. cit., p. 490.
11 A. Siegfried, *De la IIIe à la IVe République* (1956), pp. 32-3.
12 Zeldin, op. cit., vol. 1, p. 585.
13 J. Caillaux, *Mes mémoires* (1942-7), vol. 1, p. 187.
14 P. Legendre, *Histoire de l'administration de 1750 à nos jours* (1968), p. 541.
15 M. Larkin, *Church and State after the Dreyfus Affair. The Separation Issue in France* (1974), pp. 55-6.
16 G. Lefranc, *Le Mouvement syndical sous la Troisième République* (1967), p. 186.
17 E. N. Suleiman, *Politics, Power, and Bureaucracy in France. The Administrative Elite* (1974), p. 48.
18 C. M. Andrew and A. D. Kanya-Forstner, 'The French "Colonial Party"; its composition, aims and influence, 1885-1914', *Historical Journal*, xiv (1971), p. 127.
19 E. Dolléans and G. Dehove, *Histoire du travail en France. Mouvement ouvrier et législation sociale*, vol. 1 (1953), p. 392.
20 M. Gillet, *Les Charbonnages du Nord de la France au XIXe siècle* (1973), pp. 170-8.

21   M. Rebérioux, *La République radicale? 1898–1914* (1975), pp. 51, 59–60; D. Bardonnet, *Evolution de la structure du parti radical* (1960), pp. 251–4.

22   M. Augé-Laribé, *La Politique agricole de la France de 1880 à 1940* (1950), pp. 58f., 211–14.

23   R. Poidevin, *Les Relations économiques et financières entre la France et l'Allemagne de 1898 à 1914* (1969), pp. 608, 611.

24   Augé-Laribé, op. cit., pp. 161–72, 203–4.

25   C. K. Warner, *The Winegrowers of France and the Government since 1875* (1960), p. 36.

26   See C. Bellanger *et al.* (eds), *Histoire générale de la presse française. III. De 1871 à 1940* (1972).

27   Ibid., p. 169.

CHAPTER 6: REPUBLICANS AND RADICALS

1   P. Barral, *Les Fondateurs de la Troisième République* (1968), p. 68.

2   Ibid., pp. 125–6.

3   J. Gadille, *La Pensée et l'action politiques des évêques français au début de la IIIe République 1870–1883* (1967), vol. 2, p. 252.

4   Cf. Ferry, quoted in Barral, op. cit., pp. 249–53.

5   C. M. Cipolla, *Literacy and Development in the West* (1969), Table 28. Cf. R. D. Anderson, *Education in France 1848–1870* (1975), pp. 240–1.

6   Cf. J. Bouvier, 'Pour une analyse sociale de la monnaie et du crédit: XIXe–XXe siècle', *Annales*, xxix (1974), pp. 815–16, 821.

7   P. Nora, 'Ernest Lavisse: son rôle dans la formation du sentiment national', *Revue historique*, ccxxviii (1962), p. 91.

8   A. Prost, *Histoire de l'enseignement en France 1800–1967* (1968), pp. 326–8.

9   G. Bruun, *Clemenceau* (new ed., 1962), p. 67.

10   Cf. Gambetta, quoted in Barral, op. cit., pp. 51, 131.

11   J. Jaurès, *Discours parlementaires*, vol. 1 (1904), pp. 28–30, 38.

12   A. Rambaud, *Jules Ferry* (1903), p. 517.

13   R. Priouret, *La République des députés* (1959), p. 119.

14   P. Sorlin, *Waldeck-Rousseau* (1966), pp. 191–8; A. Siegfried, *Mes souvenirs de la IIIe République. Mon père et son temps. Jules Siegfried 1836–1922* (1952), pp. 91–7.

15   Quoted in Barral, op. cit., pp. 93, 119.

16   Ibid., p. 138.

17   Ibid., pp. 162, 239–44.

18   Sorlin, op. cit., pp. 164–6.

19   Barral, op. cit., pp. 235–6.

20   T. Zeldin, *France 1848–1945*, vol. 1 (1973), pp. 654f.

21   F. Goguel, *La Politique des partis sous la IIIe République* (4th ed., 1958), p. 74; C. Seignobos, *L'Evolution de la 3e République (1875–1914)* (1921), pp. 169–70.

22   J. Kayser, in *Tendances politiques dans la vie française depuis 1789* (1960), p. 74.

23   Printed in C. Nicolet, *Le Radicalisme* (3rd ed., 1967), pp. 44–8.

24   H. Hatzfeld, *Du paupérisme à la sécurité sociale. Essai sur les origines de la sécurité sociale en France, 1850–1940* (1971), p. 34.

25   Ibid., pp. 87–9, 109, 270f., 327.

26 J. Bouvier, 'Sur "l'immobilisme" du système fiscal français au XIXe siècle', *Revue d'histoire économique et sociale*, I (1972), p. 483.

27 M. Marion, *Histoire financière de la France depuis 1715*, vol. 6 (1931), pp. 318–19.

28 Kayser, *Les Grandes Batailles*, p. 238.

29 J. Caillaux, *Mes mémoires* (1942–7), vol. 1, p. 215.

30 A. Thibaudet, *Les Idées politiques de la France* (1932), p. 130.

CHAPTER 7: THE RIGHT

1 D. Halévy, *La République des ducs* (1937), p. 290.

2 Cf. J. Rothney, *Bonapartism after Sedan* (1969), pp. 295f.

3 G. Cholvy, *Géographie religieuse de l'Hérault contemporain* (1968), pp. 365–7.

4 R. R. Locke, *French Legitimists and the Politics of Moral Order in the Early Third Republic* (1974), p. 91.

5 M. Denis, 'Un aspect du conservatisme en Bretagne au début de la IIIe République: le monarchisme libéral', *Annales de Bretagne*, lxxvii (1970), pp. 391–415.

6 R. Anderson, in T. Zeldin (ed.), *Conflicts in French Society. Anticlericalism, Education and Morals in the Nineteenth Century* (1970), p. 59.

7 J. Gadille, *La Pensée et l'action politiques des évêques français au début de la IIIe République 1870–1883* (1967), vol. 2, p. 244.

8 L. de Vaucelles, *"Le Nouvelliste de Lyon" et la défense religieuse (1879–1889)* (1971), p. III.

9 G. Dupeux, in L. Desgraves and G. Dupeux, *Bordeaux au XIXe siècle* (1969), pp. 330–2; P. Guillaume, in C. Higounet (ed.), *Histoire de l'Aquitaine* (1971), pp. 426–7.

10 R. Girardet, *Le Nationalisme français 1871–1914* (1966), pp. 135–7.

11 Z. Sternhell, 'Paul Déroulède and the origins of modern French nationalism', *Journal of Contemporary History*, vi (1971), p. 64.

12 C. Bellanger *et al.* (eds), *Histoire générale de la presse française. III. De 1871 à 1940* (1972), pp. 342–3.

13 P. Sorlin, *"La Croix" et les Juifs (1880–1899). Contribution à l'histoire de l'antisémitisme contemporain* (1967), pp. 213–17.

14 Cf. E. Weber, in H. Rogger and E. Weber (eds), *The European Right. A Historical Profile* (1965), p. 92.

15 J. Bouvier, *Le Krach de l'Union générale (1878–1885)* (1960), pp. 31f.

16 J. Verdès-Leroux, *Scandale financier et antisémitisme catholique. Le krach de l'Union générale* (1969), p. 207.

17 R. Talmy, *Une Forme hybride du catholicisme social en France. L'Association catholique des patrons du Nord 1884–1895* (1962), *passim*.

18 J. M. Mayeur, *Un Prêtre démocrate, l'abbé Lemire, 1853–1928* (1968), p. 152.

19 Ibid., p. 605.

20 D. B. Ralston, *The Army of the Republic. The Place of the Military in the Political Evolution of France, 1871–1914* (1967), p. 249.

21 F. Bédarida, 'L'armée et la République: les opinions politiques des officiers français en 1876–78', *Revue historique*, ccxxx (1964), pp. 119–64.

22 G. Wormser, *La République de Clemenceau* (1961), pp. 186–7.

23 S. M. Lipset, *Political Man. The Social Bases of Politics* (1960), pp. 131, 134f.

24 Z. Sternhell, *Maurice Barrès et le nationalisme français* (1972), p. 369.

25 G. Sorel, *Reflections on Violence* (1961), p. 211.

26 *Selections from the Prison Notebooks of Antonio Gramsci* (1971), p. 395.

27 J. Benda, *La Trahison des clercs* (new ed., 1965), pp. 26, 29.

28 M. Barrès, *Scènes et doctrines du nationalisme* (n.d.), p. 81.

29 Ibid., pp. 72–3.

30 D. R. Watson, in D. Shapiro (ed.), *The Right in France, 1890–1919. Three Studies* (1962), pp. 49–84.

31 E. Weber, *Action française. Royalism and Reaction in Twentieth-Century France* (1962), pp. 63–5; P. Sorlin, *Waldeck-Rousseau* (1966), pp. 420–2; T. B. Caldwell, 'The Syndicat des employés du commerce et de l'industrie (1887–1919)', *International Review of Social History*, xi (1966), pp. 228–66.

32 G. L. Mosse, 'The French Right and the working classes: Les Jaunes', *Journal of Contemporary History*, vii (1972), p. 208.

33 R. Rémond, *La Droite en France de la première Restauration à la Ve République* (new ed., 1963), p. 182.

34 A. Olivesi, 'La droite à Marseille en 1914', *Provence historique*, vii (1957), pp. 175–99.

35 Desgraves and Dupeux, op. cit., pp. 444f.

36 Rogger and Weber, op. cit., pp. 94–5.

37 M. Anderson, in Shapiro, op. cit., pp. 123–30.

38 Quoted in E. Beau de Loménie, *Les Responsabilités des dynasties bourgeoises*, vol. 2 (1947), pp. 449–50.

CHAPTER 8: THE WORKING-CLASS MOVEMENT

1 J. Bruhat, in 'Eglise et monde ouvrier en France', *Le Mouvement social*, no. 57 (1966), p. 74.

2 S. Edwards, *The Paris Commune 1871* (1971), p. 206.

3 J. Rougerie (ed.), *1871. Jalons pour une histoire de la Commune de Paris* (1972), p. 59.

4 K. Marx and F. Engels, *Selected Works* (1962), vol. 1, p. 527.

5 G. Lefranc, *Le Mouvement syndical sous la Troisième République* (1967), p. 26.

6 D. Stafford, *From Anarchism to Reformism. A Study of the Political Activities of Paul Brousse within the First International and the French Socialist Movement 1870–90* (1971), pp. 185–7.

7 C. Willard, *Le Mouvement socialiste en France (1893–1905): Les guesdistes* (1965), pp. 28–30, 196.

8 M. Perrot, 'Archives policières et militants ouvriers sous la Troisième République. Un exemple: le Gard', *Revue d'histoire économique et sociale*, xxxvii (1959), pp. 227–8.

9 Stafford, op. cit., p. 88.

10 J. Maitron, *Histoire du mouvement anarchiste en France (1880–1914)* (1951), p. 124.

11 Lefranc, op. cit., p. 51.

12 M. Perrot, *Les Ouvriers en grève. France 1871–1890* (1974), pp. 722–5; E. Shorter and C. Tilly, *Strikes in France 1830–1968* (1974), pp. 104–5, 284–5; debate in *Annales*, xxviii (1973), pp. 888–94.

13 Willard, op. cit., pp. 246–7, 394–5, 398.

14 Ibid., p. 242.

15 J. Michel, 'Emile Basly (1854–1928)', *Revue du Nord*, lv (1973), pp. 365–83.

16 Shorter and Tilly, op. cit., pp. 286–95 (quoting and disagreeing with C. Kerr and A. Siegel); E. Allardt, in A. Pizzorno (ed.), *Political Sociology. Selected Readings* (1971), pp. 273–90.

17 J. A. Roy, *Histoire de la famille Schneider et du Creusot* (1962), pp. 97–100.

18 L. Loubère, 'Coal miners, strikes and politics in the Lower Languedoc, 1880–1914', *Journal of Social History*, ii (1968), p. 44.

19 Willard, op. cit., p. 318; P. Caron, *Histoire de l'exploitation d'un grand réseau. La Compagnie du chemin de fer du Nord 1846–1937* (1973), p. 283.

20 Shorter and Tilly, op. cit., pp. 275–6; J. W. Scott, *The Glassworkers of Carmaux* (1974), pp. 116–19.

21 S. Derruau-Boniol, 'Le socialisme dans l'Allier de 1848 à 1914', *Cahiers d'histoire*, ii (1957), pp. 115–61; Willard, op. cit., pp. 261–9.

22 Willard, op. cit., pp. 285–303.

23 H. R. Kedward, *The Dreyfus Affair. Catalyst for Tensions in French Society* (1965), pp. 100–5.

24 Cf. Appendix I. Figures given by authorities vary, e.g. for 1906 between 51 and 59 seats.

25 Printed in A. Kriegel and J. J. Becker, *1914. La guerre et le mouvement ouvrier français* (1964), p. 209.

26 M. Rebérioux, in J. Droz (ed.), *Histoire générale du socialisme. II. De 1875 à 1918* (1975), pp. 207–11.

27 S. Neumann, cited in S. M. Lipset, *Political Man. The Social Bases of Politics* (1960), pp. 85–6; cf. M. Perrot and A. Kriegel, *Le Socialisme français et le pouvoir* (1966), pp. 85–6.

28 L. Lévy (ed.), *Anthologie de Jean Jaurès* (1947), p. 120.

29 J. Jaurès, *Discours parlementaires*, vol. 1 (1904), p. 161.

30 Lévy, op. cit., p. 29.

31 J. Jaurès, *L'Esprit du socialisme* (n.d.), p. 124.

32 M. Rebérioux, *La République radicale? 1898–1914* (1975), p. 228.

33 Printed in D. Thomson, *France: Empire and Republic, 1850–1940. Historical Documents* (1968), pp. 171–2.

34 R. de Jouvenel, *La République des camarades* (new ed., 1934), p. 17.

35 G. Sorel, *Reflections on Violence* (1961), pp. 122, 157.

36 R. Brécy, *Le Mouvement syndical en France 1871–1921. Essai bibliographique* (1963), p. 9; Lefranc, op. cit., pp. 105–6.

37 R. Trempé, *Les Mineurs de Carmaux 1848–1914* (1971), pp. 537f., 636f.; M. Gillet, *Les Charbonnages du Nord de la France au XIXe siècle* (1973), pp. 166–7, 183.

38 Lagardelle in 1906, quoted in H. Dubief (ed.), *Le Syndicalisme révolutionnaire* (1969), p. 152.

39 Maitron, op. cit., p. 114.

40 R. Girardet, *La Société militaire dans la France contemporaine 1815–1939* (1953), p. 228.

41 Kriegel and Becker, op. cit., pp. 141–2.

CHAPTER 9: FRANCE AND THE WORLD

1 C. Andrew, *Théophile Delcassé and the Making of the Entente Cordiale. A Reappraisal of French Foreign Policy 1898–1905* (1968), p. 75.

2 R. D. Challener, *The French Theory of the Nation in Arms 1866–1939* (1955), pp. 38–41, 60.
3 H. Contamine, *La Revanche 1871–1914* (1957), p. 35.
4 H. Brunschwig, *Mythes et réalités de l'impérialisme colonial français 1871–1914* (1960), p. 80.
5 Ibid., p. 89; M. Rebérioux, *La République radicale? 1898–1914* (1975), p. 125.
6 Brunschwig, op. cit., p. 55. Cf. J. Ganiage, *L'Expansion coloniale de la France sous la Troisième République (1871–1914)* (1968), pp. 60–80.
7 Brunschwig, op. cit., pp. 76–7.
8 Quoted in H. Deschamps, *Les Méthodes et les doctrines coloniales de la France (du XVIe siècle à nos jours)* (1953), p. 126.
9 Brunschwig, op. cit., pp. 185–6.
10 Rebérioux, op. cit., pp. 125–33.
11 D. B. Ralston, *The Army of the Republic. The Place of the Military in the Political Evolution of France, 1871–1914* (1967), pp. 180f.
12 W. L. Langer, *The Franco-Russian Alliance 1890–1894* (new ed., 1967), pp. 260, 263.
13 R. Girault, 'Pour un portrait nouveau de l'homme d'affaires français vers 1914', *Revue d'histoire moderne et contemporaine*, xvi (1969), pp. 329–49.
14 L. C. F. Turner, *Origins of the First World War* (1970), p. 35.
15 Contamine, op. cit., p. 108.
16 C. and A. Ambrosi, *La France 1870–1970* (1971), p. 55; Challener, op. cit., p. 47 (figures for 1911).
17 Ralston, op. cit., pp. 330f.
18 Speech of 1912, quoted in G. Bonnefous, *Histoire politique de la Troisième République*, vol. 1 (2nd ed., 1965), p. 314.
19 Cf. J. Chastenet, *Raymond Poincaré* (1948), pp. 123–4, 160; G. Wright, *Raymond Poincaré and the French Presidency* (new ed., 1967), pp. 129–41.
20 Girault, loc. cit., pp. 346–8; J. T. Nordmann, *Histoire des radicaux 1820–1973* (1974), pp. 181–2. Cf. H. Goldberg, *Life of Jean Jaurès* (1962), pp. 373–4.
21 J. Caillaux, *Mes mémoires* (1942–7), vol. 2, pp. 111–12, 136–7.
22 R. Poidevin, *Les Relations économiques et financières entre la France et l'Allemagne de 1898 à 1914* (1969), pp. 727f., 767f.
23 R. Poidevin, *Finances et relations internationales 1887–1914* (1970), *passim*.
24 Poidevin, *Les Relations économiques*, pp. 811–13; J. Thobie, 'Intérêts économiques, financiers et politiques dans l'Empire ottoman (1895–1914)', *Le Mouvement social*, no. 86 (1974), pp. 49–53.

CONCLUSION

1 A. Siegfried, *De la IIIe à la IVe République* (1956), p. 13.
2 J. E. C. Bodley, *France* (new ed., 1899), p. 401, and cf. 25f., 407–8.
3 G. A. Almond and G. B. Powell, *Comparative Politics. A Developmental Approach* (1966), pp. 105f.
4 Cf. S. M. Lipset, *Political Man. The Social Bases of Politics* (1960), p. 83.
5 D. Thomson, *Democracy in France since 1870* (4th ed., 1964), p. 72.
6 S. Hoffmann, in S. Hoffmann *et al.*, *France: Change and Tradition* (1963), pp. 3f.
7 C. Seignobos, *Le Déclin de l'Empire et l'établissement de la 3e République (1859–1875)* (1921), p. 408.

Bibliography

Limitations of space mean that the bibliography must be selective, and it is designed for those who will do their basic reading in English but who wish to know about current scholarship on specialized issues. I have had to be ruthless in omitting older books, and except in a few cases have not included contemporary sources; but I have tried to indicate the books and articles which will give the reader further guidance.

(T) indicates one of the major university theses on the period. The French thesis is traditionally conceived on a large scale, and includes an exhaustive bibliography; study of such theses is the best introduction to the archive sources. (B) indicates other books with especially useful bibliographies. (S) indicates collections of source material. Two series are mentioned specially: 'Archives', published by Julliard, dealing with episodes studied through original sources, and 'Kiosque' (Colin), which looks at history from the angle of the Press. Both are especially useful for entering into the atmosphere of the period, and suited to university-level teaching.

In the case of translations from French, the original date of publication is shown, but the original title is cited only where it differs substantially from the English one.

The bibliography was compiled in 1975.

Abbreviations

Annales	*Annales. Economies, Sociétés, Civilisations*
FHS	*French Historical Studies*
IRSH	*International Review of Social History*
JCH	*Journal of Contemporary History*
JMH	*Journal of Modern History*
MS	*Le Mouvement social*
RFSP	*Revue française de science politique*
RH	*Revue historique*
RHES	*Revue d'histoire économique et sociale*
RHMC	*Revue d'histoire moderne et contemporaine*

I. GENERAL HISTORY

A. INTRODUCTORY

Apart from general histories of France, one may turn first to the classic
narrative of D. W. Brogan, *The Development of Modern France (1870–
1939)* (new ed., 1967). T. Zeldin, *France 1848–1945. I. Ambition,
Love and Politics* (1973) is a thematic treatment which provides much
information and synthesizes modern scholarship. G. Chapman, *The
Third Republic of France. The First Phase, 1871–1894* (1962) combines
narrative with analysis, and D. Thomson, *Democracy in France since 1870*
(5th ed., 1969) discusses the political system and its values. Thomson's
France: Empire and Republic, 1850–1940. Historical Documents (S, 1968)
is a rather staid collection of sources. The best brief account of the
Republic's political evolution is still F. Goguel, *La Politique des partis
sous la IIIe République* (4th ed., 1958). There are some interesting essays
in E. M. Earle (ed.), *Modern France. Problems of the Third and Fourth
Republics* (1951).

Of the standard works in French, one can recommend one old
series and one new. C. Seignobos, *Le Déclin de l'Empire et l'établissement
de la 3e République (1859–1875)* (1921) and *L'Evolution de la 3e République
(1875–1914)* (1921) (vols 7–8 of E. Lavisse (ed.), *Histoire de France
contemporaine*) have in many respects never been superseded, while
J. M. Mayeur, *Les Débuts de la Troisième République 1871–1898* (B, 1973)
and M. Rebérioux, *La République radicale? 1898–1914* (B, 1975) (vols
10–11 of a *Nouvelle histoire de la France contemporaine*) are both outstanding. J. Chastenet, *Histoire de la Troisième République* (7 vols,
1952–63; reissued in 4 vols, 1973–4) is a solid general history.

B. HISTORY BY PERIODS

For the 1870s, the best guide is R. Rémond, *La Vie politique en France
depuis 1789. II. 1848–1879* (B, 2nd ed., 1969). J. Gouault, *Comment la
France est devenue républicaine. Les élections générales et partielles à l'Assemblée
nationale 1870–1875* (1954) is an important specialized study. J. T.
Joughin, *The Paris Commune in French Politics, 1871–1880. The History
of the Amnesty of 1880* (2 vols, 1955) covers a major political issue. For
the Commune itself, see section VIII.B below. Among older books, it
is still worth reading G. Hanotaux, *Contemporary France* (4 vols, 1903–9;
orig. 1903–8), a full treatment of the years 1871–82, and the brilliant
essays of D. Halévy: *The End of the Notables* (1974; orig. 1930) and *La
République des ducs* (1937).

There is little specifically on the 1880s, though J. Gaillard offers a brief interpretation in *L'Information historique* 1957. S. A. Ashley discusses the failure of Gambetta's ministry in *FHS* 1975. On the Boulanger crisis: F. H. Seager, *The Boulanger Affair. Political Crossroad of France 1886–1889* (1969); A. Dansette, *Le Boulangisme* (1938); J. Néré, *Le Boulangisme et la presse* (Kiosque, 1964).

On the 1890s, see A. Sedgwick, *The Ralliement in French Politics 1890–1898* (1965); cf. J. M. Mayeur on *Rallié* deputies in *RHMC* 1966. A good treatment of the Panama affair is J. Bouvier, *Les deux scandales de Panama* (S, Archives, 1964).

The bibliography of the Dreyfus affair is very large. The best introduction is D. Johnson, *France and the Dreyfus Affair* (B, 1966), and H. R. Kedward provides a stimulating selection of documents in *The Dreyfus Affair. Catalyst for Tensions in French Society* (B, S, 1965). On the details of the case: G. Chapman, *The Dreyfus Case, a Reassessment* (1955), reissued in mutilated form as *The Dreyfus Trials* (1972); M. Thomas, *L'Affaire sans Dreyfus* (1961). J. P. Peter discusses its significance in *Annales* 1961. Of the books written by participants, one may pick out C. Péguy, *Notre jeunesse* (1933) and L. Blum, *Souvenirs sur l'Affaire* (1935).

J. B. Duroselle, *La France et les Français 1900–1914* (B, 1972) is a wide-ranging survey of its period. For political narrative, see G. Bonnefous, *Histoire politique de la Troisième République. I. L'avant-guerre (1906–1914)* (2nd ed., 1965), conceived as a continuation of A. Daniel (ed.), *L'Année politique*, an annual publication covering the years 1874–1905.

C. MEMOIRS AND BIOGRAPHY

E. Combes, *Mon ministère. Mémoires 1902–1905* (1956) and J. Caillaux, *Mes mémoires* (3 vols, 1942–7) reveal much of their authors' personalities, though Caillaux should be read in conjunction with R. Poincaré, *Au service de la France. Neuf années de souvenirs*, vols 1–4 (1926–7; the English tr. of 1926–8 is unreliable). C. de Freycinet, *Souvenirs 1878–1893* (1913) is unrevealing but important. Also of interest is A. Siegfried, *Mes souvenirs de la IIIe République. Mon père et son temps. Jules Siegfried 1836–1922* (1952).

Biographies are numerous, but often polemical or of mediocre quality. Indeed, the bad reputation of literary-style biographies helped make the genre taboo among professional historians. P. Sorlin's *Waldeck-Rousseau* (T, 1966) set new scholarly standards, but biography is still more favoured by 'Anglo-Saxon' historians: D. R. Watson,

Georges Clemenceau. A Political Biography (1974); G. Bruun, *Clemenceau* (1943); J. Hampden Jackson, *Clemenceau and the Third Republic* (1946) (brief but useful); J. P. T. Bury, *Gambetta and the National Defence: a Republican Dictatorship in France* (1936) and *Gambetta and the Making of the Third Republic* (1973); G. Wright, *Raymond Poincaré and the French Presidency* (1942). Among the more useful works in French are: A. Rambaud, *Jules Ferry* (1903); G. Wormser, *La République de Clemenceau* (1961); P. Miquel, *Poincaré* (1961).

D. REFERENCE AND BIBLIOGRAPHY

Valuable reference works are P. Pierrard, *Dictionnaire de la IIIe République* (1968) and the *Atlas historique de la France contemporaine 1800–1965* (1966).

The large-scale *Dictionnaire de biographie française* (1933f.) has reached the letter F. Politicians, however, are covered by A. Robert *et al.*, *Dictionnaire des parlementaires français . . . depuis le 1er mai 1789 jusqu'au 1er mai 1889* (5 vols, 1891) and J. Jolly (ed.), *Dictionnaire des parlementaires français . . . de 1889 à 1940* (1960f.); vol. 1 of the latter includes a complete list of cabinet ministers.

An index is in progress for one newspaper: *Tables du journal Le Temps* (1966f.). On the use of the Press, see J. Kayser in *RH* 1957, P. Albert in *MS* 1965.

Current work is listed comprehensively in the *Bibliographie annuelle de l'histoire de France*, whose coverage begins in 1953. For further guidance to sources, see such standard manuals as P. Renouvin *et al.*, *L'Epoque contemporaine. II. La paix armée et la grande guerre (1871–1919)* (new ed., 1960) ('Clio' series); J. B. Duroselle, *L'Europe de 1815 à nos jours. Vie politique et relations internationales* (1964) ('Nouvelle Clio'); P. Guiral *et al.*, *Guide de l'étudiant en histoire moderne et contemporaine* (1971); J. P. Brunet and A. Plessis, *Introduction à l'histoire contemporaine* (1972).

II. ECONOMIC AND SOCIAL HISTORY

A. ECONOMIC HISTORY

An authoritative history for this period is not yet available, but there is useful information in J. H. Clapham, *The Economic Development of France and Germany, 1815–1914* (4th ed., 1936); T. Kemp, *Economic Forces in French History* (1971); G. Palmade, *French Capitalism in the*

Nineteenth Century (1972; orig. 1961). The best introduction to the debate on France's economic growth is C. P. Kindleberger, *Economic Growth in France and Britain 1851–1950* (B, 1964), and F. Crouzet has a survey article in *History* 1974. Other recent articles of importance are by R. E. Cameron in *Annales* 1970; F. Crouzet in *Annales* 1970 and *Revue du Nord* 1972; M. Lévy-Leboyer in *Annales* 1968, *RH* 1968, *RHES* 1971 and *MS* 1974.

B. SOCIAL HISTORY

Valuable general surveys are G. Dupeux, *French Society, 1789–1970* (B, 1976; orig. 6th ed., 1972) and P. Sorlin, *La Société française. I. 1840–1914* (B, 1969), while the following give general interpretations of the period in social terms: J. Lhomme, *La Grande Bourgeoisie au pouvoir (1830–1880)* (1960); C. Morazé, *La France bourgeoise, XVIIIe–XXe siècles* (1946); E. Beau de Loménie's polemical *Les Responsabilités des dynasties bourgeoises*, vols 1–2 (1943–7). P. Barral, *Les Perier dans l'Isère au XIXe siècle* (1964) studies one of the 'bourgeois dynasties' through their correspondence. There are some important articles on social history in *Conjoncture économique, structures sociales. Hommage à Ernest Labrousse* (1974).

The study of French social structure has been based on the records of personal wealth: A. Daumard (ed.), *Les Fortunes françaises au XIXe siècle* (1973) brings together studies of various towns. Cf. Daumard's articles in *RHES* 1966, *RH* 1972 and (on the methodology of social history) *RHES* 1974.

C. AGRICULTURE AND THE PEASANTRY

M. Augé-Laribé, *La Politique agricole de la France de 1880 à 1940* (1950) and P. Barral, *Les Agrariens français de Méline à Pisani* (1968) cover the politics of agriculture and the syndicate movement. See also P. Houée, *Les Etapes du développement rural*, vol. 1 (1972); G. Wright, *Rural Revolution in France. The Peasantry in the Twentieth Century* (1964); N. Heber-Suffrin-Lévêque on Méline in *Annales de l'Est* 1964. On winegrowers and the alcohol lobby: R. Laurent, *Les Vignerons de la 'Côte d'Or' au XIXe siècle* (T, 2 vols, 1957–8); C. K. Warner, *The Winegrowers of France and the Government since 1875* (1960).

Other articles are by G. Cholvy on peasant mentalities in *L'Information historique* 1974; C. Marcilhacy on the veracity of Zola's peasant novel *La Terre* in *Annales* 1957; R. Hubscher on the movement of rent in the Pas-de-Calais in *RH* 1971.

D. INDUSTRY

J. Boudet (ed.), *Le Monde des affaires en France de 1830 à nos jours* (1952) is a mine of information on business firms. Recent work deals with limited sectors. On coal, see M. Gillet, *Les Charbonnages du Nord de la France au XIXe siècle* (T, 1973) and L. Trénard (ed.), *Charbon et sciences humaines* (1966); an essay by Gillet from the latter is printed in F. Crouzet *et al.* (eds), *Essays in European Economic History 1789–1914* (1969). On railways: P. Caron, *Histoire de l'exploitation d'un grand réseau. La Compagnie du chemin de fer du Nord 1846–1937* (T, 1973). On steel: C. Prêcheur, *La Lorraine sidérurgique* (T, 1959), and P. Léon on the Allevard works in *Cahiers d'histoire* 1963. J. A. Roy, *Histoire de la famille Schneider et du Creusot* (1962) is good on the 'company town' atmosphere. F. Crouzet has two articles on the arms industry in *RH* 1974. On the motor industry: P. Fridenson, *Histoire des usines Renault. I. Naissance de la grande entreprise 1898–1939* (1972), and special no. of *MS* 1972.

J. Bouvier, *Le Crédit Lyonnais de 1863 à 1882* (T, 2 vols, 1961) is a major work on banking, reissued in abridged ed. as *Naissance d'une banque: le Crédit Lyonnais* (1968). Cf. Bouvier's *Un siècle de banque française* (1973); *Histoire économique et histoire sociale. Recherches sur le capitalisme contemporain* (1968) (collected articles); article on the sociology of money in *Annales* 1974.

E. ECONOMIC AND SOCIAL POLICIES

On the Freycinet plan: Y. Gonjo in *RH* 1972. On tariff questions: E. O. Golob, *The Méline Tariff: French Agriculture and Nationalist Economic Policy* (1944), and articles by D. Salem in *RHES* 1967, R. Poidevin in *RH* 1971. On public finance, the standard but boring work is M. Marion, *Histoire financière de la France depuis 1715*, vols 5–6 (1928–31). The subject is beginning to attract new attention: R. Schnerb (ed.), *Deux siècles de fiscalité française XIXe–XXe siècle* (1973) is a collection of articles, and see also Schnerb in *Annales d'histoire économique et sociale* 1938, J. Bouvier in *RHES* 1968 and 1972, and (on the income-tax battle) P. Callet in *Cahiers d'histoire* 1962. Municipal finance is neglected, but see Callet's article on the abolition of the octroi at Lyons in *Cahiers d'histoire* 1962.

H. Hatzfeld, *Du paupérisme à la sécurité sociale. Essai sur les origines de la sécurité sociale en France. 1850–1940* (B, 1971) is a pioneering study of social-security legislation. There is information on housing in R. H. Guerrand, *Les Origines du logement social en France* (1967), on labour legislation in J. A. Tournerie, *Le Ministère du travail (origines et premiers développements*) (1971), and on the population question in R. Talmy, *Histoire du mouvement familial en France (1896–1939)* (2 vols, 1962); cf. J. C. Hunter on the birth-rate problem in *FHS* 1962.

III. REGIONAL AND LOCAL STUDIES

A. ELECTORAL SOCIOLOGY

An indispensable guide, consisting essentially of maps, is F. Goguel, *Géographie des élections françaises sous la Troisième et la Quatrième République* (1970); P. Barral synthesizes recent work in valuable articles in *L'Information historique* 1962 and *RH* 1967. Cf. F. Goguel and G. Dupeux, *Sociologie électorale. Esquisse d'un bilan. Guide de recherches* (1951). Electoral sociology as an approach is discussed by G. Dupeux in *British Journal of Sociology* 1955, A. Lajusan in *Annales* 1949, R. Arambourou in *RFSP* 1951. J. Rougerie points out some of the weaknesses of localized studies in *Annales* 1966.

B. REGIONAL

A. Siegfried's pioneering *Tableau politique de la France de l'Ouest sous la Troisième République* (1913) should now be read in conjunction with P. Bois, *Paysans de l'Ouest. Des structures économiques et sociales aux options politiques depuis l'époque révolutionnaire dans la Sarthe* (T, 1960; abridged ed. with same title, 1971); cf. Bois's article in *Annales historiques de la Révolution française* 1961. On the political role of the landed class and its electoral influence, see also J. Bécarud in *RFSP* 1973.

M. Agulhon, *La République au village. (Les populations du Var de la Révolution à la Seconde République)* (1970) describes the 'sociability' of Provence. On clubs, cafés, etc. see also Agulhon in *RH* 1971 and C. Garron-Gasquy in *Provence historique* 1970. In *Annales* 1973, Agulhon discusses civic enthusiasm for the Republic as expressed in statues and symbols.

Other regional studies – some ending before 1870, but relevant to understanding the Third Republic – are A. Armengaud, *Les Populations de l'Est-Aquitain au début de l'époque contemporaine* (T, 1961); G. Garrier, *Paysans du Beaujolais et du Lyonnais 1800–1970* (T, 2 vols, 1973); J. Lovie, *La Savoie dans la vie française de 1860 à 1875* (T, 1963); L. A. Loubère, *Radicalism in Mediterranean France. Its Rise and Decline, 1848–1914* (1974); *Recherches sur les forces politiques de la France de l'Est depuis 1787* (1966); special no. of *Revue du Nord* 1974 on political life in the north in the twentieth century; P. Vigier, *La Seconde République dans la région alpine* (T, 2 vols, 1963).

The 'Univers de la France' series of regional histories usually has good sections on the modern period. Useful examples are E. Baratier (ed.), *Histoire de la Provence* (1969); C. Higounet (ed.), *Histoire de l'Aquitaine* (1971); L. Trénard (ed.), *Histoire des Pays-Bas français* (1972).

C. DEPARTMENTAL

The department is the classic unit for electoral sociology. A. Siegfried himself produced *Géographie électorale de l'Ardèche sous la IIIe République* (1949), and sketched the history of the Aude in *Société d'histoire de la Troisième République. Bulletin* 1939. The outstanding recent works are P. Barral, *Le Département de l'Isère sous la Troisième République, 1870–1940. Histoire sociale et politique* (T, 1962) and G. Dupeux, *Aspects de l'histoire sociale et politique du Loir-et-Cher, 1848–1914* (T, 1962). Other useful studies are P. Bernard, *Economie et sociologie de la Seine-et-Marne 1850–1950* (1953); M. Denis, *L'Eglise et la République en Mayenne, 1896–1906* (1967); R. Long, *Les Elections législatives en Côte d'Or depuis 1870. Essai d'interprétation sociologique* (1958); J. Merley, *La Haute-Loire de la fin de l'ancien régime aux débuts de la Troisième République* (T, 2 vols, n.d.); J. Micheu-Puyou, *Histoire électorale du département des Basses-Pyrénées sous la IIIe et la IVe République* (1965); J. Pataut, *Sociologie électorale de la Nièvre au XXe siècle (1902–1951)*, vol. 1 (1956); J. F. Viple, *Sociologie politique de l'Allier* (1967). Among available articles are M. Bordes on the Gers in *L'Information historique* 1961; G. Désert on the Calvados in *Annales de Normandie* 1971; S. H. Elwitt on the Loire 1869–73 in *FHS* 1969; H. Goallou on the Ille-et-Vilaine in *Annales de Bretagne* 1965 and *L'Information historique* 1974; J. P. Landrevie on the Tarn-et-Garonne 1869–77 in *Annales du Midi* 1972; G. Lenormand on the Somme 1870–77 in *RH* 1946; P. Mansire on the Seine-Inférieure in *Annales de Normandie* 1956; B. Phan on the Calvados in *Annales de Normandie* 1970.

D. VILLAGE STUDIES

On the Republic at the grass roots, there is nothing to rival R. Thabault, *Education and Change in a Village Community* (1971; orig. *Mon village*, 1945). See also R. Arambourou on communes in the south-west in *Annales du Midi* 1953 and in F. Goguel (ed.), *Nouvelles études de sociologie électorale* (1954). L. Lévi-Strauss gives an example of kinship networks in village politics in *Annales* 1975.

E. URBAN STUDIES

The 'Univers de la France' series includes some histories of towns, e.g. E. Baratier (ed.), *Histoire de Marseille* (1973); J. Meyer (ed.), *Histoire de Rennes* (1972); P. Wolff (ed.), *Histoire de Toulouse* (1974). Other general histories are L. Desgraves and G. Dupeux, *Bordeaux au XIXe siècle* (1969); C. Fohlen (ed.), *Histoire de Besançon*, vol. 2 (1965); A. Kleinclausz (ed.), *Histoire de Lyon. III. De 1814 à 1940* (1952); P. Pierrard, *Lille et les Lillois* (1967). More detailed political history is in J. Ameye, *La Vie politique à Tourcoing sous la Troisième République* (1963); R. Fruit, *La Croissance économique du pays de Saint-Amand (Nord) 1668–1914* (1963); E. Ginestous, *Histoire politique de Bordeaux sous la IIIe République* (1946); P. Gonnet on Nice in *Cahiers d'histoire* 1968; special no. of *Cahiers d'histoire* 1971 on Lyons; C. Marie, *L'Evolution du comportement politique dans une ville en expansion. Grenoble 1871–1965* (1966).

The politics of Paris after the Commune are neglected by historians, but there are some hints in A. Sutcliffe, *The Autumn of Central Paris. The Defeat of Town Planning, 1850–1970* (1970). M. Agulhon studies a suburban commune in *Etudes sur la banlieue de Paris. Essais méthodologiques* (1950).

IV. POLITICAL INSTITUTIONS

A. GENERAL INTERPRETATION

Books which provide stimulating ideas about the political system are C. Morazé, *The French and the Republic* (1958; orig. 1956); R. Priouret, *La République des députés* (1959); A. Siegfried, *De la IIIe à la IVe République* (1956); A. Thibaudet, *Les Idées politiques de la France* (1932); J. E. C. Bodley's opinionated *France* (new ed., 1899) is still very readable. R. de Jouvenel, *La République des camarades* (1914) was an influential pamphlet. M. Duverger, *La Démocratie sans le peuple* (1967) develops ideas on 'centrism' first put forward in *RFSP* 1964.

B. THE PARLIAMENTARY SYSTEM

On the workings of Parliament, see standard authorities like W. L. Middleton, *The French Political System* (1932) and R. K. Gooch, *The French Parliamentary Committee System* (1935). R. A. Winnacker discusses the *délégation des gauches* in *JMH* 1937. On the Senate: J. P. Marichy,

La Deuxième Chambre dans la vie politique française depuis 1875 (1969), and D. Salem in *RHES* 1972. On the Cabinet system, the classic and complementary treatises of A. Soulier, *L'Instabilité ministérielle sous la Troisième République (1871–1938)* (1939) and J. Ollé-Laprune, *La Stabilité des ministres sous la Troisième République 1879–1940* (1962). Little work has been done on parties, but there is material on France in M. Duverger, *Political Parties* (3rd ed., 1964; orig. 1951) and R. Michels, *Political Parties* (1915).

The 'Centre de recherches sur l'histoire du XIXe siecle' at the Sorbonne has begun the application of quantitative methods to the politics of the 1880s. A. Prost and C. Rosenzveig analyse the voting patterns of deputies in *RFSP* 1971 and 1973. A. Prost, *Vocabulaire des proclamations électorales de 1881, 1885 et 1889* (1974) analyses the content of 'Barodet', the officially published collection of deputies' election statements. Cf. his article in *Cahiers de lexicologie* 1969; the pioneer of this approach was J. Dubois, *Le Vocabulaire politique et social en France de 1869 à 1872* (1962).

C. ELECTIONS

There is no compilation of election results, but P. Campbell, *French Electoral Systems and Elections since 1789* (2nd ed., 1965) gives brief results as well as procedures. M. T. and A. Lancelot, *Atlas des circonscriptions électorales en France depuis 1875* (1970) includes a guide to sources. On two specialized aspects: J. P. Charnay, *Les Scrutins politiques en France de 1815 à 1962. Contestations et invalidations* (1964) and A. Lancelot, *L'Abstentionnisme électoral en France* (1968). Some articles on elections in particular constituencies are by J. P. T. Bury in *Historical Journal* 1967, J. Chouvy in *RFSP* 1970, G. Jacquemet in *RHMC* 1971, J. C. Liedot in *Annales de l'Est* 1961, Y. Malartic in *Provence historique* 1962 (Clemenceau in 1893), P. Mansire in *Annales de Normandie* 1957, D. Percheron in *Revue du Nord* 1968.

D. DEPUTIES

The expert here is M. Dogan. His essay on the nature and origins of the political elite in D. Marvick (ed.), *Political Decision-makers* (1961) is expanded in *Revue française de sociologie* 1967 and discussed by J. Charlot in *Archives européennes de sociologie* 1973. Cf. Dogan on the turnover of deputies in *RFSP* 1953. The dominance of lawyers is documented in Y. H. Gaudemet, *Les Juristes et la vie politique de la IIIe République* (1970). J. Bousquet-Mélou, *Louis Barthou et la circonscription d'Oloron (1889–1914)* (1972) is interesting on a deputy's relations with his constituency.

E. THE ADMINISTRATION

The best introduction is P. Legendre's original and suggestive *Histoire de l'administration de 1750 à nos jours* (B, 1968). Little has been done on local administration, but there is much of relevance in L. Girard *et al.*, *Les Conseillers généraux en 1870. Etude statistique d'un personnel politique* (1967); cf. J. L. Mestre on the *conseil général* of the Bouches-du-Rhône in *Provence historique* 1971.

F. THE PRESS

There is now an excellent standard history: C. Bellanger *et al.* (eds), *Histoire générale de la presse française. III. De 1871 à 1940* (B, 1972). On cartoons, see J. Lethève, *La Caricature et la presse sous la IIIe République* (Kiosque, 1961), and on the 1881 Press law I. Collins, *The Government and the Newspaper Press in France 1814–1881* (1959). This is now a very active field of research. The fullest study of a single paper is F. Amaury, *Histoire du plus grand quotidien de la IIIe République. Le Petit Parisien 1876–1944* (T, 2 vols, 1972). Others are C. Hirtz, *L'Est républicain 1889–1914* (1973); E. and M. Dixmier, *L'Assiette au beurre. Revue satirique illustrée 1901–1912* (1974); L. de Vaucelles, '*Le Nouvelliste de Lyon*' *et la défense religieuse (1879–1889)* (1971).

V. RELIGIOUS AND INTELLECTUAL LIFE

A. THE CHURCH: GENERAL HISTORY

J. McManners, *Church and State in France, 1870–1914* (B, 1972) is an excellent introduction; A. Dansette, *Religious History of Modern France* (2 vols, 1961; orig. 1948–51) is a standard history. The place of the Church in society is discussed in T. Zeldin (ed.), *Conflicts in French Society. Anticlericalism, Education and Morals in the Nineteenth Century* (1970).

On the political attitudes of the clergy, a pioneering study is J. Gadille, *La Pensée et l'action politiques des évêques français au début de la IIIe République 1870–1883* (T, 2 vols, 1967). L. Capéran, *L'Anticléricalisme et l'Affaire Dreyfus 1897–1899* (1948) defends the Catholic record in the affair. For the affair and the Separation crisis, see M.

Larkin, *Church and State after the Dreyfus Affair. The Separation Issue in France* (1974); cf. Larkin's article on the workings of the Concordat in *English Historical Review* 1966. J. M. Mayeur, *La Séparation de l'Eglise et de l'Etat* (S, Archives, 1966) illustrates the inventories crisis, on which see also his article in *Annales* 1966. L. V. Méjan, *La Séparation des Eglises et de l'Etat. L'Oeuvre de Louis Méjan* (1959) is interesting on the evolution of the 1905 law, while L. Capéran, *L'Invasion laïque. De l'avènement de Combes au vote de la Séparation* (1935) is good on anti-clerical ideology. For the impact in the provinces: G. Laperrière, *La 'Séparation' à Lyon (1904–1908). Etude d'opinion publique* (1973).

F. Boulard provides *An Introduction to Religious Sociology. Pioneer Work in France* (1960; orig. *Premiers itinéraires en sociologie religieuse,* 1954). There are many monographs in this field – one may pick out G. Cholvy, *Géographie religieuse de l'Hérault contemporain* (T, 1968) – and Y. M. Hilaire summarizes some of them in *L'Information historique* 1963. E. G. Léonard, *Le Protestant français* (B, 1955) is an interesting introduction to Protestantism; cf. S. R. Schram, *Protestantism and Politics in France* (1954).

B. SOCIAL CATHOLICS AND CHRISTIAN DEMOCRATS

Much of the work in this field is of limited interest to the general historian. But J. M. Mayeur, *Un Prêtre démocrate, l'abbé Lemire, 1853–1928* (T, 1968) throws much light on the political role of Christian democracy; cf. his article on Christian democrat congresses in *RHMC* 1962, and R. Rémond, *Les deux congrès ecclésiastiques de Reims et de Bourges 1896–1900* (1964). Other work of particular value is J. Caron, *Le Sillon et la démocratie chrétienne 1894–1910* (1967); C. Molette, *L'Association catholique de la jeunesse française 1886–1907* (T, 1968); R. Talmy, *Une Forme hybride du catholicisme social en France. L'Association catholique des patrons du Nord 1884–1895* (T, 1962); S. Wilson on the *Union Nationale* movement in *JCH* 1975. T. B. Caldwell in *IRSH* 1966 and M. Launay in *MS* 1969 examine the Catholic white-collar trade union.

C. EDUCATION

A. Prost, *Histoire de l'enseignement en France 1800–1967* (B, 1968) is the best introduction, and M. Ozouf, *L'Ecole, l'Eglise et la République 1871–1914* (Kiosque, 1963) illustrates the conflicts of this period. M. Gontard, *L'Oeuvre scolaire de la Troisième République. L'enseignement primaire en France de 1876 à 1914* (n.d.) deals with primary education;

cf. G. Vincent in *Revue française de sociologie* 1972. G. Bonheur, *Qui a cassé le vase de Soissons?* (1963) is an amusing evocation of the values of French education – a French equivalent of *1066 and All That*. P. Nora in *RH* 1962 is good on Ernest Lavisse and nationalism in school textbooks; P. Bois assesses the impact of secular education on politics in *Annales* 1954.

On the teachers as a social group, see J. Ozouf (ed.), *Nous les maîtres d'école. Autobiographies d'instituteurs de la Belle Epoque* (S, Archives, 1967), based on recorded interviews; cf. Ozouf in *MS* 1963, and G. Duveau, *Les Instituteurs* (n.d.). On the secondary teachers, see P. Gerbod, *La Condition universitaire en France au XIXe siècle* (T, 1965), and articles by G. Vincent in *RHMC* 1966 and *MS* 1966, and V. Karady in *Revue française de sociologie* 1972 and 1973. A. Thibaudet, *La République des professeurs* (1927) first analysed the invasion of politics by the teachers. For higher education, there is a useful brief account by T. Zeldin in *JCH* 1967; cf. R. J. Smith on the politics of the *Ecole normale* in *RHMC* 1973.

D. POLITICAL THOUGHT

A useful guide is J. Touchard *et al.*, *Histoire des idées politiques. II. Du XVIIIe siècle à nos jours* (B, 6th ed., 1973). Standard works are J. P. Mayer, *Political Thought in France from the Revolution to the Fifth Republic* (3rd ed., 1961); R. Soltau, *French Political Thought in the Nineteenth Century* (1931); J. A. Scott, *Republican Ideas and the Liberal Tradition in France 1870–1914* (1951).

VI. REPUBLICANS AND RADICALS

The best introduction to the ideas of the Opportunists is P. Barral's anthology *Les Fondateurs de la Troisième République* (S, 1968). The general history of anti-clericalism is given in G. Weill, *Histoire de l'idée laïque en France au XIXe siècle* (1925), and on the Republic's anti-clerical legislation see: E. M. Acomb, *The French Laic Laws (1879–1889)* (1941); L. Capéran, *Histoire contemporaine de la laïcité française* (2 vols, 1957–60); J. Gadille on the idea of 'republican defence' in *Bulletin de la Société d'histoire moderne* 1967; L. Legrand, *L'Influence du positivisme dans l'oeuvre scolaire de Jules Ferry* (1961).

Scholarly writing on freemasonry is rare, but see M. J. Headings, *French Freemasonry under the Third Republic* (1949) and D. Ligou, *Frédéric Desmons et la franc-maçonnerie sous la 3e République* (1966).

A useful brief history of Radicalism is C. Nicolet, *Le Radicalisme* (3rd ed., 1967) and a fuller one J. T. Nordmann, *Histoire des radicaux 1820–1973* (1974). J. Kayser, *Les Grandes Batailles du radicalisme. Des origines aux portes du pouvoir, 1820–1901* (1962) includes a number of documents; cf. Kayser on Radicalism in *Tendances politiques dans la vie française depuis 1789* (1960). D. Halévy, *La République des comités* (1934) was a scathing pamphlet about the party. D. Bardonnet, *Evolution de la structure du parti radical* (1960) deals with the organizational side, and there are interesting articles on the local activists by R. Vandenbussche in *Revue du Nord* 1965 and P. Polivka in *RHMC* 1975.

Radical views on social questions before 1900 are discussed by L. A. Loubère in *IRSH* 1962, *FHS* 1963, *American Journal of Legal History* 1964, and *RHES* 1964; 'solidarism' is examined by J. E. S. Hayward in *IRSH* 1959, 1961 and 1963.

VII. THE RIGHT

A. GENERAL

The starting-point must be R. Rémond, *The Right Wing in France. From 1815 to de Gaulle* (B, 2nd ed., 1969; orig. 3rd ed., 1968). Also valuable are M. Anderson, *Conservative Politics in France* (1974) and the essays in D. Shapiro (ed.), *The Right in France 1890–1919. Three Studies* (1962). J. S. McClelland (ed.), *The French Right (from de Maistre to Maurras)* (S, 1970) is an anthology. R. Girardet, *Le Nationalisme français 1871–1914* (S, 1966) is an excellent collection of documents; cf. his important article on nationalism in *RFSP* 1958. Some interpretative ideas are put forward by E. Weber in *American Historical Review*, vol. lxv (1959–60) and in H. Rogger and E. Weber (eds), *The European Right. A Historical Profile* (1965).

On some miscellaneous aspects: J. M. Roberts, *The Paris Commune from the Right* (1973); A. Olivesi on the Right at Marseilles in 1914 in *Provence historique* 1957; R. Sanson on the cult of Joan of Arc in *RHMC* 1973.

Two good books on the army and politics are D. B. Ralston, *The Army of the Republic. The Place of the Military in the Political Evolution of France, 1871–1914* (1967) and R. Girardet, *La Société militaire dans la France contemporaine 1815–1939* (1953); cf. F. Bédarida in *RH* 1964 on the opinions of officers in 1876–8.

B. ROYALISM

There are several recent studies of this, especially in the 1870s: S. M. Osgood, *French Royalism since 1870* (2nd ed., 1970); M. L. Brown, *The Comte de Chambord* (1967); R. R. Locke, *French Legitimists and the Politics of Moral Order in the Early Third Republic* (1974); J. Rothney, *Bonapartism after Sedan* (1969). For the local context, see A. Bonafous in *Revue du Nord* 1965 (royalists and the *Ralliement*), M. Denis in *Annales de Bretagne* 1970 (liberal Legitimism in Brittany).

C. THE 'NEW RIGHT' OF THE 1880S AND 1890S

On Boulangism and its offshoots: C. S. Doty in *The Historian* 1970 (Boulangist deputies after 1889); P. H. Hutton in *JCH* 1976 (popular Boulangism); P. M. Rutkoff in *FHS* 1974 (the *Ligue des Patriotes*); Z. Sternhell in *JCH* 1971 (Déroulède). See also G. L. Mosse on the 'jaunes' trade-union movement in *JCH* 1972.

R. F. Byrnes, *Antisemitism in Modern France. I. The Prologue to the Dreyfus Affair* (1950) is an introduction to this subject, but has not been continued. Recent work has focused on Catholic attitudes: P. Pierrard, *Juifs et catholiques français. De Drumont à Jules Isaac (1886–1945)* (B, 1970); P. Sorlin, '*La Croix*' *et les Juifs (1880–1899)* (T, 1967); J. Verdès-Leroux, *Scandale financier et antisémitisme catholique. Le krach de l'Union Générale* (B, 1969). On this last scandal, cf. J. Bouvier, *Le Krach de l'Union Générale (1878–1885)* (T, 1960). S. Wilson studies the anti-Semitic riots in 1898 in *Historical Journal* 1973, and M. R. Marrus breaks new ground with *The Politics of Assimilation. A Study of the French Jewish Community at the time of the Dreyfus Affair* (1971). For left-wing anti-Semitism, see E. Silberner in *Jewish Social Studies* 1953 and *Historia Judaica* 1954.

D. THE NEW NATIONALISM

Barrès has attracted considerable recent attention, and the best book is Z. Sternhell, *Maurice Barrès et le nationalisme français* (1972); cf. his article in *JCH* 1973. See also R. Soucy, *Fascism in France. The Case of Maurice Barrès* (1972) and *Maurice Barrès. Actes du colloque organisé par ... l'Université de Nancy* (1963). Barrès himself anthologized his political writings in *Scènes et doctrines du nationalisme* (n.d.); a similar collection for Maurras is F. Natter and C. Rousseau (eds), *De la politique naturelle au nationalisme intégral* (1972).

On Maurras and his movement, E. Weber, *Action Française. Royalism*

and Reaction in Twentieth-Century France (1962) is generally better than
E. R. Tannenbaum, *The Action Française* (1962), though Tannenbaum
is rather fuller on the pre-1914 period. See also E. Nolte, *Three Faces of
Fascism. Action Française, Italian Fascism, National Socialism* (1969).
M. Curtis, *Three Against the Third Republic. Sorel, Barrès, and Maurras*
(1959) compares the ideas of the three thinkers. On the influence of
nationalism among students, see 'Agathon', *Les Jeunes Gens d'aujourd'hui*
(1913), and P. Bénéton in *RFSP* 1971.

E. Weber, *The Nationalist Revival in France, 1905–1914* (1968)
concentrates on 'Poincarist' nationalism. Weber has also discussed the
political implications of sport in *JCH* 1970 and *American Historical
Review* 1971; cf. R. D. Anderson in *History of Education* 1973.

VIII. THE WORKING-CLASS MOVEMENT

A. SOCIALISM: GENERAL HISTORY

The best brief survey is the essay on France by M. Rebérioux in
J. Droz (ed.), *Histoire générale du socialisme. II. De 1875 à 1918* (1975).
G. Lefranc, *Le Mouvement socialiste sous la Troisième République (1875–
1940)* (1963) and D. Ligou, *Histoire du socialisme en France (1871–1961)*
(1962) are standard works, and there is material on France in G. D. H.
Cole, *A History of Socialist Thought*, vols 2–3 (1954–6). A. Noland, *The
Founding of the French Socialist Party (1893–1905)* (1956) is good on the
unification period; for the years around 1900 see also L. Derfler in
RHMC 1963 and J. Pinset in *RHES* 1958. On the later years, see
J. J. Fiechter, *Le Socialisme français: de l'Affaire Dreyfus à la Grande
Guerre* (1965). J. Maitron discusses Socialist students in *MS* 1964,
C. Sowerwine Socialist feminism in *MS* 1975.

Socialist attitudes towards the State are discussed in M. Perrot and
A. Kriegel, *Le Socialisme français et le pouvoir* (1966), and by M. Rebérioux
in *MS* 1968. J. Maitron has a valuable article on the psychology of
Socialist activists in *MS* 1960–1. For Socialist views on religion, see
special no. of *MS* 1966; on education, M. Ozouf in *MS* 1963; on
population, A. Armengaud in *Annales de démographie historique* 1966;
on patriotism, M. Winock in *RHMC* 1973; on colonies, A. Olivesi in
MS 1964 and F. Bédarida in *MS* 1974.

On the 1914 crisis, a vivid introduction is A. Kriegel and J. J. Becker,
1914. La guerre et le mouvement ouvrier français (Kiosque, 1964). Cf. essays
in A. Kriegel, *Le Pain et les roses. Jalons pour une histoire des socialismes*
(1968); Kriegel in *RHES* 1965; J. J. Becker, *Le Carnet B. Les pouvoirs*

publics et l'antimilitarisme avant la guerre de 1914 (1973); special no. of *MS* 1964 on 1914. Two articles on local anti-militarists are Y. Rinaudo in *Provence historique* 1970 and R. Andréani in *RHMC* 1973.

B. THE COMMUNE

The best account in English is now S. Edwards, *The Paris Commune 1871* (B, 1971); R. L. Williams, *The French Revolution of 1870–1871* (1969) sets it in a wider context; E. Schulkind, *The Paris Commune of 1871* (B, 1971) is a 'Historical Association' pamphlet. Documents are available in E. Schulkind, *The Paris Commune of 1871. The View from the Left* (B, S, 1972); S. Edwards, *The Communards of Paris, 1871* (S, 1973); J. Rougerie, *Paris libre 1871* (1971) (with linking commentary); J. Rougerie, *Procès des communards* (S, Archives, 1964) (good on the social background of the insurgents; cf. his article in *MS* 1964). Marx's 'The Civil War in France' is available in K. Marx and F. Engels, *Selected Works* (2 vols, 1962), and other editions. For a modern Marxist account, lavishly illustrated, see J. Bruhat *et al.* (eds), *La Commune de 1871* (B, 2nd ed., 1970).

The centenary produced much writing, which is assessed in articles by J. Rougerie in *RH* 1971, J. Gaillard in *Annales* 1973 and J. Estèbe in *MS* 1974. Useful colloquia, originally special nos. of *MS* and *IRSH* respectively in 1972, are *Colloque universitaire pour la commémoration du centenaire de la Commune de 1871* (1972) and J. Rougerie (ed.), *1871. Jalons pour une histoire de la Commune de Paris* (1972).

On the composition and ideas of the Commune, see C. Rihs, *La Commune de Paris. Sa structure et ses doctrines* (2nd ed., 1973). Articles on various aspects of this are by R. D. Price in *Historical Journal* 1972, E. W. Schulkind in *FHS* 1960, R. Wolfe in *Past and Present* 1968.

J. Gaillard, *Communes de province, Commune de Paris 1870–1871* (1971) is an introduction to the question of the provincial movements, and L. M. Greenberg, *Sisters of Liberty. Marseille, Lyon, Paris and the Reaction to a Centralized State, 1868–1871* (1971) stresses 'decentralist' tendencies. Cf. J. Archer on Lyons in *MS* 1971; J. Girault, *La Commune et Bordeaux (1870–1871)* (1971); P. Guillen (ed.), *Grenoble à l'époque de la Commune* (1972); M. Moissonnier, *La Première Internationale et la Commune à Lyon (1865–1871)* (1972); A. Olivesi, *La Commune de 1871 à Marseille et ses origines* (1950).

C. VARIETIES OF SOCIALISM

(i) Guesdism. C. Willard, *Le Mouvement socialiste en France (1893–1905)*.

Les guesdistes (T, 1965) is a model study. On early Marxism, see also S. Bernstein, *The Beginnings of Marxian Socialism in France* (1933), and on various aspects of Guesdism and Guesde's action L. Derfler in *IRSH* 1967, P. H. Hutton in *FHS* 1971, C. Landauer in *IRSH* 1961.

(ii) Blanquism. Blanqui's career largely precedes 1870, but see M. Dommanget, *Auguste Blanqui au début de la IIIe République (1871–1880)* (1971); cf. Dommanget's *Edouard Vaillant* (1956). On Blanquists and Vaillant in the 1880s, see P. H. Hutton in *JMH* 1974, J. Howorth in *MS* 1970.

(iii) Possibilism. See D. Stafford, *From Anarchism to Reformism. A Study of the Political Activities of Paul Brousse within the First International and the French Socialist Movement 1870–90* (1971). C. Landauer discusses the origins of reformism in *IRSH* 1967, and M. Winock the Allemanist split in *MS* 1971.

(iv) Jaurès. H. Goldberg, *Life of Jean Jaurès* (1962) is an excellent biography; J. Hampden Jackson, *Jean Jaurès. His Life and Work* (1943) is also still worth citing. Selections from Jaurès are available in *L'Esprit du socialisme* (n.d.); *Textes choisis. I. Contre la guerre et la politique coloniale* (1959); L. Lévy (ed.), *Anthologie de Jean Jaurès* (1947). Jaurès's *Discours parlementaires*, vol. 1 (1904) includes an interesting study of politics in the 1880s.

For essays on Jaurès, see *Actes du colloque Jaurès et la nation* (1965); *Jean Jaurès, présenté par Vincent Auriol* (1962); special no. of *MS* 1962; M. Rebérioux on Jaurès's early years at Toulouse in *Annales du Midi* 1963. G. Lefranc discusses *Jaurès et le socialisme des intellectuels* (1968); cf. G. Ziebura, *Léon Blum et le parti socialiste 1872–1934* (1967).

(v) Anarchism. J. Maitron, *Le Mouvement anarchiste en France* (T, 2 vols, 2nd ed., 1975; title of 1st ed. differs slightly) is a fundamental thesis. See also Maitron's vivid *Ravachol et les anarchistes* (S, Archives, 1964), and his article on the anarchist mentality in *MS* 1973. Cf. also G. Woodcock, *Anarchism* (1962). Articles on local anarchist groups are by J. Polet in *Revue du Nord* 1969 and J. Masse in *MS* 1969.

D. TRADE UNIONISM AND LABOUR CONDITIONS

The standard work is G. Lefranc, *Le Mouvement syndical sous la Troisième République* (1967); also useful is V. R. Lorwin, *The French Labor Movement* (1954). M. Guilbert assembles material about women's unionism in *Les Femmes et l'organisation syndicale avant 1914* (1966).

Scholars have generally studied particular groups of workers rather than trade unionism itself, and the most impressive recent work is

R. Trempé, *Les Mineurs de Carmaux 1848–1914* (T, 2 vols, 1971). Carmaux is also the subject of J. W. Scott, *The Glassworkers of Carmaux* (1974), and is interesting as Jaurès's constituency; cf. Trempé on his opponent Solages in *Annales du Midi* 1959. Other work on miners: special no. of *MS* 1963; R. Trempé on the reformism of miners in *MS* 1968; L. Loubère on the Languedoc miners in *Journal of Social History* 1968; J. Julliard on the Pas-de-Calais in *MS* 1964; M. Gillet on the 'convention of Arras' in *Revue du Nord* 1957; J. Michel on Emile Basly in *Revue du Nord* 1973 and *MS* 1974.

Other workers to attract attention are those in metallurgy – see C. Gras in *MS* 1965 and 1971 – and the railwaymen: G. Thuillier in *MS* 1969; F. Caron in *MS* 1965; G. Chaumel, *Histoire des cheminots et de leurs syndicats* (1948).

On agricultural trade unionism see P. Gratton's *Les Luttes de classes dans les campagnes* (1971) and his essays in *Les Paysans français contre l'agrarisme* (1972). Other articles are by R. Braque in *MS* 1963, and in a special no. of *MS* 1969.

E. STRIKES

Two recent works open up new perspectives on this subject: M. Perrot, *Les Ouvriers en grève. France 1871–1890* (T, 2 vols, 1974), a fundamental thesis, and E. Shorter and C. Tilly, *Strikes in France 1830–1968* (B, 1974), interesting for its quantitative approach. Related articles by Shorter and Tilly are in *MS* 1971 and *Annales* 1973. Other articles on the study of strikes in general are by J. Néré in *RHES* 1956, Y. Lequin in *Cahiers d'histoire* 1967, and P. N. Stearns in *IRSH* 1974. Stearns has also studied the employers' reaction to strikes after 1900 in *JMH* 1968.

On the connection between strikes and economic fluctuations, see special no. of *MS* 1968, and articles by J. Bouvier in *MS* 1964, J. M. Flonneau in *MS* 1970.

Among the work on individual strikes, one may mention N. Papayanis in *IRSH* 1971 (Hennebont, 1906), G. Désiré-Vuillemin in *Annales du Midi* 1971 and 1973 (strikes at Limoges), M. Lartigue in *Provence historique* 1960 (Marseilles dockers), C. Geslin in *MS* 1973 (Fougères).

F. REVOLUTIONARY SYNDICALISM

The best introduction is H. Dubief's collection *Le Syndicalisme révolutionnaire* (S, 1969). J. Julliard, *Clemenceau briseur de grèves. L'affaire de Draveil-Villeneuve-Saint-Georges* (S, Archives, 1965) illustrates one major crisis. The theories are discussed in J. Joll, *The Anarchists* (1964) and F. F. Ridley, *Revolutionary Syndicalism in France* (1970). J. Julliard's *Fernand Pelloutier et les origines du syndicalisme d'action directe* (1971) includes a selection of Pelloutier's writings; cf. A. B. Spitzer on Pelloutier in *IRSH* 1963. For a later CGT leader, see B. Georges *et al.*, *Léon Jouhaux*, vol. 1 (1962).

G. LOCAL STUDIES

These vary a good deal in quality. A selection covering both Socialism and unionism is: G. Baal on revolutionary syndicalism in Brest in *MS* 1973; R. P. Baker on Socialism in the Nord in *IRSH* 1967; J. Charles, *Les Débuts du mouvement syndical à Besançon* (1962); P. Cousteix on the Limousin in *L'Actualité de l'histoire* 1957; S. Derruau-Boniol on the Allier in *Cahiers d'histoire* 1957; T. Judt on the Var in *Historical Journal* 1975; Y. Lequin on Lyons in *MS* 1969; M. Perrot on the Gard in *RHES* 1959; R. Pierreuse and N. Quillien on Roubaix in *Revue du Nord* 1969; D. Vasseur, *Les Débuts du mouvement ouvrier dans la région de Belfort-Montbéliard (1870–1914)* (1967).

H. BIBLIOGRAPHY AND REFERENCE

The review *Le Mouvement social* is the best guide to current work, and useful bibliographical articles are by A. Kriegel in *RH* 1966 and M. Perrot and J. Maitron in *MS* 1968. See also E. Dolléans and M. Crozier, *Mouvements ouvrier et socialiste. Chronologie et bibliographie. Angleterre, France, Allemagne, Etats-Unis (1750–1918)* (1950). R. Brécy, *Le Mouvement syndical en France 1871–1921. Essai bibliographique* (1963) contains both bibliography and details of trade-union organizations and congresses; cf. J. A. Clarke on Socialist congresses in *JMH* 1959. An important reference work is J. Maitron (ed.), *Dictionnaire biographique du mouvement ouvrier français* (1964f.).

IX. FOREIGN AND COLONIAL POLICY

A. FOREIGN POLICY

There is no up-to-date general survey, but one can still use E. M. Carroll, *French Public Opinion and Foreign Affairs 1870–1914* (1931) and F. L. Schuman, *War and Diplomacy in the French Republic. An Inquiry into Political Motivations and the Control of Foreign Policy* (1931); on parliamentary control, see also J. C. Cairns on 1911–14 in *Canadian Historical Review* 1953.

The standard work on the Franco-Russian alliance is W. L. Langer, *The Franco-Russian Alliance 1890–1894* (1929); cf. P. Renouvin on its revision in 1900–1 in *Revue d'histoire diplomatique* 1966. On the Entente Cordiale, see C. Andrew, *Théophile Delcassé and the Making of the Entente Cordiale. A Reappraisal of French Foreign Policy 1898–1905* (1968); P. J. V. Rolo, *Entente Cordiale* (1969); P. Guillen in *Revue d'histoire diplomatique* 1968.

The financial and economic side of foreign relations has attracted most attention recently. The documents in R. Poidevin, *Finances et relations internationales 1887–1914* (S, 1970) form an interesting introduction, and for French investments in general see R. E. Cameron, *France and the Economic Development of Europe 1800–1914* (1961) and H. Feis, *Europe the World's Banker, 1870–1914* (1930). Two major theses are R. Poidevin, *Les Relations économiques et financières entre la France et l'Allemagne de 1898 à 1914* (T, 1969) and R. Girault, *Emprunts russes et investissements français en Russie 1887–1914* (T, 1973). Related articles by Girault are in *RHMC* 1966, *RHMC* 1969, and *Revue du Nord* 1975; in *RH* 1975 he studies Franco-Russian relations in the Balkans on the eve of 1914. Cf. D. N. Collins in *Historical Journal* 1973 on France and Russian railways. For French interests in the Ottoman empire in the 1900s, see J. Thobie in *RH* 1968 and *MS* 1974, and W. I. Shorrock in *European Studies Review* 1974. P. Guillen studies the economic penetration of Morocco in *Les Emprunts marocains 1902–1904* (n.d.), *RH* 1963, and *Revue d'histoire diplomatique* 1965; in *RH* 1972 he considers the role of colonial questions generally in Franco-German relations on the eve of war.

B. COLONIAL POLICY

A very clear presentation of the facts is J. Ganiage, *L'Expansion coloniale de la France sous la Troisième République (1871–1914)* (B, 1968). H. Brunschwig, *French Colonialism 1871–1914, Myths and Realities* (1966; orig. 1960) discusses the question of motivation, and the 'colonial party'. J. Bouvier surveys the question in *MS* 1974.

On Ferry and the reorientation of policy around 1880: T. F. Power, *Jules Ferry and the Renaissance of French Imperialism* (1944); F. Pisani-Ferry, *Jules Ferry et le partage du monde* (1962); J. Ganiage, *Les Origines du protectorat français en Tunisie (1861–1881)* (T, 1959); J. P. T. Bury on Gambetta's attitudes in *English Historical Review* 1967. No attempt can be made here to cover expansion in the various territories, but one study which emphasizes links with internal politics is R. G. Brown,

Fashoda Reconsidered. The Impact of Domestic Politics on French Policy in Africa 1893–1898 (1969)

C. M. Andrew and A. S. Kanya-Forstner have valuable articles on the colonial party in *Historical Journal* 1971 and 1974. Business pressures are examined by S. M. Persell in *Historical Journal* 1974 (the 'Union Coloniale') and J. F. Laffey in *FHS* 1969 (colonialism at Lyons). J. J. Cooke, *New French Imperialism 1880–1910: the Third Republic and Colonial Expansion* (1973) is mainly about Etienne.

R. Girardet, *L'Idée coloniale en France de 1871 à 1962* (1972) is excellent on attitudes to colonialism. On the 1870s, cf. A. Murphy, *The Ideology of French Imperialism 1871–1881* (1948), and J. Valette in *RHMC* 1967. C. R. Ageron, *L'Anticolonialisme en France de 1871 à 1914* (S, 1973) is a collection of documents.

C. MILITARY QUESTIONS

The best guide to France's military planning is H. Contamine, *La Revanche, 1871–1914* (1957). On the politics of conscription, see R. D. Challener, *The French Theory of the Nation in Arms 1866–1939* (1955). On the military background to 1914: S. R. Williamson, *The Politics of Grand Strategy. Britain and France prepare for War, 1904–1914* (1969), and J. C. Cairns on the army's views about international politics in *JMH* 1953.

The French navy seems entirely neglected by historians, but the basic facts are in J. Tramond and A. Reussner, *Eléments d'histoire maritime et coloniale contemporaine (1815–1914)* (new ed., 1947), and P. Masson's article in *Revue maritime* 1968.

Index

NOTE Periods of office as prime minister (*PM*) and president are shown. Other offices held are shown only when they are of some significance.

Action française movement, 26, 70, 86, 110, 113, 115–16, 118, 152, 201–2
Action libérale, 21, 72, 117, 170–3
Adam, Juliette (1836–1936), 147
affaire des fiches, 25, 150
agriculture: politics of, 65, 83–5, 191; statistics, 31–2, 39–40; *see also* land-owners; peasants
Allemane, Jean (1843–1935), and Allemanism, 126–8, 131, 175
Alliance communiste, 175
Alliance démocratique, 22, 72, 172
Amiens charter, 136–7
anarchism, 16, 120, 123–4, 126–31, 137, 139, 175, 204
André, Louis (1838–1913), *minister war May 1900–November 1904*, 25, 112
anti-clericalism, 2, 10–13, 19–25, 56–8, 67, 71, 89–91, 122, 133, 198–9
anti-militarism, 26, 92, 133, 138–9, 150–151
anti-Semitism, 17, 20, 38, 100, 107–10, 115–17, 133, 201
Anzin, 16, 35, 131
Appel au peuple group, 165, 167
army, 20–1, 25, 63, 82, 111–12, 117–18, 120, 147, 149–53, 200, 208
army laws: 1872, 144–5; 1889, 147; 1905, 151; 1913 (three-year law), 28–9, 80, 98, 118, 135, 151–3
Arras, Convention of, 130
Association catholique de la jeunesse française, 110
Association catholique des patrons du Nord, 109
Assumptionists, 20, 23, 103, 106, 109, 111
Aube, Théophile (1826–90), *minister marine January 1886–May 1887*, 153

Audiffret-Pasquier, Duc d' (1823–1905), 9
Bakunin, Michael (1814–76), 123
'Barodet', 196
Barrère, Camille (1851–1940), 143
Barrès, Maurice (1862–1923), 15, 107, 112, 114–15, 117
Barthou, Louis (1862–1934), *PM 1913*, 22, 28, 174
Basly, Emile (1854–1928), 130
bataillons scolaires, 92
Belleville programme, 88–9
Benda, Julien (1867–1956), 114
Bergson, Henri (1859–1941), 113
Bert, Paul (1833–86), *minister public instruction November 1881–January 1882*, 89, 92
Biétry, Pierre (1872–1918), 117
Blanc, Louis (1811–82), 88
Blanqui, Auguste (1805–81), and Blanquism, 106, 119–20, 122–3, 126–8, 131–3, 175, 204
Bloc, 22, 25, 28, 71–2, 78, 133–4, 157, 172–3
Blum, Léon (1872–1950), 134
Bodley, John E. C. (1853–1925), 66, 75, 157
Boisdeffre, Raoul de (1839–1919), 148
Bonapartism, 1–2, 10, 44, 47, 51, 53, 56, 58–9, 86, 100–1, 104, 107, 115, 164–6, 201
Bontoux, Eugène (1820–1905), 108
Bordeaux, 6, 59, 107
Bordeaux pact, 7
bouilleurs de cru, 85
Boulanger, Georges (1837–91), *minister war January 1886–May 1887*, 14–15
Boulanger crisis, 14–15, 18, 68, 91, 95, 106, 112, 118, 121, 142, 147–8, 189

Boulangism, 14–17, 20, 44, 52–3, 70, 106–7, 110, 113–14, 116, 125–6, 132, 168–9, 189, 201

Bourgeois, Léon (1851–1925), *PM 1895–6, foreign minister March–October 1906 and June 1914*, 18, 76, 78, 95–6, 150, 170

bourses du travail, 127–8, 131, 176

Brazza, Pierre Savorgnan de (1852–1905), 149

Brest, 52, 56

Briand, Aristide (1862–1932), *PM 1909–11 and 1913, minister public instruction March 1906–January 1908, minister justice January 1908–July 1909 and January 1912–January 1913*, 27–8, 66, 68, 79, 93, 118, 127, 139, 172–4

Brisson, Henri (1835–1912), *PM 1885–6 and 1898*, 167, 170

Broglie, Albert, Duc de (1821–1901), *PM 1873–4 and 1877*, 9–10, 69, 93, 101, 165

Brousse, Paul (1844–1912), 124–6, 128; *see also* Possibilism

Broutchoux, Benoît (1879–1944), 130

Brunetière, Ferdinand (1849–1906), 113

Buffet, Louis (1818–98), *PM 1875–6*, 165

Buisson, Ferdinand (1841–1932), 81, 91

bureaucracy, *see* civil servants

businessmen and politics, 13, 34–6, 59, 63, 67, 83, 93, 98, 103, 105, 138, 142

Cabinet system, 75, 77–9, 196

Cabrières, François-Marie-Anatole de (1830–1921), 104

Caillaux, Joseph (1863–1944), *PM 1911–12, minister finance June 1899–June 1902, October 1906–July 1909, March–June 1911 and December 1913–March 1914*, 27–9, 68, 81, 87, 93, 98, 151, 154–5, 174

Calmette, Gaston (1858–1914), 87

Calvignac, Jean-Baptiste (1854–1934), 135

Cambon, Paul (1843–1924), 142, 154

Cambon, Jules (1845–1935), 143

Carmaux, 16, 132, 135

Carnet B, 139, 202–3

Carnot, Sadi (1837–94), *president 1887–1894*, 16, 167

Casimir-Perier, Jean (1847–1907), *PM 1893–4, president 1894–5*, 17, 35, 169–70

Cassagnac family (Bernard de Granier

de, 1806–80; Paul de Granier de, 1842–1904), 58, 86

Centre Left, 8, 10, 34, 93, 164–9

Centre Right, 164–5

Chalon-sur-Saône, 133

Chambord, Comte de ('Henri V') (1820–83), 9, 104, 108

Châtellerault, Socialist congress at, 175

chevau-légers, 165

Christian democrat movement, 16, 107, 109–10, 198

Church, political views and influence of, 2–3, 10, 16–17, 20–1, 47–51, 56, 59, 61–3, 69–70, 90, 103–4, 106, 109–10, 116–17, 144, 197–8; *see also* Ralliement; religious orders

Cissey, Ernest de (1810–82), *PM 1874–5*, 165

civil servants, 12, 27, 35–6, 39, 52, 64, 81–2, 197

Clemenceau, Georges (1841–1929), *PM 1906–9, minister interior March 1906–July 1909*, 11, 13, 16–17, 19, 27, 29, 66, 72, 80, 89, 92–5, 98, 112, 134, 137, 145, 151, 155, 173

Cochery, Adolphe (1829–1900), *minister posts February 1879–April 1885*, 78

colonial party, 82–3, 149, 152, 207–8

colonial policy, 13–14, 26, 82–3, 105, 141f, 207–8

Combes, Emile (1835–1921), *PM 1902–1905, minister public instruction November 1895–April 1896*, 22, 24–6, 56, 64, 66, 71, 77, 80, 105, 112, 153

Comité central des houillères de France, 83

Comité de l'Afrique française, 82, 149

Comité des forges, 83

Comité du Maroc, 150

Comité républicain du commerce et de l'industrie, 83

Comité révolutionnaire central, 123, 175

Commentry, 132

committees, parliamentary, 80–1, 84, 195

Commune of 1871, 2, 7–8, 11, 16, 23, 37–8, 57, 88, 102, 119, 121–4, 126, 159, 203

Comte, Auguste (1798–1857), 89

concentration républicaine, 26, 167, 170, 173–4

Concordat of 1801, 13, 24, 81, 90, 198

Confédération générale du travail (CGT), 25–7, 119, 128, 130, 136–40, 176

conjonction des centres, 165

conscription, *see* army laws

conseils d'arrondissement, 66, 75
conseils généraux, 62–3, 66, 75, 197
constitution of 1875, 8–10, 12, 74–5
Constitutionnel group, 164–5
Courrières, 27
Croix, La, 20, 106, 108, 111, 201

Decazes, Duc de (1819–86), *foreign minister November 1873–November 1877*, 9, 144
Decazeville, 16
Delcassé, Théophile (1852–1923), *under-secretary colonies January–December 1893, minister colonies May 1894–January 1895, foreign minister June 1898–June 1905, minister marine March 1911–January 1913, minister war June 1914*, 22, 71, 78, 82, 149–50, 152, 154
délégation des gauches, 22, 77, 195
Dépêche, La, 86
deputies: background, 62, 66, 196; functions, 73, 76–80, 83, 87
Déroulède, Paul (1846–1914), 17, 20, 70, 107, 110, 115, 139
Desmons, Frédéric (1832–1910), 64
Dion, Marquis de (1851–1946), 34
Doumergue, Gaston (1863–1937), *PM 1913–14*, 174
Dreyfus, Alfred (1859–1935), 18–19, 23
Dreyfus affair, 5, 18–23, 25–6, 42, 67, 70, 82, 90, 109f, 118, 121, 133–4, 139, 150, 153, 170, 189
Droite constitutionnelle, 169
Droite républicaine, 169
Drumont, Edouard (1844–1917), 20, 86, 107–9
Duclerc, Eugène (1812–88), *PM 1882–3*, 167
Dufaure, Jules (1798–1881), *PM 1871–3, 1876 and 1877–9*, 165–6
Dumay, Charles (1843–1906), 81
Dupuy, Charles (1851–1923), *PM 1893, 1894–5 and 1898–9*, 169–70
Dupuy, Jean (1844–1919), 85
Durkheim, Emile (1858–1917), 91, 134

Ecole libre des sciences politiques, 81
Ecole normale supérieure, 126, 199
education, 3, 12–13, 24, 38, 62, 70, 89–92, 105, 114, 124, 127, 160, 198–9; *see also* teachers
elections: *1871*, 6, 163–4; *1876*, 10, 164; *1877*, 10, 46, 69–70, 164–5; *1881*, 11, 93, 166; *1885*, 14, 56, 68, 166; *1889*, 15–16, 106, 168; *1893*, 16–17, 22, 78–9, 110, 126, 168; *1898*, 19–21, 79, 98, 116, 168–9; *1902*, 22–4, 46, 56, 116, 170; *1906*, 24, 134, 171; *1910*, 171; *1914*, 28, 132, 134–5, 151, 158, 171–2
electoral sociology, 44–53, 193
electoral system, 28, 62, 67–70, 76, 78–9, 135, 196
employers, *see* businessmen
Engels, Friedrich (1820–95), 124, 126
Eschasseriaux, René (1823–1906), 58
Esterhazy, Marie-Charles-Ferdinand (1847–1923), 19
Etienne, Eugène (1844–1921), *under-secretary colonies May–December 1887 and February 1889–February 1892, minister war November 1905–October 1906 and January–December 1913*, 83, 150
Extreme Left, 11, 164–7

Fallières, Armand (1841–1931), *PM 1883, president 1906–13*, 167, 173
Fashoda incident, 83, 118, 142, 144, 148–9, 153
Faure, Félix (1841–99), *president 1895–9*, 20, 169
Fédération communiste révolutionnaire anarchiste, 175
Fédération des bourses du travail, 128, 136, 176
Fédération des Gauches, 28, 171–2
Fédération des syndicats, 125, 127–8, 176
Fédération des travailleurs socialistes français, 175
Fédération du Livre, 125, 131, 138
Fédération du parti des travailleurs socialistes de France, 123, 175
Fédération républicaine, 171–2
Ferroul, Ernest-Joseph (1853–1921), 132
Ferry, Jules (1832–93), *PM 1880–1 and 1883–5, minister public instruction February 1879–November 1881 and January–August 1882*, 11–14, 18, 26, 56, 58, 74, 80, 82, 89, 91–5, 105, 142, 145–7, 165, 167
Figaro, Le, 29, 85, 87
Floquet, Charles (1828–96), *PM 1888–9*, 167
Fontaine, Arthur (1860–1931), 81
foreign ministry, 78, 81–2, 86, 142–3, 155, 177
Fourmies, 16, 125

France, Anatole (1844–1924), 134
Franco-Russian alliance, 38, 82, 87, 141, 143–4, 147–8, 150, 152, 154–5, 207
freemasonry, 20, 25, 70–1, 108, 115, 132, 199
Freppel, Charles (1827–91), 49, 106
Freycinet, Charles de (1828–1923), *PM 1879–80, 1882, 1886 and 1890–2, minister public works December 1877–December 1879, foreign minister April 1885–December 1886, minister war April 1888–January 1893 and November 1898–May 1899*, 14, 74, 92–3, 147–148, 166–7, 169
Freycinet plan, 13, 93, 192

Galliéni, Joseph (1849–1916), 149
Galliffet, Marquis de (1830–1909), *minister war June 1899–May 1900*, 23, 25, 133
Gambetta, Léon (1838–82), *PM 1881–2*, 5–6, 9–13, 22, 36, 51, 61, 65, 67–8, 70, 72, 74–5, 78, 81, 88–9, 93–5, 142–3, 146–8, 165, 167
Garnier, Théodore (1847–1920), 109
Gauche démocratique: (Radical group), 169, 172–3; (moderate group), 172–3
Gauche progressiste, 169
Gauche radicale, 167, 169, 171–3
Gauche républicaine, 165–7
Gayraud, Hippolyte (1856–1911), 49, 109
Goblet, René (1828–1905), *PM 1886–7*, 167
Government of National Defence, 5–7, 57, 93, 165
Grandmaison, Louis de, 153
Grenoble, 56, 59
Grévy, Jules (1807–91), *president 1879–1887*, 11, 15, 74–5, 167
Griffuelhes, Victor (1874–1923), 138
groups, parliamentary, 72, 76–7, 80, 125, 163f
Guérin, Jules (1860–1910), 108
Guesde, Jules (1845–1922), and Guesdism, 23, 72, 123f, 139, 175–6, 203–4

Halévy, Daniel (1872–1962), 101
Hanotaux, Gabriel (1853–1944), *foreign minister May 1894–November 1895 and April 1896–June 1898*, 149
Henry, Hubert (1846–98), 19
Herr, Lucien (1864–1926), 126
Herriot, Edouard (1872–1957), 67

Hervé, Gustave (1875–1944), 139
Herz, Cornelius, 17
Hugo, Victor (1802–85), 88
Hugues, Clovis (1851–1907), 125
Hulst, Maurice d' (1841–96), 49
Humanité, L', 86, 135

income-tax, 18, 27–8, 37, 76, 81, 84, 95–6, 98, 118, 132, 192
Independent Republican group, 169
Independent Socialists, 29, 72, 171–4, 175
intellectuals, 19, 67, 70–1, 113–14, 124, 126, 134
interpellations, 77
inventories crisis, 24, 57, 198

Jaurès, Jean (1859–1914), 16, 22, 26, 28–9, 51, 63, 72, 86, 92, 113, 126, 133–6, 139–40, 151
Jesuits, 12, 90, 111
Joffre, Joseph (1852–1931), 153
Jouhaux, Léon (1879–1954), 140, 206
Jouvenel, Robert de (1881–1924), 137
Jura Federation, 123

Keufer, Auguste (1851–1924), 131

Lafargue, Paul (1843–1911), 124–6
La Grand'Combe, 131
landowners, political influence of, 2, 33–5, 37, 40, 47–8, 57, 61–3, 65, 103–4, 193
Languedoc, disturbances in, 27, 84–5, 132
La Tour du Pin, René de (1834–1924), 109
Laval, Pierre (1883–1945), 66
Lavigerie, Charles (1825–92), 16
Lavisse, Ernest (1842–1922), 92
laws: 1872, against International (*loi Dufaure*), 122; 1874, child labour, 97; 1875, Catholic universities, 13; 1880, girls' education (*loi Camille Sée*), 13; 1881–2, primary education, 12–13, 91; 1881, Press, 12, 86; 1881, public meetings, 12; 1884, trade unions, 12, 125; 1884, local government, 12; 1884, divorce (*loi Naquet*), 12; 1886, primary education, 13; 1892, hours of work, 97; 1894, anti-anarchist (*lois scélérates*), 16, 132; 1898, accident insurance, 97; 1900, hours of work (*loi Millerand-Colliard*), 97; 1901,

associations, 23–4; 1904, teaching orders, 24, 105; 1905, separation of Church and State, 24; 1906, hours of work, 97; 1910, pensions, 27, 97–8; *see also* army laws
Le Creusot, 57, 63, 131, 138, 192
Legitimism, 1, 3, 6, 8–10, 16, 33, 49, 57, 62, 90, 100–6, 108, 164–5, 167, 201
Le Havre, Socialist congress at, 123, 175
Lemire, Jules (1853–1928), 59, 109
Lens, 130
Leo XIII (1810–1903), *Pope from 1878*, 16, 111
Le Play, Frédéric (1806–82), 103
Leroy-Beaulieu, Paul (1843–1916), 146
Lesseps, Ferdinand de (1805–94), 17
Libre Parole, La, 86, 107–8
libre pensée movement, 71
Ligue antisémitique, 108
Ligue des Antipatriotes, 139
Ligue des Droits de l'Homme, 70–1, 81
Ligue de l'Enseignement, 70–1, 81
Ligue du Midi, 57
Ligue de la Patrie française, 70, 112, 116
Ligue des Patriotes, 20, 70, 107
Lille, 125–6
Limoges, 57
Limoges, Socialist congress at, 139
Loubet, Emile (1838–1929), *PM 1892, president 1899–1906*, 169, 173
Lyautey, Hubert (1854–1934), 150
Lyons, 7, 56–7, 59, 67, 106, 130
Lyons, congresses at, 125, 175

Macé, Jean (1815–94), 70
MacMahon, Comte de (1808–93), *president 1873–9*, 9–11, 69, 90, 101, 112, 165
Maistre, Joseph de (1753–1821), 103
Marchand, Jean-Baptiste (1863–1934), 149
Marseilles, 7, 56–7, 59, 118, 125, 143
Marseilles, congresses at, 123, 126, 175
Marx, Karl (1818–83), 39, 122–5
Marxists, French, *see* Guesde
Maurras, Charles (1868–1952), 26, 86, 112–16
Mazières-en-Gâtine, 65
Méline, Jules (1838–1925), *PM 1896–8, minister agriculture February 1883–April 1885*, 17–19, 21–2, 41, 58, 65, 84, 110, 118, 132, 167, 170
Menier family, 63
métayage, 40, 47, 57, 84, 132
Michel, General, 153

Michelet, Jules (1798–1874), 89, 136
Millerand, Alexandre (1859–1943), *minister commerce June 1899–June 1902, minister war January 1912–January 1913*, 22–3, 28, 96–7, 118, 126, 133
miners, 27, 63, 97, 125, 130–2, 135, 138, 205
Monis, Ernest (1846–1929), *PM 1911*, 174
Montluçon, 132
moral order, 9, 104, 165
Morès, Marquis de (1858–96), 108
Morocco question, 26, 28, 83, 118, 142–5, 149–51, 154–5
Mun, Albert de (1841–1914), 49, 109–10, 118, 139

Nancy, 107, 114
Nancy, Radical congress at, 96
Nantes, 59
Nantes, trade-union congress at, 176
Napoleon III (1808–73), 1–3, 5, 7, 41, 57–8, 104
Napoleon, Prince (Jérôme-Napoléon Bonaparte) (1822–91), 104
Narbonne, 57, 132
National Assembly, 6–9, 11, 62, 74, 90, 97, 101, 144, 163–4
National Socialist party, 117
nationalism: general, 15, 26, 28, 91–2, 95, 151, 200, 202; integral, 112–17; nationalist deputies, 21, 26, 116–17, 168, 170–2; right-wing, 15, 20, 22–4, 38, 52–3, 59, 100, 106, 110f, 155
navy, 82, 143, 153–4, 208
N'Goko Sangha affair, 151

Œuvre des cercles, 109
Opportunists, 5, 11–16, 53, 68, 71, 88f, 105, 107, 147, 166–7, 169, 199
Orleanism, 1–2, 8–10, 33–4, 95, 100–2, 105, 164–5
Orléans, Philippe, Duc de (1869–1926), royalist pretender from 1894, 115

Panama scandal, 17–18, 86, 107–8, 132, 169, 189
Paris, congresses at, 123, 133, 175–6
Paris, local politics of, 5–8, 14, 38, 59, 95, 116, 120, 124, 126; *see also* Commune of 1871
Paris, Philippe, Comte de (1838–94), Orleanist pretender, 9
Parti ouvrier (Allemanist), 175

Parti ouvrier (Guesdist), *see* Guesde
Parti ouvrier socialiste révolutionnaire, 175; *see also* Allemane
Parti socialiste de France, 133, 175
Parti socialiste français, 133, 175
Parti socialiste révolutionnaire, 175; *see also* Blanqui
parties, development of, 42–5, 61–2, 70–3, 76–8, 134, 157, 196
patronage, 61, 63–5, 68–9, 73, 81
Pau, Radical congress at, 28, 71
peasants, 2–3, 9, 18, 32, 35, 39–41, 47–8, 50, 53, 57, 65, 94, 98, 126, 132, 160, 191, 205; *see also* winegrowers
Péguy, Charles (1873–1914), 113–14
Pelletan, Camille (1846–1915), *minister marine June 1902–January 1905*, 34, 153–4
Pelloutier, Fernand (1867–1901), 127–8
pensions question, 27, 76, 96–8, 192
Petit Parisien, Le, 85, 197
Picquart, Georges (1854–1914), *minister war October 1906–July 1909*, 19
Piou, Jacques (1838–1932), 17, 169
Pius IX (1792–1878), *Pope from 1846*, 2, 103
Pius X (1835–1914), *Pope from 1904*, 24, 109
Poincaré, Raymond (1860–1934), *PM 1912–13, president 1913–20*, 22, 28, 58, 74–5, 118, 151, 154–5, 173–4
Possibilism, 123–4, 126, 175, 204
Pouget, Emile (1860–1931), 127
presidency, 9, 74–5, 82
Press, 12, 16–17, 19–20, 68–70, 76, 85–7, 108, 142, 190, 197
prime minister, position of, 74, 77, 79, 177
Prince Imperial (Eugène Bonaparte) (1856–79), 104
Progressists, 21, 42, 58, 100, 117–18, 170–4
proportional representation, *see* electoral system
protectionism, *see* tariff questions
Protestantism, 20, 46, 49, 108, 115, 198
Proudhon, Pierre-Joseph (1809–65), 120–1, 123–4

Quai d'Orsay, *see* foreign ministry
Quinet, Edgar (1803–75), 91

Radicalism: general development, 5, 11f, 21f, 46, 68–9, 75, 79, 126, 132, 134–6; geography, 56–9; nature and ideas, 3, 38, 44, 53, 64, 76, 88, 90, 93f, 106, 113, 118, 147, 150–1, 159–60; Radical groups and party, 26, 70–2, 83, 167–74, 200
railwaymen, 26–7, 97, 125, 131, 138, 205
railways, 13, 27, 34, 37, 63, 95–6
Ralliement, Ralliés, 5, 16–18, 63, 79, 100, 109–10, 117, 135, 168–70, 189; *see also Action libérale*
Ravachol, François (1859–92), 127
Reille, René (1835–98), 135
Reinach, Jacques (1840–92), 17
religious orders, 12–13, 23–4, 90, 112, 141–2
Renan, Ernest (1823–92), 91, 102
Renouvier, Charles (1815–1903), 91
Républicains de gauche, 21, 171–3
Républicains socialistes, 173, 175
revolutionary syndicalism, *see* syndicalism
Ribot, Alexandre (1842–1923), *PM 1892–3, 1895 and 1914, foreign minister March 1890–January 1893*, 74, 169–70, 174
Roanne, Socialist congress at, 175
Rochebouët, Gaétan de (1813–99), *PM 1877*, 166
Rochefort, Henri (1830–1913), 86, 94, 106
Roubaix, 126
Rouvier, Maurice (1842–1911), *PM 1887 and 1905–6, minister finance February 1889–December 1892 and June 1902–January 1905*, 81, 150, 167, 173
royalism, 1–3, 8–10, 15, 21, 23, 53, 58, 70, 86, 100f, 115, 117, 131, 163–7, 201; *see also* Legitimism, Orleanism

Saint-Etienne, 57
Saint-Etienne, congresses at, 175–6
Saint-Mandé speech, 133
Sangnier, Marc (1873–1950), 110
Sarraut family, 86
Sarrien, Jean (1840–1915), *PM 1906*, 173
Say, Léon (1826–96), *minister finance December 1872–May 1873, March 1875–May 1877, December 1877–December 1879 and January–August 1882*, 81
Schnaebelé affair, 14, 147
Schneider company and family (Henri, 1840–98; Eugène, 1868–1942), 63, 131, 148, 155, 192

Section française de l'Internationale ouvrière (*SFIO*), *see* Socialism
Seize Mai crisis, 10, 74, 90, 112, 164
Senate, 9–12, 18, 25, 27, 66, 74–6, 98, 195–6
Separation of Church and State, 24, 88–9, 116, 159, 197–8
Séré de Rivière, Raymond (1815–95), 145
Siegfried, André (1875–1959), 44f, 60, 63, 73, 79–80, 93, 100, 157
Sillon movement, 109–10, 198
Simon, Jules (1814–96), *PM 1876–7, minister public instruction February 1871–May 1873*, 10, 165
Social Catholic movement, 16, 107, 109, 198
Socialism: bibliography, 202–4; geography, 46, 56–60, 128f; political development, 16, 18–19, 22f, 42, 44, 46, 53, 61, 71, 76, 96, 119f, 167–73, 175; *SFIO* party, 4, 25, 28, 57, 68, 72–3, 77, 119, 134f, 158, 171–3, 175
Société des agriculteurs de France, 65
Société nationale d'encouragement a l'agriculture, 65
Solages family, 63, 135
solidarism, 95–6, 98, 200
Sorel, Georges (1847–1922), 113, 137
strikes, 16, 25–7, 61, 112, 119–20, 125, 128, 130–1, 133, 135–9, 205
syndicalism, 25, 113, 125, 127–8, 131, 136–9, 158, 205–6

Taine, Hippolyte (1828–93), 102, 114
tariff questions, 18, 84, 95, 146, 192
teachers and politics, 13, 27, 36, 39, 64–5, 67, 71, 91–2, 126, 139, 199
Temps, Le, 86, 98
Thalamas, Amédée, 116
Thiers, Adolphe (1797–1877), *president 1871–3*, 6–9, 35, 144, 165
Thivrier, Christophe (1841–95), 132
three-year law, *see* army laws
Tirard, Pierre (1827–93), *PM 1887–8 and 1889–90*, 167, 169

Tocqueville, Alexis de (1805–59), 102
Tortelier, 128
Toulouse, 56–7, 86
Toulouse, Socialist congress at, 135
Tours, delegation of, 5
Tours, Radical congress at, 71
trade unions, development of, 16, 25–7, 38–9, 109, 117, 119f, 204–5

Union coloniale française, 82
Union démocratique: (of 1880s), 167; (of 1900s), 172
Union des droites, 167
Union des gauches, 167
Union générale bank, 108, 201
Union libérale, 169
Union progressiste, 169, 172
Union républicaine: (of 1880s), 165–7; (of 1900s), 172–3
Unité socialiste révolutionnaire, 175
universités populaires, 134
Uzès, Duchesse d' (1847–1933), 106

Vaillant, Auguste (1861–94), 16
Vaillant, Edouard (1840–1915), 123–4, 134, 139
Veuillot, Louis (1813–83), 86
Viviani, René (1863–1925), *PM 1914–15, minister labour October 1906–November 1910*, 29, 154, 174

Waddington, William (1826–94), *PM 1879, foreign minister December 1877–December 1879*, 167
Waldeck-Rousseau, René (1846–1904), *PM 1899–1902, minister interior November 1881–January 1882 and February 1883–April 1885*, 22–4, 77, 93, 97–8, 110, 133, 138, 173
Wallon amendment, 9
Watrin, 16
Wilson, Daniel (1840–1919), 15
winegrowers and politics, 27, 40–1, 50, 84–5, 191

Zola, Emile (1840–1902), 16, 19, 21, 116